A Biblical Chronology

From Adam to Christ

New Revised Edition

Don T. Phillips

"A Biblical Chronology from Adam to Christ, Revised Edition," by Don T. Phillips. ISBN 978-1-62137-121-2.

Published, 2012 2014 by Virtualbookworm.com Publishing Inc., P.O. Box 9949, College Station, TX 77842, US.

Manufactured in the United States of America.

Preface

This book is a result of 8 years part time study directed to a complete construction of a biblical chronology from the year that Adam and Eve were expunged from the Garden of Eden until the Crucifixion of our Lord Jesus Christ. This manuscript has evolved from a casual study of existing Biblical chronologies to an intense study of the Holy Scriptures. In the initial stages of this study I found myself both amazed and confused at how many different chronologies had been developed over the last 600 years, and how each that I studied rendered different starting points and used different sources of information. It was disturbing to me that when the Holy Bible failed scholarly inquiry, various chronologists simply threw in the towel … claiming incomplete records, scribal errors or errors in translation. Being a biblical literalist, I was convinced that with dedicated study, much prayer, and guidance from the Holy Spirit that a complete Chronology from Adam to Christ could be achieved. There were several critical assumptions that had to be made and all are discussed in Chapter 1. However, one deserves immediate explanation. I had to decide which version of the Holy Scriptures to use.

The oldest known manuscripts are the Old Testament Hebrew, Aramaic and Greek manuscripts. The collection of ancient writings became known as the *Tanakh*, which were compiled in three different books: (1) the five books of the *Torah* ("teaching" or "law"), (2) the *Nevi'im* ("prophets"), containing the historic account of ancient Israel and Judah and (3) the *Ketuvim* ("writings"): poetic and philosophical works such as the Psalms and the Book of Job. These manuscripts were meticulously hand copied by Jewish scribes through hundreds of years. These earliest manuscripts were preserved by a group known as the *Masoretes*, who gathered the original manuscripts into a text now known as the *Masoretic Text*. Modern evacuations of the Dead Sea scrolls have uncovered a wide array of ancient Biblical texts. The modern Christian Bible is divided into two parts. The first is called the *Old Testament*, containing the (minimum) 39 books of Hebrew Scripture, and the second portion is called the *New Testament*, containing a set of 27 books. The oldest surviving Christian Bibles are Greek manuscripts from the 4th century; the oldest complete Jewish Bible is a Greek translation, also dating to the 4th century. The oldest complete manuscripts of the Hebrew Bible (the Masoretic text) date from the middle Ages. The bible was separated into chapters in the 13th century by Stephen Langton, who eventually became a Roman Catholic Archbishop, and into verses in the 16th century by Robert Estienne, a French printer.

During the three centuries following the establishment of Christianity in the 1st century, Church Fathers compiled Gospel accounts and letters of apostles into a Christian Bible which became known as the New Testament. The first four books of the New Testament form the Canonical gospels which recount the life of Jesus. Christian Bibles include the books of the Hebrew Bible, but arranged in a different order. The Old and New Testaments together are commonly referred to as *The Holy Bible* (τὰ βιβλία τὰ ἅγια). Many Christians consider the text of the Bible to be divinely inspired, and cite passages in the Bible itself as support for this belief. The Old Testament canon entered into Christian use in the *Greek Septuagint* translations and original books. Around 400 AD Jerome produced a definitive Latin edition of the Bible which was called the *Latin Vulgate*, the canon of which at the insistence of the Pope was in accord with the earliest manuscripts available. A definitive list of what constituted the canon of scripture did not come from an Ecumenical Council until the Council of Trent (1545). The most widely used and respected bible is probably the Authorized King James Bible, which was an English rendering of the canon of scripture.

The *Authorized Version*, commonly known as the *King James Version* (KJV) or *King James Bible* (KJB) is an English translation of the Christian Bible by the Church of England begun in 1604 and completed in 1611.The translation we use today was done by 47 scholars, all of whom were members of the Church of England. In common with most other translations of the period, the New Testament was translated from Greek and the Old Testament was translated from Hebrew text, By the first half of the 18th century, the *Authorized King James Version* was effectively unchallenged as the English translation used in Anglican and Protestant churches. Over the course of the 18th century, the *KJV* supplanted the Latin Vulgate as the standard version of scripture for English speaking scholars.

It is obvious that the King James Bible has stood as the source of Biblical Truth for over 400 years. It is my opinion that the KJV was compiled by learned scholars who were divinely inspired and guided by the Holy Spirit. It is my belief that God would not allow millions of Christians to be deceived or misled by faulty translation. Hence, I have chosen to use the King James Bible as the primary source of all biblical dates and historical records. Having said that let me state that I have no problem whatsoever using additional sources of information from archeological records or from other biblical manuscripts, as long as they do not contradict or replace the Biblical Records. Hence, the reader will see that the ancient book of Jasher (which is referenced by Jesus Himself) was used to establish when Abraham was born. In addition, it will become necessary to use ancient Jewish, Egyptian and Assyrian records to establish when the prophecy of Daniel's 70 weeks of years began and ended. Other uses of extra-biblical sources will be presented and justified as necessary to confirm Biblical accounts. It should be stated with great conviction that the main contributions of this manuscript are: (1) To establish that the Biblical record of the King James Bible is both reliable and historically accurate. (2) Present a methodology that can be repeated and used if different scholars wish to make different assumptions. The chronology which is offered will span almost 4000 years, beginning with when Adam and Eve were expunged from the Garden of Eden and ending at the crucifixion of our Lord Jesus Christ. Finally, I am very aware of the following warning considering what I have written in trying to provide a new and biblically based chronology of mankind.

> *"And the Spirit and the bride say, Come. And let him that heareth say, Come. And let him that is athirst come. And whosoever will, let him take the water of life freely. For I testify unto every man that heareth the words of the prophecy of this book, If any man shall add unto these things, God shall add unto him the plagues that are written in this book: And if any man shall take away from the words of the book of this prophecy, God shall take away his part out of the book of life, and out of the holy city, and from the things which are written in this book."*   Rev 22:17-19

I have tried to interpret the scriptures without compromising either content or meaning. I hope that in some way, the words in this book will lead a soul to Christ, and for others strengthen their belief that the Bible is accurate and historically correct. I encourage anyone who reads this book to seek the Holy Spirit in forming their own opinions; take nothing as an absolute truth without intense investigation; and always… always… let the scriptures themselves speak the truth. God will hold me accountable for what I have written and knows that I have done the best that I can. As time goes by and informed people offer suggestions and criticisms, I am sure that I may be led to offer alternate or new interpretations. In some cases, it is probable that the further interpretations await new discoveries.

Acknowledgements

The material presented in this book was largely compiled by the author as a hobby. I was interested in seeing if the Biblical records could be used to produce a coherent and unbroken record of mankind from Adam to Christ. I soon discovered that this goal was much more difficult to achieve than I ever realized. At that point, I began to turn to *giants in the field upon whose shoulders I might stand.* It did not take long to discover that past efforts by multiple brilliant scholars were almost universally in disagreement. The reasons why are discussed in Chapter 1, but for now let me state that there was much wisdom and understanding gained by studying historical efforts. In particular, the monumental work of James Ussher in 1658 provided a framework to move forward; the works of Sir Isaac Newton and Sir Robert Anderson were very helpful. Modern scholars such as Dwight D. Pentacost, M. J. Agee and Martin Anstey all provided inspiration and truth. These fine scholars are all acknowledged for their contributions. Much later I discovered the Doctoral dissertation of Dr. Floyd Nolan Jones. His approach, conclusions and enduring belief that the Biblical records are God inspired and inerrant greatly reinforced my own beliefs. Although we disagree on several key points, his conclusions were remarkably close to my own. Dr. Jones deserves special recognition.

I have saved my most sincere and heartfelt thanks for the last. My main supporter in writing this book; my severest critic; and the person who continually challenged my scriptural understanding of prophecy; is my wife: Candyce J. Phillips. She suffered through countless hours of editing, reading, challenging and inquiring the pages of this manuscript. She patiently endured my long hours of study and my writing style.

The last acknowledgements are to my family who at times could not understand why I would not leave my desk for long periods of time.

To those that matter most in my life……….

    Candy Phillips

    Ronald Alan Phillips (Ron)

    Don T. Phillips, III (Donnie)

    …….and *"The Mouse"*

In the beginning,

God created the heavens and the earth.

Genesis 1:1

The heavens declare the glory of God;

and the firmament sheweth his handywork.

Psalms 19:1

Table of Contents

Let the **words of my mouth**,

and the meditation of my heart,

be acceptable in thy sight, O LORD,

my strength, and my redeemer.

Psalms 19:15

Throughout recorded history, man has been engaged in a quest to find the origin of human life. A raging debate has evolved between creationists and evolutionists. Spurred on by the work of Charles Darwin in the mid 1800's, and his classic work on the theory of evolution; there are many who believe that life emerged through a onetime event by which life simply appeared from basic microorganisms, and developed into homo sapiens over millions of years. The antithesis of this basic theory is that held by most Christians, who hold the belief that man was created by an omnipotent and omnipresent God. The fundamental basis for most creationists is the Holy Bible. The Bible opens with two simple but definitive statements.

> ***"In the beginning God created the heaven and the earth"***   Genesis 1:1

> ***"And the LORD God formed man of the dust of the ground, and breathed into his nostrils the breath of life; and man became a living soul"***   Genesis 2:7

For the Biblical literalist, this is enough to settle the issue. However, the Holy Bible never says exactly when the heavens and earth were created … It only says that they were made by the hand of God *in the beginning*. The Holy records also never say when in time man was created; only that it was on the 6th day (Gen1: 26-31). Within the sphere of creationalists, there are two fundamental lines of belief. The first is that if one carefully follows the genealogies contained in the Holy Bible, the numbers will lead to about 4000 years from Gen 1:1 to the birth of Christ. This gives rise to the belief that the earth is now about 6000 years old, and that all mankind in the world today has emerged from two of God's subsequent creations … Adam and Eve. The second line of belief is that the geological records indicate that the world is millions of years old, and so there must have been a large chasm of time that elapsed between when God created the heaven and earth and when Adam and Eve were created. This is generally called the *gap theory*; and it is based upon an unspecified amount of time between Genesis 1:1 and Genesis 1:2. This Biblical Chronology is not concerned with how to analyze or settle this debate, but is focused to the sequence of events which were faithfully recorded between Genesis 1:2 and the Crucifixion of our Lord Jesus Christ.

Ancient and modern theologians have created many partial or full biblical chronologies, but most have started at the time when God created Adam. The *age of man* is therefore determined by two factors: (1) How long did Adam (and Eve) stay in the Garden of Eden and (2) when should an unbroken biblical chronology begin and end? The first issue of how long Adam stayed in the Garden of Eden is pure conjecture: Some have used 40 years (the Biblical number for trial and testing): Others have used 7 years (The Biblical number of perfection). Still others have used a time period based upon other written records outside the Canon of scripture. The use of 40 years based upon *trial and testing* seems to be misplaced, since God did not create Adam and Eve to test and taunt them… Satan used that approach. The use of 7 years is even more farfetched, since if 7 (the Biblical number of perfection) is the duration of time spent in the Garden of Eden, there is nothing perfect about the sin and fall of Adam and Eve at all; it was a tragic end for what had been planned to last eternity. On the other hand, an unbroken genealogy of Adam between when he was expunged from the Garden of Eden until the death of Joseph is clearly delineated in the

Holy records. Linkage to subsequent major events in Biblical history can be linked to the death of Joseph by carefully examining the written records which follow. In any case, the chronology which will be developed in this text chooses to avoid any argument as to when the earth was created, when Adam was created or how long that Adam and Eve lived in Eden by starting at the year when Adam and Eve *left* the Garden of Eden. We will call this year AY 1…. **Adam Year 1**. Most chronographers will use the notation *year AM*; Anno Mundi (Latin: in the year of the world). We choose **AY** to stress that this is not the beginning of the world, but the first year that Adam entered the world in the flesh. Consistent with almost all modern beliefs, this same year will be *Year 0* of Adam's earthly age. The first year of a newborn is always year zero, and when someone has a birthday and is *one year old,* during the subsequent year the actual age is between one year- one day and 1 year- 365 days. Hence, when Genesis 5:3 states that Adam had a son called Seth at age 130, this occurred sometime in year AY 131. The passing of time through important Biblical events is subsequently recorded as AY years. It will be seen that the holy inspired word of God augmented by reliable archeological discoveries provide an unbroken record between when Adam and Eve left the Garden of Eden and when our Lord and Savior Jesus Christ was crucified. Although the Biblical record is complete and reliable, uncovering the correct sequence of chronological milestones and the AY year in which key events occurred is not an easy process. The only remaining task after following the Biblical record is to find any event recorded in the Bible which can be 100% correlated to either a Julian or Gregorian year. Once this has been found, using the AY year when that event occurred; and the associated Julian calendar date as an *anchor point*; all other AY years can be definitively associated with a calendar year both forward and backward through time.

God's plan for mankind has never changed. It started with a personal, sinless relationship with Adam and Eve in the Garden of Eden, and it will end in the same way after the 1000 year millennial kingdom when Christ will establish a new heaven and a new earth. Since the Holy Bible is divinely inspired and recorded by men under the guidance of the Holy Spirit, one would certainly expect to find an inerrant record of the sequence of events which are recorded between the first book of the Bible (*Genesis*) and the last (*Revelation*). We believe that this is true, and that by carefully studying and following the Scriptures, a continuous sequence of key events that have occurred between the year that Adam and Eve were expunged from the Garden of Eden and the crucifixion of Christ can be constructed.

Several biblical scholars have attempted construction of a complete biblical chronology. Those of James Ussher, Martin Anstey and Sir Isaac Newton represent efforts going back to the 16th century AD. More recently; Floyd Nolan Jones, Daniel Gregg, Willis Beecher, M.J. Agee and others have published various chronologies. The work presented here is largely the result of independent investigations and biblical research by the author, but there is general agreement within certain periods of time across all other published chronologies; particularly in the sequential ordering and yearly counts of the Old Testament patriarchs between Adam and the death of Joseph. The basic premise accepted by this offered chronology is that the biblical records are sequential, complete, and without error. The basis of all biblical records used in this study is the *Authorized King James Bible*. The author's choice of using the Authorized King James Version of the Holy Scriptures will surely be challenged by some theologians, pastors and Christians. It is wonderful to read the gospel message in the NIV; the New American Standard and other modern translations; but an inescapable fact is that some modern translations have changed the original meaning of the King James Bible in offering liberal, contemporary translations. A comparison of almost any liberal translation of the original Greek manuscripts, such as the Common English Bible (2011), to the KJV will verify this assertion. This is not to say that modern versions which followed the original manuscripts are not trustworthy and sound presentations of the Gospel message, but if any biblical student wishes to study the Greek, Hebrew and Aramaic original meaning of Old Testament and New Testament scripture the King James Version is indispensable. Such reference texts as the Strong's Concordance and the Vines Biblical Dictionary are written to understand where the English text of the KJV originated. Aside from social considerations, it is a historical fact that in the fullness of time the modern printing press was invented by Johannes Gutenberg in 1440, and the time had come for every English speaking individual to own his/her own Bible. So God moved King Henry VIII and the Church of England to charter a team of biblical experts to write an English version of the Biblical text. Begun in 1604 and completed in 1611, the result was the 1611 BC version of the Holy Bible known as the Authorized King James Bible (KJV). It is a fact that for over 400 years the KJV remains a written record of God's plan for salvation available to millions of common people. It is my conviction that God would not confuse his people for over 400 years without an inerrant record of his creation and the salvation offered by His son, our Lord Jesus Christ. For this reason, I have chosen to use the Authorized King James Bible as the primary source of Biblical record for this chronology. However, I will also state that I have no reason to fully reject historical records from sources such as the Jewish historian Josephus; other non-canonical Biblical writings such as the Book of Jasher; or archeological findings from the ancient Assyrian, Babylonian, Greek and Roman empires, provided that such historical records do not stand in conflict with those given in the Holy word. When conflicts arise, non-biblical sources should always give way to the inspired word of God. We will demonstrate that if these principles are followed, the validity and inerrancy of God's Holy Word can be verified and accepted as the truth. This is my own personal world view, and one which will be followed throughout the development of this chronology. Nevertheless, the conclusions reached and the methodologies employed in reaching a coherent and biblically consistent chronology will hopefully aid other investigations. This chronology does not claim inerrancy or uniqueness in its structure or interpretation; but it does claim to always be guided by the biblical records.

Beginning: Where?

A fundamental point of contention, and one that differentiates each chronology from another, is where the chronology should start. Some biblical chronologies start with when the world was supposedly created; others start with when the first man Adam was created. As previously indicated, there are three fundamental constructions that have been offered. The *first* is that the calendar of years starts with the creation of the world. The *second* is that the calendar of years starts with the birth of Adam. The *third* is that the calendar of years starts from the year in which Adam was expelled from the Garden of Eden. The problem with each starting point is that nowhere in the Holy Scriptures are we told when these events occurred. In fact, the way years are distinguished today (2014 AD, for example) is a creation of man and not God. Years are divided into two categories: BC and AD. It is commonly taught that BC stands for *before Christ* and AD stands for *after death*. This is only partially correct. How could the year 1 BC have been *before Christ* and 1 AD been after death? BC does stand for before Christ, but AD actually stands for the Latin phrase *anno domini*, which means *in the year of our Lord*. The BC/AD dating system is not taught in the Bible. A 6th century monk named Dionysius Exiguous invented the BC/AD terminology. The issue of where to start a chronology is further complicated by the fact that we are not told how long Adam and Eve spent in Eden before the fall. Some chronologists have used 40 years, others seven years, and still others seem to have a particular reason for choosing one number or another. However, as we will demonstrate, if we start at AY 1 all other AY dates can be established with reasonable certainty. In referencing secular dates, the old Roman Julian Calendar will be used. To associate each AY date with a Julian year, a secular *anchor event* or secular date must be identified to match a particular AY year. Once this has been accomplished, any other AY date in time can be matched to a Julian year both forward and backward through time provided AY linkages exist.

Certain periods of Biblical time present more difficulties than others. Many chronologists have been confounded in the quagmire of having to calculate the time span consumed by the *period of the judges* and the *period of the Kings of the Southern Kingdom of Judah* and the *Northern Kingdom of Israel*. To show how these problems can influence a particular chronology (Jones), the following table shows what is often referred to as the *Date of Creation* by several respected chronologists, although this may not be strictly true as previously discussed.

Name	Year (BC)	Name	Year (BC)	Name	Year (BC)
J. Africanus	5501	H. Spondanus	4051	Becke	3974
G. Syncellus	5492	M. Anstey	4042	Krentzeim	3971
J. Jackson	5426	M. Lange	4041	W. Dolen	3971
W. Hales	5411	E. Reinholt	4021	E. Reusnerus	3970
Eusebius	5189	J. Cappellus	4005	J. Claverius	3968
M. Scotus	4192	J. Ussher	4004	P. Melanchthon	3964
L.Condomanus	4141	E. Greswell	4004	J. Haynlinus	3963
L. Lydiat	4103	F. Jones	4004	A. Salmeron	3958
M. Maestlinus	4079	E. Faulstich	4001	J. Scaliger	3949
J. Ricciolus	4062	D. Petavius	3983	M. Beroaldus	3927
J. Salianus	4053	F. Klassen	3975	A. Helwigius	3836

In conclusion, in order to avoid making an assumption as to when God created the earth, or how long that Adam and Eve were in the Garden of Eden, the chronology which we offer will begin with the first year that Adam and Eve left the Garden of Eden. All years after that year will be called an AY (Adam's Year) year. Some may wish to call the first year *Year 0*, but we will not. Because we do not know from the biblical record how long that Adam was in the Garden of Eden, we choose to make the year of expulsion equal to AY=1. This anchors what we will call a *relative chronology*. This will result in our AY count being one year longer than those that start at Year 0.

Epochs of Recorded Time

Ancient Biblical time can be divided into *five* main *epochs*. The *first* is the time which was recorded between when Adam and Eve were expelled from the Garden of Eden to the Exodus out of Egypt. The *second* was between the Exodus out of Egypt and the 4th year of King Solomon's reign. This epoch can be further subdivided into four sub-periods of time: (1) The 40 years which elapsed between the departure out of Egypt led by Moses, (2) the reign of Joshua as Moses' successor and commander- in- chief until his death; (3) the time of the *elders* and (4) the time between the elders and the 4th year of King Solomon. This period of time contains the confusing and complicated *reign of the judges*. The *third* epoch of time is between the 4th year of King Solomon and the end of the divided Kingdom of the Northern and Southern tribes. This period of time contains the last 36 years of King Solomon's reign and the years in which the Northern Kingdom of Judah and the Southern Kingdom of Israel existed. The *fourth* epoch is the period of time between the end of the divided kingdom and the decree which initiated the 490 years of Daniel's 70 week of years. The *fifth* epoch is between the initiation of Daniel's 490 year prophecy and the crucifixion of Jesus Christ.

The Architecture of a Biblical Chronology

Before we launch off into the depths of a biblically based chronology, it is believed that a short discussion of the architecture of the offered chronology will be most desirable before the details unfold. The architecture will summarize the major events which drive the Chronology, the AY identification, and the Julian calendar year that was determined for each event. As years unfold in the Biblical records, an AY year number is determined for each event included in the chronology. It will be demonstrated that by carefully following the Biblical records, an unbroken, verifiable sequence of AY numbers can be identified all the way from AY 1 to AY 3358; which was the year that the Southern Kingdom of Judah and the Holy City of Jerusalem fell to the Babylonian empire. The **Rosetta stone** which unlocks the identification of Julian years for each event is that this event is now widely accepted to have occurred on July 18, 586 BC. In *Chapter 4* we will arrive at AY 3358 as the AY year that Jerusalem fell. By interlocking AY 3358 to 586 BC, any other event both forward and backward through time can be assigned a Julian year date. The journey from AY 1 to AY 3358 will be described in great detail in *Chapters 2-4*. The sequence of key events and their AY count will provide a point of reference as each date is determined. Please note that the association of each AY year with a specific Julian year cannot actually be determined until the AY year that Jerusalem fell is firmly established. However, in following the regnal years of both the Northern and Southern Kings of the Divided Kingdom it will be much clearer if *a'priori* Julian years and AY years are both used. We will use this convention in *Chapter 4*.

The Duration of AY Years

A critical chronological assumption, and one that is hotly deliberated, is in which Hebrew and calendar year month was the world created. In the following discussion, we will refer to the *Hebrew Civil* year and the *Hebrew Religious* year. The Civil year begins on Tishri 1 in either the modern month of September or October, and the Religious year begins on Nisan 1 in either March or April. The Biblical record is silent on whether the world was created on Tishri 1 or on Nisan 1. Finegan in δ169 quotes Rabbi Eleazar from the Tractate *Rosh Hashanah* 10b-11a: *In Tishri the world was created; in Tishri the patriarchs (Abraham and Jacob) were born.* Finegan continues: *In the reckoning of years from the creation of the world it was generally considered that the start should be made from Tishri.*

We agree with his conclusion. In this chronology, we will use the duration of each AY year to be Tishri 1 to Adar 29, which for convenience will be referenced as Tishri 1 (Sept/Oct) to Tishri 1 (Sept/Oct). This naturally follows the assumption that the world was created on Tishri 1.

Records of Time

The final point to be made before moving on is the relationship between any Hebrew calendar year and the corresponding ancient Julian or modern Gregorian calendar year. This issue will later be discussed in some detail, but for now we simply note that the ancient (and modern) Hebrew calendar consists of 12 months (13 in a *Leap Year*). This calendar is called a *Lunar-Solar Calendar*. The months follow a lunar cycle of approximately 29.53 days from new moon to new moon, and the 12 (13) month year is constructed to closely align with the Solar cycle of roughly 365.2422 days. This synchrony is achieved by the periodic insertion of a 13th month called a *Leap Month* seven times over a 19 year period. The Hebrew year can be further characterized as either a *Civil Year* or a *Religious Year*. The Civil Year always starts in September or October on the Julian (or Gregorian) calendar, and the Religious Year starts in the month of March or April. Prior to the return from Babylonian captivity in about 539 BC, the months were often referred to only by number and not name. The Hebrew Civil year started in Sept/ Oct and that month was called *Month 1*. When the exodus occurred, Got instructed the Children of Israel to renumber the months so that the 7th month was to be the 1st month. This was to constantly remind Israel of God's deliverance in March or April of that year. The 1st month of the Civil year is now called Tishri, and the 1st month of the Religious year is now called Nisan. The Religious year, which begins on Nisan 1 in March or April, is used to mark and ordain the Seven Holy Convocations or Feasts of Israel which were given to the Nation of Israel at Mt Sinai when Moses received the Ten Commandments. Since the Civil year clearly preceded and existed before the Exodus as the only known cylindrical year, we have chosen to associate the year called AY 1 with September/October to September/October on the ancient Julian calendar. This decision is not without controversy. Other chronographers have equated AY 1 (or AY 0) to a Nisan 1 (March/April) to Nisan 1 (March/April) year. Either way, any one AY year will obviously span two Julian years. For example, Jerusalem and the Temple of Solomon fell in AY 3358 on July 18, 586 BC. We will show that AY 3358 is identical to Sept/Oct, 587 BC – Sept/Oct, 586 BC. The table shown below reflects these chronological choices.

AY and Julian Dates from the Fall of Adam & Eve to End of the Divided Kingdom		
Event	**AY Year**	**Julian Years**
Adam and Eve leave the Garden of Eden	1	Sept/Oct 3944-Sept/Oct 3943 BC
The Great Flood (Noah is 600 years old)	1657	Sept/Oct 2288-Sept/Oct 2287 BC
Abraham Leaves Haran @ Age 75	2024	Sept/Oct 1921-Sept/Oct 1920 BC
Jacob Dies	2256	Sept/Oct 1689-Sept/Oct 1688 BC
Joseph Dies	2310	Sept/Oct 1635-Sept/Oct 1634 BC
Moses Born	2374	Sept/Oct 1571-Sept/Oct 1570 BC
Exodus from Egypt	2454	March/April 1490 BC
Law is Given @ Mt. Sinai	2454	April/May 1490 BC
Moses dies at Age 120	2494	Feb/March 1450 BC
Exodus Ends & River Jordan is Crossed	2494	March/April 1450 BC
Promised Land is Conquered and Divided	2500	Summer 1444 BC
First Sabbatical Year	2507	Sept/Oct 1438-Sept/Oct 1437 BC
First Jubilee Year	2550	Sept/Oct 1395-Sept/Oct 1394 BC
First Year of King Solomon's Reign	2930	Sept/Oct 1015-Sept/Oct 1014 BC
4th Year of King Solomon's Reign[1]	2933	Sept/Oct 1012-Sept/Oct 1011 BC
Solomon's Temple Started in Month of Ziv	2933	April/May 1011 BC
Last Year of King Solomon's Reign	2969	Sept/Oct 976-Sept/Oct 975 BC
First Year of Divided Kingdom	2970	Sept/Oct 975-Sept/Oct 974 BC
Last Year of Northern Kingdom of Israel	3358	Sept/Oct 587-Sept/Oct 586 BC
Jerusalem Falls to the Babylonian Empire	3358	July 8, 586 BC[2]
1 We will later show that Solomon likely died in late spring or early summer of 975 BC		
2 This is a widely accepted date, verified by solar eclipse records and the Babylonian Chronicles		

The AY years shown for each event and the corresponding Julian calendar dates will be justified in subsequent chapters of this book. The following table provides a second example of how the AY years are linked to a particular Julian calendar year for selected major milestones.

AY Year		Julian Dates
1	Year Adam left Eden	Sept/Oct, 3944-Sept/Oct, 3943
		2454 Years
2454	Year of the Exodus	Sept/Oct, 1491-Sept/Oct, 1490
2454	Exodus	Sept/Oct, 1491-Sept/Oct, 1490
		480 Years
2933	Solomon's 4th Year	Sept/Oct, 1012-Sept/Oct, 1011
2930	Solomon's 4th Year	Sept/Oct, 1012-Sept/Oct, 1011
		4 Years
2933	Solomon's 1st Year	Sept/Oct, 1015-Sept/Oct, 1014
2930	Solomon's 1st Year	Sept/Oct, 1015-Sept/Oct, 1014
		40 Years
2969	Solomon's 40th Year	Sept/Oct, 976-Sept/Oct, 975
2970	Divided Kingdom (Judah)	Sept/Oct, 975-Sept/Oct, 974
	Jerusalem fell, July 18, 586 BC	389 Years
3358	Last Year of Judah	Sept/Oct, 587-Sept/Oct, 586
3358	Last Year of Judah	Sept/Oct, 587-Sept/Oct, 586
		129 Years
3487	Start of Daniel's Prophecy	Sept/Oct, 458 Tishri 1
3487	Start of Daniel's Prophecy	Sept/Oct, 458-Sept/Oct, 457
		483 Years
3970	End of Daniel's 69th Week	Sept/Oct, 25 AD-Sept/Oct, 26 AD
3971	Beginning: Ministry of Christ	Sept/Oct, 26 AD-Sept/Oct, 27 AD
		3.5 Jewish Years
3974	*Crucifixion of Christ*	Nisan 14, 30 AD
		Wednesday, April 5

The AY years are represented as Hebrew Calendar *Civil Years* which span Tishri 1 to Tishri 1, using non-inclusive reckoning and September 1 - September 1 for clarity and convenience. Julian calendar equivalence is also shown for future reference. These dates and AY years will be derived in subsequent chapters. Please be aware that the Julian calendar shown in the third column was not introduced until 45 BC. It is common practice to extend Julian years back in time beyond when the calendar was formally put into use. Such an extension is called a *Proleptic calendar*.

We will now show that the Biblical record contains an uninterrupted and traceable record of the generations between Adam and the end of the Divided Kingdom. The period of time between the final fall of Jerusalem and the destruction of the Southern Kingdom to the death of Jesus Christ will also be reconstructed, but silence of the biblical records over this period of history forces a co-dependency upon ancient Assyrian, Babylonian and Egyptian records. Let us now begin this exciting journey through recorded time.

Thoughts and Things………

Chapter 2
Epoch 1
Adam to the Exodus

"This is the book of the generations of Adam."   Gen 5:1

"And Adam lived an hundred and thirty years, and begat a son in his own likeness, after his image, and called his name Seth."   Gen 5:3

Starting in Genesis 5, there are references to the generations and events which follow Adam. Genealogies are detailed throughout Genesis, Exodus and Leviticus. Of particular interest are Gen 5 and Gen 11, which lists the generations of Adam to Noah. From Noah to Joseph requires a bit more detective work but the information is in the Holy Scriptures. From the biblical records, one can construct Table 1.

Name	Lived (Yrs)	Had Son	At Age		AY YEAR Year Born	Biblical Reference
Adam	930	Seth	130	Creation Yr	1	Gen 5:3
Seth	912	Enosh	105		131	Gen 5:6
Enosh	905	Cainan	90	Methusalah	236	Gen 5:9
Cainan/Kenan	910	Mahalalel	70	Dies	326	Gen 5:12
Mahalalel	895	Jared	65	1657	396	Gen 5:15
Jared	962	Enoch	162	Creation	461	Gen 5:18
Enoch	365	Methuselah	65	Year of Flood	623	Gen 5:21
Methuselah	969	Lamech	187	1657	688	Gen 5:25
Lamech	777	Noah	182	Shem Birth	875	Gen 5:28
Noah-600 @ Flood	950	Shem	502	1559	1057	Gen 5:32
Shem-Gen 11:10-Lived 600 yrs	600	Arphaaxed	100	Arphaaxed Birth	1559	Gen 11:10
Arphaaxed-Born 2Yrs after flood	438	Salah	35	1659	1659	Gen 11:12
Selah	433	Eber	30	Abram Covenant	1694	Gen 11:14
Eber	464	Peleg	34	1729	1724	Gen 11:16
Peleg	239	Reu	30	Abram 75 when	1758	Gen 11:18
Reu	239	Serug	32	enters Canaan	1788	Gen 11:20
Serug	230	Nabor	30	2024	1820	Gen 11:22
Nahor	148	Terah	29	Terah died in	1850	Gen 11:24
Terah	205	Abraham	70	2084	1879	Gen 11:26
Abraham...75 entered Canaan	175	Isaac	100	Abram 100 when	1949	Gen 21:5
Isaac	180	Jacob & Esau	60	Issac born	2049	Gen 25:26
Jacob	147	Joseph	91	2049	2109	See Below
Joseph	110				2200	Gen 50:22

Table 1
AY years from Adam to the Death of Joseph

There are some details that should be clarified. The AY dates given in Table 1 establish that the great flood occurred in AY 1657. A review of many other chronologies will result in a corresponding date of AM 1656. This is because most chronologists choose to start with the first

AY/AM year defined as year zero. We use AY 1 to designate the first year Adam left the Garden of Eden. While not without controversy, we will also equate AY 1 to the *earthly birth year* of Adam. Adam was created by God in His own image (Gen 1:27). A mate was created by God to be with Adam as his wife (Gen 2:18-25). Both Adam and Eve were created to commune with God and live in the Garden of Eden forever; free from sin. Both Adam and Eve were created to live forever in the Paradise of God, and they were sustained by a Tree of Life (Gen 2:9). However, Adam and Eve both fell from grace by eating fruit from the Tree of the Knowledge of Good and Evil (Gen 2:17). The penalty was swift and sure: *in the day that thou eatest thereof, thou shalt surely die* (Gen 2:17). Hence, from the day that Adam and Eve ate of the fruit, they both began to die. So it is with all mankind: when a person is born into this world he/she begins to die. The expulsion of Adam and Eve from the Garden of Eden was both a death to Paradise, and a birth into this world. Hence, as in most modern lifespan designations the first year of Adam's life after he was expunged from the Garden of Eden is called his *birth year*. This is in no way a conflict with his *creation year*, which is not given in the Holy Writ. So, when Adam had a son called Seth at age 130; this was in year AY 131. Other Chronologies which do not use this convention will differ by one year. Most use a common count of years called AM years. Others may significantly differ from Table 1 if the AY/AM count is started before Adam and Eve were cast out of Eden. We reject the arbitrary choice of any other starting date because there is no Biblical basis for establishing any year other when Adam left the Garden of Eden and was *born* into the world. However, it should be clearly understood that AY (AM) dates are strictly for incrementing time in terms of years elapsed to some point in time at which a unique biblical event marked by a unique AY date can be absolutely associated to a Julian calendar date. Once that is achieved, all other calendar dates can be assigned to AY/AM dates both forward and backward through time. Hence, whether one begins with AY=1 or AY=0 or any other number is a matter of choice and nothing else. We will determine the AY dates for every major Biblical event and later recover the calendar year for all AY years/events.

A second major difference in AY/AM dates is often due to the age at which Terah fathered Abram (Abraham). The controversy revolves around which version of the Holy Bible is used to establish this event. The King James Authorized Bible seems to indicate that Terah was 70 years old when Abram was born (Gen 11:26). This was in the year AY 1879. The standard Masoretic text of the Hebrew Bible places the birth of Abraham when Terah was 120 years old. To confound the issue, the translated Greek Septuagint and the Samaritan version of the Torah both have different dates: All agree that Abraham died at the age of 175. The choice of Terah being 70 or 120 years old when Abram is born, coupled with the convention of whether the AY dates start at Creation or departure from the Garden of Eden, can cause significant chronological counting differences.

A major consideration of whether to use 70 or 120 as the age of Abram's birth is the subsequent impact on when Methuselah died. All scholars agree that Methuselah died prior to the flood. Methuselah died at age 969, and using Terah's age as 70 when Abram was born then Methuselah died in AY 1657, which was the year of the great flood. One objection turns on the observation that if Methuselah died in the year of the flood, then he might have drown…. and that could never be true. The problem does not rest on using the age of Terah as 70 at Abram's birth, but is in failing to properly discern the biblical account of the flood and when it occurred. It doesn't matter if Nisan 1 or Tishri 1 is used to start the biblical year of the flood, either Jewish calendar date would cause the perceived problem. In this chronology, we have argued that Tishri 1 (September/October) is the correct calendar date to begin both AY and ancient Jewish years, so we will reference that as the point of departure. In Gen 7:11 we are told that the rains came on the 17th day of the 2cd month; 7 days after the Lord commanded Noah to load the ark. It is obvious that Methuselah could have died between the 1st day of the 1st month and the 10th day of the 2cd month. Hence, the problem of Methuselah having to die in the year of the flood but before the flood started is resolved. Of course, if Terah is 120 years old when Abram was born then there would be no problem at all. At this point, we will assume that Terah was 70 years old when his son Abram was born, and not 120 years old. We will defer a detailed justification for this age until later in this chapter.

To conclude this discussion, again note in Table 1 that Adam is shown to leave the Garden of Eden in *Year 1,* and this is designated as AY 1. We choose to use the convention that the first year that Adam was cast out of the Garden of Eden was his *birth year into the world.* This is because that while he was in the Garden of Eden, and ate of the Tree of Life; his body would never decay or die. God intended that he would walk and talk with Adam forever (Gen 1:15-17). When Adam sinned, he began to die (Gen 2:17). This is how every man is born of the flesh. From the moment he exits the womb of a woman, his body starts to function and die until the actual time of his death. Consistent with accepted convention, the *birth year of his life* is counted as *Year 0,* not year one. So when Adam had a son Seth at age 130 (Gen 5:3), it was in AY year 131, and not AY year 130. By following the sequence of birth dates recorded in Genesis, and knowing that Moses was 80 years old at the exodus; one can determine that the Exodus occurred in AY 2454. Table 2 depicts the years between when Joseph was sold into slavery by his jealous brothers at age 17 and when the exodus occurred in terms of AY years. The AY date of the exodus is determined as follows.

After being sold into slavery at age 17, scriptures tell us that Joseph was brought before the pharaoh at age 30 and asked to interpret a dream. God showed him the meaning of the dream after all of the Pharaoh's soothsayers had failed. The dream depicted an immediate period of seven years of plenty, followed by seven years of extreme famine (Gen 41:1-48). The Pharaoh was so pleased he put Joseph in charge of all the grain in Egypt, and instructed him to stockpile grain during the seven years of plenty for use in the seven years of famine. In the second year of famine, Joseph's father Jacob (Israel) moved himself and his entire family to Egypt at age 130 (Gen 47:9) in AY 2239. Joseph then divinely became the *kinsman redeemer*, a type of Jesus Christ. Jacob remains in Egypt until he died at age 147 in AY 2256. Joseph dies at age 110 in AY 2310 (Gen 50:26). At this point many

Biblical Event	AY Year
Joseph sold into slavery at age 17	2217
13 Yrs later at age 30 he is called	
before Pharoh (Gen 41:46).............	2230
7 Years of Plenty follow	2237
Followed by 7 by years of famine	2244
Jacob moves to Egypt at age 130 in	
second year of famine..........	2239
Jacob lives for 17 Yrs in Egypt, then dies	
at age 147 [enters at 130, (130 +17)]=147	2256
Joseph lives to age 110, and then dies in Yr	2310
The number of years between	
Josephs death & Moses birth is 64	2374
Moses is 80 years old at the Exodus	2454
Years between when Joseph moved his family to Egypt and the Exodus occurred....	215

Table 2
The AY Year of the Exodus

chronologists falter, since there is no continuing linkage to the Exodus from Egypt. Here we must do some detective work to find the AY Year of the Exodus. The key is found in Gen 12:40-41.

"Now the sojourning of the Children of Israel, who dwelt in Egypt, was 430 years. And it came to pass at the end of the 430 years, even the selfsame day it came to pass, that all the hosts of the Lord went out from the land of Egypt." Exodus 12:40-41.

Paul affirmed this period of time in Gal 3:15-17. The *Children of Israel* is a generic term used for the nation of Israel, starting with Abraham and continuing to those who followed Moses out of Egypt. The 430 years apply to the total sojourn of Abraham and his descendants from when Abraham left Mesopotamia to the Exodus from Egypt. The last day of the 430-year period of time was the same day that the Exodus occurred, which was Nisan 15 on the Hebrew Calendar. This passage might also imply that the starting day of the 490-year period and the day of the Exodus was on the same day of the week: *Thursday*.

The offered chronology clearly shows that the Exodus occurred in AY 2454. It can also be stated with certainty that the Exodus occurred shortly after midnight on Nisan 15 (Note that Hebrew days start and end at 6:00 pm, not at midnight). Hence, we can calculate that the 430-year period started in the Year AY 2024 (AY 2454-430 years). Is this date significant in our chronology? *YES*, it is the year that Abraham answered the call of God to leave Haran at age 75.

"Now the Lord had said onto Abram, get thee out of thy country (Haran), and from thy kindred, and from thy father's house, unto a land that I will show thee (Land of Canaan). And I will make of thee a great nation, and I will bless thee and make thy name great; and thou shalt be a blessing (Gen 12:1-2). So Abram departed, as the Lord had spoken unto him, and Lot went with him, and Lot was seventy and five years old when he departed out of Haran." Genesis 12:4.

So how long did the *Children of Israel* spend in Canaan? That is easily determined. Abraham left Haran at age 75 in AY 2024. Jacob moved the nation of Israel to Egypt in AY 2239. Hence, the nation of Israel spent 215 years in Haran (AY 2239-AY 2024). Since the total sojourn of Israel in both Canaan and Egypt was 430 years, this solves a problem that has long been debated. Israel spent *exactly 215 years in Egypt* (AY 2454 - AY 2239). As a second witness, we can calculate the 215 years spent in Egypt another way. The 430-year period began when Abram was 75 years old. From the call of Abram to the birth of Isaac is 25 years (Gen 12:4). From the birth of Isaac to Jacob's birth is 60 years (Gen 25:26). From Jacob's birth to his death is 147 years (Gen 47:28). From the death of Jacob to the death of Joseph is 54 years (Gen 41:46- Gen 50:22). The total is 286 years. Subtracting 286 from the total of 430 years we obtain 144 years to the Exodus. Note that since Moses was 80 years old at the Exodus, there is (144-80) = 64 years from Joseph's death to the birth of Moses, and 61 years to the birth of Aaron. Now, Jacob came to Egypt with his family and stayed 17 years before his death at age 147 (Gen 47:9, Gen 47:28). Seventeen years to the death of Jacob plus 54 years to the death of Joseph plus 144 years from the death of Joseph to the Exodus totals 215 years. Hence, the sojourn of Abraham and his descendants in Canaan was also 215 years.

Gen 15:16 records that **they** (the seed of Abraham) **will come hither again in the 4th generation**. This implies that the Children of Israel must leave Canaan and then return again. They left Canaan when Jacob came to Egypt with his family. When did they return again? They left at the exodus; which was 215 years later. The four generations were Jacob to Levy; Levy to Kohath;

Kohath to Amran; and Amran to Moses (Gen. 35:23, Exod. 6:16, 6:18, and 6:20). There are two other biblical clues which can now lead to a complete chronology from Adam's departure out of the Garden of Eden to the exodus out of Egypt.

> *"Then he said to Abram: Know certainly that your descendants will be strangers in a land that is not theirs, and will serve them, and they will afflict them four hundred years."*
> Gen 15:13

We have shown that the Israelites spent only 215 years in Canaan, and 215 more years in Egypt. Hence, this length of time (400 years) cannot be equivalent to that period of time (430 years). The key to interpreting this verse is that it pertains to *Abraham's descendants*, and not to Abraham. We now need to notice that Abraham entered the land of Canaan at age 75 (Gen 12:4). He was 86 years old when Ishmael was born to Hagar, but Ishmael was not the child of promise (Gen 17:21). Isaac was the offspring who would begin the line of descendants which would lead to Jesus Christ (Mat 1:2-16). Isaac was born to Sarah when Abraham was 100 years old (Gen 21:5). Many biblical chronologists state that Isaac was weaned at age 5, and that event started the 400 year count in Gen 5:13. The following logic is often stated.

Isaac was born in AY 2049, which was 25 years after Abram left Haran for the land of Canaan. When Isaac is age 5, there was a great feast held in Canaan (Gen 21:8). Ishmael was jealous of Isaac and *scoffed him*. Hearing this, Sarah said to Abraham: *cast out this bondwoman* (Hagar) *and her son (Ishmael) for the son of this bondwoman shall not be heir with my son, even with Isaac* (Gen 21:10). At this point in time, Ishmael lost any claim to his birthright as the oldest son. This event occurred 30 years after Abraham left Haran and it was at this point in time that the 400 year period of time given in Gen 15:13 started. The *seed* referred to in Gen 15:13 and Acts 7:6 is Isaac, and later Jacob; starting when Isaac became heir to the promise when Ishmael was cast out for mocking Isaac (Gen 21:8-10). This turn of events was a fulfillment of Gen 17:21 when God told Abram that Isaac was to be heir to the promises, and not Ishmael. The terminus of the 400 years in Gen 15:13 is the Exodus. This then solves the problem of correctly identifying the 400 year period as part of the 430-year period. Both have the same *terminus ad quem*.

At this point, we need to revisit the birth of Abram (Abraham). As previously discussed, when Terah birthed his son Abram (later called Abraham) it is recorded in the King James Bible that *Terah lived 70 years and begat Abram, Nahor and Haran* (Gen 11:26). But how old was Terah when Abram was born? The KJV text seems to indicate that Abram was born first when Haran was 70 years old, but this is not conclusively stated. In the book of Acts, Stephen stated that *Then he* (Abram) *came out of the land of the Chaldeans* (Mesopotamia); *and dwelt in Charan* (Haran); *and from thence, when his father was dead, he removed him into this land* (Canaan) *wherein you* (Israel) *now dwell* (Acts 7:4). The record of Acts 7:4 seems to indicate that Abraham was already living in Haran when his father died, and when he learned of his death he (Abraham) went to retrieve his body to bury it in Haran. This does not match the belief that Abraham did not leave for Haran until *after* his father died. In Genesis, Moses recorded that *and the days of Terah were 205 years; and Terah died in Haran* (Gen 11:32). Terah did certainly die at the age of 205 and this would be in AY 2084. This might lead one to believe that Abraham did not depart for Haran until his father died. Other scholars have taken Abram to be born when

Terah was age 70: This would make Terah age 145 when Abram left at age 75, and he would have been alive 25 years later when Isaac was born. So what age was Terah when Abram was born? How important is it? Again note that the birth of Abram when Terah was 70 years old or when he was 130 years old is only important for properly liking the birth and death AY dates of a particular chronology. Assuming that Terah was 130 years old at the birth of Abram simply pushes all AY dates after AY 2009 forward 60 AY years. Nevertheless, we would like to have a second witness to confirm whether Abram was born in year AY 2009 or in year AY 2069. Can we find other support to justify the *short chronology*? One source of additional information is the ancient book of Jasher. Jasher is not just one of many non-canonical biblical records; it is mentioned twice in the Old Testament.

"*Is it not written in the Book of Jasher?*"	Josh 10:13
"*Behold, it is written in the Book of Jasher*"	II Sam 1:18

These two references in the KJV seem to lend credibility to the witness of Jasher. The Book of Jasher contains a remarkably detailed record of the generations of the patriarchs from Adam to the death of Joseph. It also contains information not found anywhere else, including the names of other wives and sons. The following statement is interesting: **Terah was 70 years old when he begat Abram** (Jasher 7:51). This is a second witness to the almost identical statement in KJV; **Terah lived 70 years and begat Abram, Nahor and Haran** (Gen 11:26), but it is very specific and unambiguous. We have taken the time to carefully study the Book of Jasher and traced the following sequence of AY years for events which emerge using AY 1879 as the birth date of Abram when his father Haran was 70 years old.

Terah Age	The Book of Jasher	KJV AY Year	Abram's Age	Noah's Age
	Terah Born in................	1879		
70	Terah's age when Abram is born.. [70]	1949	0	892
80	Abram hides for 10 Yrs in a cave from Nimrod................	1959	10	902
80	Sarah is born this same Year................	1959	10	902
119	Abram now moves to Noah's house in Shinar and stays 39 Yrs.........	1998	49	941
120	Abram leaves Noah at age 50, returns to father Terah in Shinar................	1999	50	942
122	Abram stays in Shinar 2 Yrs, at which time Nimrod threatens his life. He moves back to Noah's house................	2001	52	944
122	After one month in Noah's house, Terah comes to see Abram and Abram convinces him to go to Canaan with him.........	2001	52	944
125	But they stop in Haran and remain 3 Yrs.........	2004	55	947
125	After these three Yrs, God appears to Abram for the first time and tells him to move on to Canaan................	2004	55	947
128	Abram & Terah dwell in Canaan for 3 Yrs, then Noah dies at age 950...350 Yrs after the flood occurred. Abram is 58 Yrs old. when Terah returns to Haran................	2007	58	950
140	After 12 more Yrs (15 Yrs in Canaan), God gives all the promised land to Abram........	2019	70	
145	"At that time"...Abram returns to Haran to tell his father Terah...He stays 5 Yrs.........	2024	75	

Section 1

Terah Age		AY Year	Age of Abram	Age of Issac
145	The lord now appears to Abram a second time and says, " 20 years ago I told you to go to Canaan…now you do it". Abram now leaves a SECOND TIME for Canaan. Before leaving he takes Sarah as his wife and convinces his brother Lot to come with him…	2024	75	
169	Abram lives with Lot in Canaan for 24 years, then God institutes the ritual of circumcism..	2048	99	
169	The same Year, the destruction of Sodom and Gomorah occur……………………..	2048	99	
170	One year later, Issac is born…Abram is 100 years old……………………………	2049	100	0
175	Issac becomes the child of promise at age 5 and Terah attends a great feast	2054	105	5
205	Terah dies at age 205 when Issac is 35 years old.He is buried in Haran…………………..	2084	135	35
	Two years later when Issac is 37 years old, the "binding of Issac" occurs………………..	2086	137	37

Section 2

Jacob Age		AY Year	Age of Abram	Age of Issac
	Issac takes a wife (Rebecca) 3 yrs later at age 40………………………	2089	140	40
0	When Issac is 60 yrs old, Rebecca has Jacob & Esau…………………..	2109	160	60
15	15 Yrs later, Abraham dies at age 175……….	2124	175	75
16	1 yr later (Jacob & Esau are 16), Esau goes hunting…he is attacked by Nimrod, and Esau kills Nimrod…Nimrod is 215 yrs old, and has reigned for 185 years…………………	2125		76
18	2 years later, Selah son of Arphaxad dies at age 483 yrs old……………………………	2127		78
50	"at that time", Jacob is sent to the house of Shem where he stays for 32 years………………………………	2159		110
50	"at that time" Shem dies at age 600. Jacob then returns home to Hebron………………….	2159		110

Note ….Shem was born 98 years before the flood, and was 100 years old when Arphaxed was born. (Gen 11:10). He died exactly 500 yrs after the birth of Arphaxed (Gen 11:11)

Section 3

Jacob		AY Year	Age of Joseph	Issac
63	13 years after the death of Shem, Rebecca & Jacob "steal" the birthright from Esau. Jacob and Esau now 63 yrs old……………….	2172		123
64	Ishmael dies one yr later………………….	2173		124
77	Esau vows to kill Jacob, and he flees to Eber's house where he hides for 14 years……………………………	2186		137
77	After hiding for 14 yrs, Jacob finally returns to Hebron but Esau still wants to kill him, so he now flees to Laban's house in Canaan….	2186		137
79	2 yrs later, Eber son of Shem dies at age 464..	2188		139
91	Joseph is born when Jacob is 91 yrs old	2200	0	151
97	Jacob spends 20 yrs at Laban's house. He marries both Leah & Rachel during this period of time. …………………………	2206		157
107	When Jacob is age 107, in 10th yr after leaving Laban's house Leah dies at age 51….	2216		167
108	In the following year, Joseph is sold into Egyptian slavery at age 17……………….	2217	17	168

Note….If Jacob is now age 108, and Joseph is age 17, Jacob had son Joseph at age 91.

Jacob		AY Year	Joseph	Issac
109	At age of 18, he encounters the sexual advances of Potifar's wife. He is accused of attacking her & thrown in prison...............	2218	18	169
120	Issac dies at age 180.................................	2229	29	180
121	Joseph stays in prison for 12 yrs..................	2230	30	
121	At age 30, Joseph is called before the Pharoh to interpret his dreams..................	2230	30	
128	7 Yrs of plenty follow........................	2237	37	
130	After 2 yrs of famine, Jacob moves his entire family to Egypt..........................	2239	39	
135	5 more yrs of famine follow.........................	2244	44	
147	Jacob lives in Egypt for 17 yrs, and then dies. He is 147 yrs old.............................	2256	56	
	Joseph dies at age 110.............................	2310	110	
	Jacob was born in yr 2169. He dies at age 147...in yr (2169+ 147) = 2316			
	Abram leaves Haran at age 75........................	2024		
	430 years later: Exodus occurs.....................	2454		
	Moses was therefore born in........................	2374		
	Joseph died in creation year..........................	2310		
	Years between death of Joseph and birth of Moses........................		64	Years

Note......Creation year 2024 was the SECOND departure of Abram for Canaan and Haran was alive at this time

Jasher Chronology

It was amazing to find that the sequence of events recorded in the book of Jasher between when Terah was born and the exodus occurred exactly coincide with the AY dates independently determined from the KJV records. The Jasher Chronology is therefore accepted as being valid to this study. There are several interesting details that emerge from the Book of Jasher that are not recorded in the KJV narrative, but none contradict the KJV records.

> ➤ Terah was born when Noah was age 822 years old, and Abram was able to learn from him until Noah's death when Abram was age 58.
> ➤ Abram actually stayed in Noah's house for 39 years as a young adult.
> ➤ Abram is told to leave Mesopotamia and go to Canaan at age 70. He leaves but stops in Haran for 5 years.
> ➤ Abram is told a SECOND time to go to Canaan at age 75. This time he leaves with Lot and Sarah. His father Terah worshipped idols: He refuses to go and stays in Haran. Abram is 75 years old when he leaves Haran for Canaan.
> ➤ Terah lives another 60 years and dies in Haran.
> ➤ Acts 7:4 simply records that Abraham moves his body to Canaan and buries him there.
> ➤ Isaac is anointed the child of promise at age 5; not at his weaning ceremony but at a great feast. Isaac is chosen as a result of jealousy by Ishmael, which resulted in his expulsion.
> ➤ Isaac is 60 years old when Jacob and Esau are born.

All indications are that the chronological record, and the sequence of events recorded in the Book of Jasher, can be accepted as authentic when synchronized to the KJV narrative. If this premise is accepted, then Jasher provides much more detail to the KJV chronology. It is particularly interesting to now realize that Abram did not leave for the promised land of Canaan after his father Terah died. Terah died when Abraham was age 135 and Isaac is age 35; which was 60 years after Abram/Abraham left for Canaan. In addition, the age of Terah at the birth of Abram is now firmly established as 70; not 130. It is also interesting to know that God had to tell Abram to leave for the Promised Land *twice* before he finally obeyed His command.

Having firmly established that the exodus took place on Nisan 15 in AY 2454, we are now ready to address the 2cd major epoch of time; the time between when the exodus out of Egypt took place and the 4th year of King Solomon's reign.

Thoughts and
Things………

Chapter 3
Epoch 2
The Exodus out of Egypt to the Fourth
Year of Solomon's Reign

The additional information brought to light by the combined chronologies from the King James Bible and the Book of Jasher seem to conclusively show that the exodus started on Nisan 15 (March/April) in AY 2454. This establishes that the 40-year exile and wanderings in the desert ended on the same day in AY 2494 after all of the males were circumcised. We are now ready to project these dates forward using a remarkable set of biblical clues.

The key biblical passage which can be used to unlock the time which transpired between the exodus from Egypt and the reign of King Solomon is found in a remarkable passage.

> *"And it came to pass in the 480th year after the children of Israel were come out of the land of Egypt, in the fourth year of reign of Solomon's reign over Israel, in the month of Ziv, which is the second month, that he began to build the house of the Lord."*
> I Kings 6:1

The Hebrew calendar referred to in I Kings 6:1 is the Religious Hebrew calendar. Both the Civil and Religious calendars are shown below. The month of *Ziv* referred to in I Kings 6:1 is the ancient Hebrew name for the 2cd month of the Religious calendar, which has the modern name of *Iyar*. Ziv (Iyar) occurs in April or May on both the Julian and Gregorian calendar.

The Religious Calendar				The Civil Calendar			
No.	Name	Days	Months	No.	Name	Days	Months
1	Nisan	30	Mar/April	7	Tishri	30	Sept/Oct
2	Iyar/Ziv	29	April/May	8	Heshvan	29	Oct/Nov
3	Sivan	30	May/June	9	Kislev	30	Nov/Dec
4	Tammuz	29	June/July	10	Tevet	29	Dec/Jan
5	Av	30	July/Aug	11	Shavuot	30	Jan/Feb
6	Elul	29	Aug/Sept	12	Adar	29	Feb/Mar
7	Tishri	30	Sept/Oct	1	Nisan	30	Mar/April
8	Heshvan	29	Oct/Nov	2	Iyar/Ziv	29	April/May
9	Kislev	30	Nov/Dec	3	Sivan	30	May/June
10	Tevet	29	Dec/Jan	4	Tammuz	29	June/July
11	Shavuot	30	Jan/Feb	5	Av	30	July/Aug
12	Adar	29	Feb/Mar	6	Elul	29	Aug/Sept

A month called Adar 2 is added periodically to keep the Hebrew 354 day Lunar Calendar in sync with the 365.2425 day solar calendar. This was likely done in ancient times by observing the barley & wheat in the ear on Nisan 1. Today Adar 2 is inserted 7 times over a 19 year cycle using a set of sophisticated rules.	*The Hebrew Civil Calendar was used from creation until the exodus in AY 2454. At that time God told Moses to renumber the months, referring to Nisan 1 as month number 1. Tishri was referred to as month 7 after the exodus. The names of each month were adopted from the Babylonian calendar after the 70 year exile.*

The scriptural account of I Kings 6:1 has been under fire by non-biblical literalists for over 1500 years. However, it states with authority and without ambiguity that 480 years elapsed between when the children of Israel left Egypt to the fourth year of King Solomon's reign, at which time King Solomon began construction on the first permanent temple of God in Jerusalem. The holy scribe goes on to say exactly when this historical event occurred, in the month of Ziv. Ziv is identified as the second month, which begins in either April or May. Recall that when Moses led the children of Israel out of Egypt, the Lord re-numbered the Jewish months. The first month, the month of new beginnings, was declared to be the Hebrew month of Nisan. Nisan occurs in either March or April on both the ancient Julian and the modern Gregorian calendars. The Seven Holy Feasts of Israel were initiated when God gave the Law to Israel and followed this new calindrical designation. Recall that the first month of the year up until this time began on Tishri 1 (September/October). From the exodus until today, the Hebrew calendar has had two different calendar years. The first is called the *civil year* and runs from Tishri 1 to Tishri 1. The second is the *religious year*, which runs from Nisan 1 to Nisan 1. The biblical student should be aware that in the Holy Scriptures, any reference to a Hebrew year by number after the exodus from Egypt is always numbered from Nisan 1 and not Tishri 1.

The 480-year period of time between the exodus from Egypt and the fourth year of King Solomon contains four sub-periods of time which have caused many a chronographer to stumble and fall. The first sub-period of time is between when the nation of Israel crossed over the River Jordan after the 40-year exodus to when the period of the Judges began. This period of time includes: (1) the rule of Joshua as commander in chief of the nation of Israel from when Moses died until the death of Joshua, (2) a short period of time known as the Period of the Elders, (3) the time of the judges between the 1st judge Othniel and the last judge Samuel, and (4) the time between when Samuel died and the fourth year of the reign of King Solomon. This last period of time initiates the Period of the Kings, which started with Saul and ended 120 years later with the death of King Solomon. The biblical records over these four periods are sometimes confusing and seemingly contradictive, but we will show that these periods of time can all be mapped into the 480 years given in I Kings 6:1. Before we start to unravel this mysterious 480 years, it should be noted that using only the testimony of I Kings 6:1, the AY years from the year that the exodus occurred (AY 2454) can now be extended through the fourth year of King Solomon. The purpose of this chapter is to validate and vindicate the statement of I Kings 6:1 within this framework. The graphic on the next page provides AY year dates for the exodus and the fourth year of King Solomon. This graphic will now be explained in some detail.

Framing the 480 Years

The correct mapping of the 480 years of I Kings 6:1 requires the recognition that the exodus started in March/April of AY 2454 on Nisan 15, but AY years start in September/October and end in September/October. Hence, it is crucial to observe that immediately after leaving Egypt, the *first year after the exodus,* started in March/April of AY 2554 and ended in March/April of AY 2455.

The *second year after the exodus* started in March/April of AY 2455 and ended in March/April of AY 2456. The following graphic shows that the 480th year after the exodus started in March/April of AY 2933 and ended in March/April of AY 2934.

The 480 years of I Kings 6:1 began in March/April on Nisan 15 in AY 2454
AY 2454 started 6 months earlier in Sept/Oct

The 480th year after the exodus began in March/April of AY 2933

Mar/April	2454	2455
		479 Yrs
Mar/April	2932	2933

480th Yr.... Mar/April, 2933-Mar/April, 2934

AY Year....
Sept/Oct, 2933-Sept/Oct, 2934

Construction of the Temple started in month of Ziv(April/May). Hence construction started between 479 yrs, 2 weeks - 479 yrs, 6 weeks after the exodus began. The AY year of 2933 (Sept/Oct - Sept/Oct included the month of Ziv.

March/April, AY 2454 - March/April, AY 2455.......Year 1
March/April, AY 2455 - March/April, AY 2456.......Year 2

March/April, AY 2933 - March/April, AY 2934........Year 480

2cd Month, Ziv (April/May) is in AY 2933...4th Year of Solomon
AY 2933 is Sept/Oct - Sept/Oct

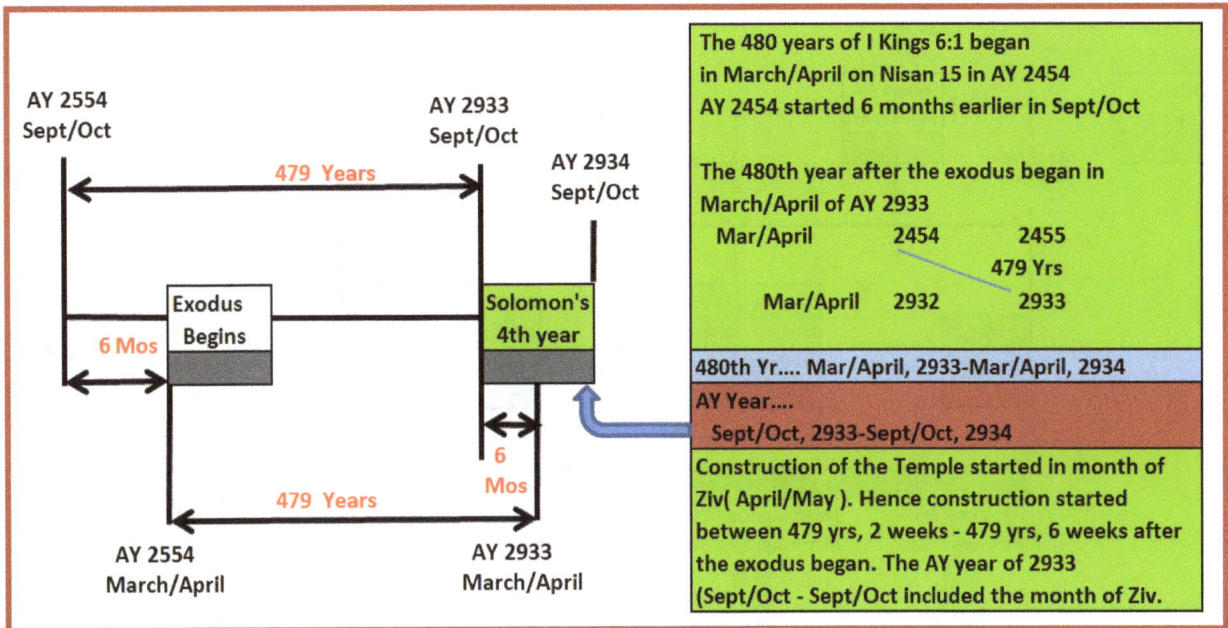

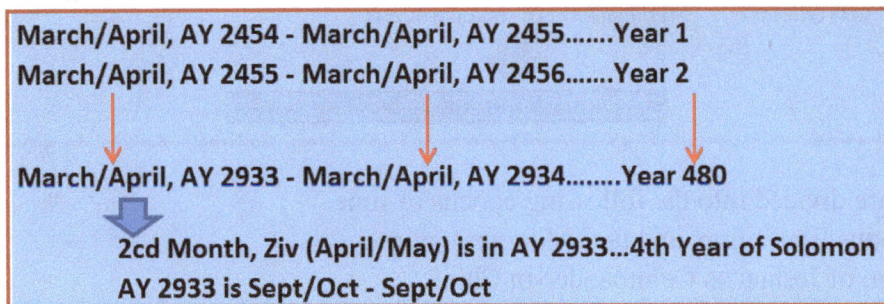

The record of I Kings 6:1 clearly states that Solomon began construction on the 1st temple in the 2cd month of the religious calendar, which is specifically identified as Ziv. From the previous graphics, it is clear that Ziv (April/May) will fall into AY 2933. This fences in the 480 years of I Kings 6:1 as starting in AY 2454 (Sept/Oct-Sept/Oct) and ending in AY 2933 (Sept/Oct-Sept/Oct). It is important to realize that the scribe of I Kings 6:1 is almost certainly referring to a 480 year period which begins in March/April of AY 2454, and ends in the 480th year of AY 2933. It will also be extremely important to the derived chronology to know that this same 480th year after the exodus fell within the 4th year of King Solomon's reign. We will later establish beyond reasonable doubt that King Solomon used a Tishri 1-Tishri 1 regnal year system, which corresponded to our AY years. Finally, note that the total number of actual Nisan 15-Nisan 15 years which passed until Solomon's temple began construction in the 4th year of King Solomon's reign was actually 479 years and less than 6 week's time. The graphic on the next page summarizes these key observations.

AY 2454
Sept/Oct

First AY Year Begins

March/April AY 2554

AY 2455
Sept/Oct

Second AY Year Begins

March/April AY 2555

AY 2456
Sept/Oct

Third AY Year Begins

March/April AY 2556

AY 2933
Sept/Oct

480th AY Year begins

March/April AY 2933

Exodus Begins

1st Year after Exodus ends | 2cd Year after Exodus begins

2cd Year after Exodus ends | 3rd Year after Exodus begins

479th Year after Exodus ends | 480th Year after Exodus begins

Exodus started in March/April of AY 2454

1st Exodus Year: March/April, AY 2454 - March/April, 2455
2cd Exodus Year: Match/April, AY 2455 - March/April, 2456

480th Exodus Year   March/April, AY 2933 - March/April, 2934

Temple started in 2cd Month (April/May, AY 2993)

Temple Started in April/May of 480th AY Year and in the 480th Exodus Year

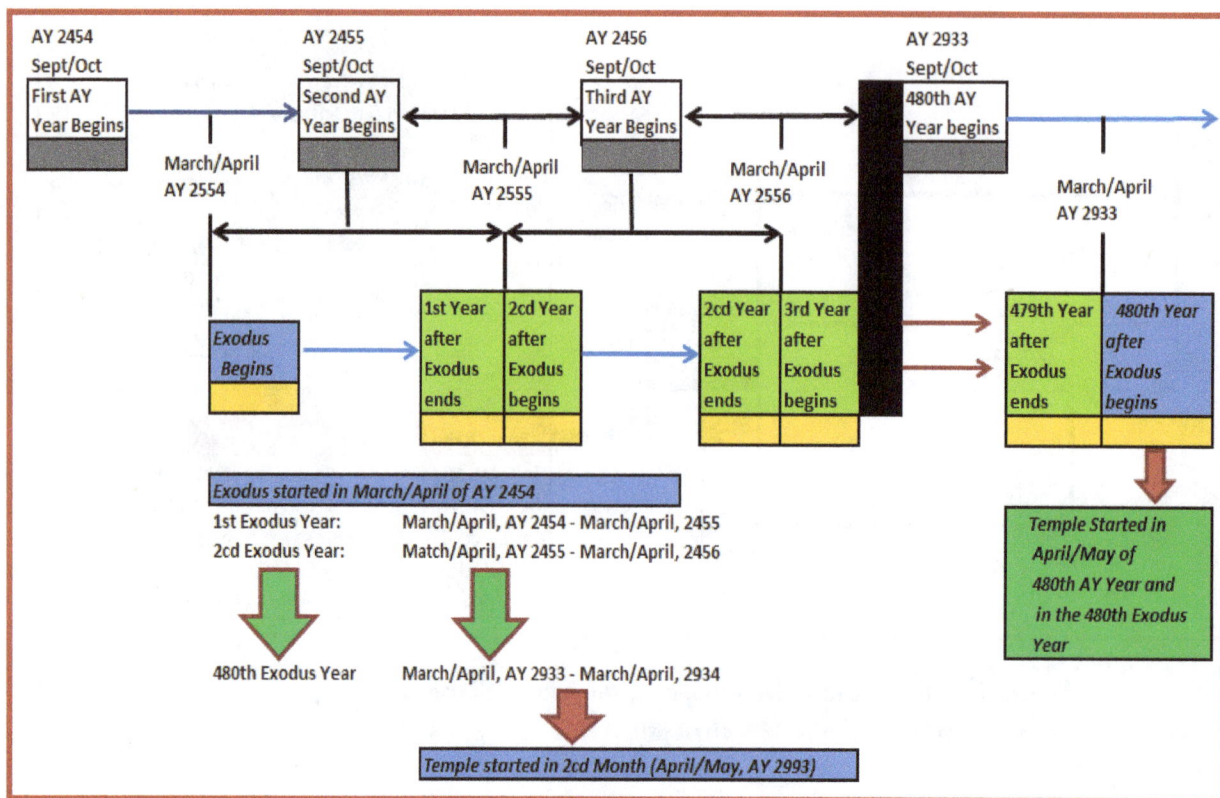

The 480 years are divided into the following epochs of time.

- The exodus from Egypt and the wilderness journey
- The reign of Joshua as Commander-in Chief
- The time of the elders
- The time of the judges
- The rule of King Saul and King David
- The 1st four years of King Solomon

Having shown that the exodus occurred in AY 2454, and Solomon's Temple was started in AY 2933 in the fourth year of King Solomon's reign, were now ready to map out this 480 year period of time. The 480 years between when the exodus took place and the fourth year of Solomon is a period of biblical time that has caused many chronographers to simply throw in the towel and state that this period of time cannot be verified. We will show that is not true. The problem which arises is that if one sequentially sums all of the years listed in the Holy Bible for all of these time periods, one will arrive at almost 600 total years which is 120 years too long. This conundrum is often called a *Gordian knot* which is a *metaphor* for a seemingly intractable problem which can only be solved by a bold stroke (cutting the Gordian knot). We will now demonstrate how this knot can be severed consistent with the biblical records.

The Forty Year Exodus

The biblical records are clear as to how long the exodus from Egypt took from when the children of Israel left Egypt on Nisan 15 until they crossed the Jordan River on Nisan 10. The length of time was only 5 days short of 40 years. The following table provides a summary of the biblical records.

Timeline	Event	Reference
1st Day....Nisan 15	Exodus starts just after midnight	Ex 12:40-42, Num 33:3
47 Day journey	Arrival at Mt Sinai	Ex 19:1
50th day after departure	God speaks the 10 commandments	Ex 20:1-20, Deut 5:22
2nd year, 1st Month, First Day	Tabernacle set up after 7 Months, 3 days Construction	Ex 40:2, 40:17
2nd year, 2nd month, 20th Day	Depart from Mt. Sinai 50 days after tabernacle is completed	Num 10:11
2nd year, 3rd Month, Day 8	Arrive at Kadesh-barnea after a 18 day journey including a 7 day delay to heal Miriam. Spies sent out to Promised Land	Deut 1:2, Num 12:15
2nd year, fourth Month, 18th Day	Spies return. Only Joshua & Caleb give a good report. God condemns them to wander 40 years (total since Exodus) in the wilderness.....One year for each day.	Num 13:25
	Moses stays at Kadesh-barnea for almost 9 Months	Deut 1:46 Deut 2:14
3rd year, 15st Day, 1st Month	Moses departs Kadesh-barnea for 38 years in the Wilderness	Deut 2:14
40th year, 5th Month, Day 1	Aaron dies and is buried on Mt. Hor	Num 33:38
40th year, 12th month, 1st Day	Moses dies and is taken to Mt. Nebo by God. He recites all of the law to Israel before he is taken away. He anoints Joshua as the new leader	Deut 34:1, Deut 34:7-8 Josh 1:1-5
41st year, Month 1, Day 1	Camp at River Jordan....Spies sent out a second time	Deut 34:8 Josh 2:1
41st year, Month 1, Day 10	River Jordan is crossed on Nisan 10 All men circumcised	Josh 4:19 Josh 5:2-5
	Exodus completed....Manna ceases	Josh 5:12
41st year, Month 1, Day 14		

After the death of Moses on Adar 1, Joshua became the leader and commander-in-chief. The full 40 years expired 45 days later on Nisan 14 after all of the men were circumcised. The manna which fed them during their wilderness journey ceased on the next day. Subtracting this 40 years from the 480 year AY total number of years leaves 440 years.

The Reign of Saul, David and Solomon

The exodus lasted 40 years, beginning in March/April of AY 2454 and ending in March/April of AY 2494. Rather than immediately addressing the reign of Joshua as Commander-in-Chief and the time of the elders, we will move to more solid ground: the reigns of Saul, David and Solomon. Samuel was the last judge to reign over Israel, and during his judgeship the people complained to Samuel that they had no king to rule over them as did the other nations. It is interesting and sad that Israel did not want God to intervene in their affairs, but they wanted to be like any other (pagan) nation. Samuel (I Sam 8:1-22) addressed the people and warned them what would happen:

> "*A King would take the sons away from their parents; he would take away their grain and corn; he would give their land to his servants; and he would levy a 10% tax on all their possessions….*" But Israel still said **"Nay, but we will have a king over us"** (I Samuel 8: 10-17).

And so Samuel inquired of God and appointed Saul as their first king. Saul was succeeded by David who reigned 40 years (II Samuel 5:4), and David was succeeded by Solomon who also reigned 40 years (I Kings 11:42). The problem is that nowhere in the Old Testament does it say how long Saul reigned as king; however, in his discourse at Antioch, the apostle Paul said:

> "*…and God gave unto them Saul the son of Cis, a man of the tribe of Benjamin, by the space of 40 years*" Acts 13:21

Paul's ministry was appointed by Christ himself, and in the natural Paul was a learned Jew who was schooled by one of the most respected teachers of his day… *Gamaliel*. There is no reason to doubt Paul's statement. So, we are on solid ground to precede the 40 years of Solomon's reign with the 40-year kingship of David which in turn was preceded by the 40-year reign of Saul. No one doubts that David reigned as king for 40 years, but some scholars have suggested an overlap of one or more regnal years of David with Saul. This will be discussed in some detail later. For now we will assume that Saul reigned 40 years followed by 40 years of David as King.

At first, it appears that the 84 years that elapsed between when Saul was anointed king by Samuel and the end of the 4th year of Solomon's reign can simply be subtracted from 480 years leaving 396 undetermined years. This is true, but confusing and apparent conflicts concerning timing and sequencing surface when the regnal years between the exodus and the first year of David's reign are closely examined. Before proceeding, the issue of how Hebrew kings counted their regnal years need to be addressed.

In Chapter 4 we will examine in detail how the united kingdom of King Solomon split into two parts; the Northern Kingdom which was ruled by the descendents of David and the Southern Kingdom ruled by a series of non-Davidic kings. The issue to be addressed here is: In which month did each Davidic king began and ended their regnal years? In a landmark study, Edwin Theile produced evidence that each king in the Southern Kingdom, all of whom were descendents of King David, started their regnal years on Tishri 1(Sept/Oct) and ended each regnal year on Elul 29 (August/Sept). Although a few scholars disagee (Jones), this has now been widely accepted (Finnegan) and is used in this book. Notice that this being assumed, the regnal years of Southern Kingdom monarchs coincide with AY years as defined in this study. The critical question is when was this system institutionalized? Did it begin with King Saul or King David or King Solomon? First, we should note that God promised David that the House of David was annointed to rule over Judah perpetually as long as Israel existed as a nation. The ultimate fulfillment of this covenant with David will be when David returns to rule over the earthly kingdom of Judah during the 1000 year millennial kingdom. We can therefore safely conjecture that the Tishri 1-Tishri 1 system was started by David when he became king after the death of Saul, and continued uninterrupted until Jerusalem and Israel fell to the Babylonian empire on July 18 in 586 BC. Why would this be a reasonable and logical assumption?

Saul became King of all Israel during the reign of Samuel, after the people said *give us a king so we can be like every other nation* (I Samuel 8:20). We propose that Saul became the first king of Israel on or very near Nisan 1 (March/ April) in AY 2849. His reign lasted for 40 years, at which time he was killed in AY 2889. At that point in time, a power struggle ensued between a son of Saul called Ishbosheth and David (II Samuel 2:8-11. Ten tribes of Judah followed after Ishbosheth, and the tribes of Judah nd Levi followed after David. Ishbosheth became King over the 10 tribes and ruled over the Northern Kingdom for 2 years after Saul's death (II Samuel 2:10). Note that this 2 years was in parallel with the reign of David in the Southern Kingdom of Judah. This same division of the nation of Israel into two kingdoms would occur again after the death of King Solomon and continue for about 255 years until the Northern Kingdom of Israel fell to the Assyrian Empire in AY 3224. It is conjectured that David did not formally establish himself as King of Judah until Tishri 1(Sept/Oct) 6 months later. Perhaps David needed 6 months to assemble the entire nation around him …… perhaps God instructed him to start his reign on Tishri 1. We may never know unless the lost *Books of the Chronicles of the Kings* are someday discovered. In any case, this appears to be when the Tishri 1-Tishri 1 regnal system of the Davidic dynasty was initiated. This conjecture is supported by a very difficult passage of scripture which is seldom addressed. In II Samuel 5:4 the following sequence of events is recorded.

> ***"Then came all the tribes of Israel to David unto Hebron, and spake, saying, Behold, we are thy bone and thy flesh. Also in time past, when Saul was king over us, thou wast he that leddest out and broughtest in Israel: and the LORD said to thee, Thou shalt feed my people Israel, and thou shalt be a captain over Israel. So all the elders of Israel came to the king to Hebron; and king David made a league with them in Hebron before the LORD: and they anointed David king over Israel. David was thirty years old when he began to reign, and he reigned forty years. In Hebron he reigned over Judah seven years and six months: and in Jerusalem he reigned thirty and three years over all Israel and Judah. "*** II Samuel 5: 1-5

II Samuel 5:1-5 completes the story started in II Samuel 2:8-11. After about 2 years, Ishbosheth came to David and proposed that all of the 12 tribes of Israel unify under David. It is implied in II Sam 5:2 that Ishbosheth may have realized that David was annointed by God to rule over His chosen people. In any case, the tribes united in Hebon and David became sole monarch at that time. II Samuel 5:5 clearly states that he (David) reigned over Judah 7 years and 6 months, and in Jerusalem he reigned thirty and three years over all Israel and Judah. Two difficulties immediately arise: (1) David evidently reigned for 7.5 years over *only Judah*… then 33 years over *all 12 tribes*. This straightforward statement must be measured against II Samuel 2:10 which records that Ishbosheth reigned over the 10 Northern tribes for 2 years. The Northern tribes were without a king who reigned in Jerusalem for 7.5 years before all 12 tribes were finally united under King David. For unknown reasons, David simply chose to remain in Hebron for these 7.5 years before moving to Jerusalem. (2) The record of II Samuel 5:1-5 clearly states that King David reigned 40 years, then immediately says that he reigned 40.5 years! Of course, the solution to this impossible situation is not impossible at all. The entire purpose of the previous lengthy, difficult analysis was to show that David transitioned to a Tishri 1-Tishri 1 regnal year system following a 6 month period of time following the death of Saul. Of course, David was functioning as the King of Judah during the entire 40.5 year period of time, but was formally credited with only 40 years of reign in the biblical records since the 6 months between Saul's death and the initiation of a Tishri 1-Tishri 1 regnal year system by David was a transition period. This strange way of counting regnal years is an *accession yrear system*. More on this later. Starting with the first official year of King David's reign on Tishri 1 in AY 2890, this method of recording the official reign of any king in the line of David continued until the Southern Kingdom of Judah fell to the Babylonian empire some 470 years later and was never abandoned. In fact, in Chapter 4 we will see that without using a Tishri 1-Tishri 1 regnal system, a chronology which synchronizes the reign of kings in the Divided Kingdom cannot fall into place. It has already been pointed out that Solomon's temple was started in the 4th year of King Solomon's reign in the 480th year after the exodus. The years between the exodus from Egypt and the 4th year of Solomon's reign are measured from Nisan1(March/April) to Nisan 1(March/April). Fitting I Kings 6:1 into a Tishri 1-Tishri 1 AY year framework is a problem which had to be solved. The following graphic can be used to explain this *mystery*.

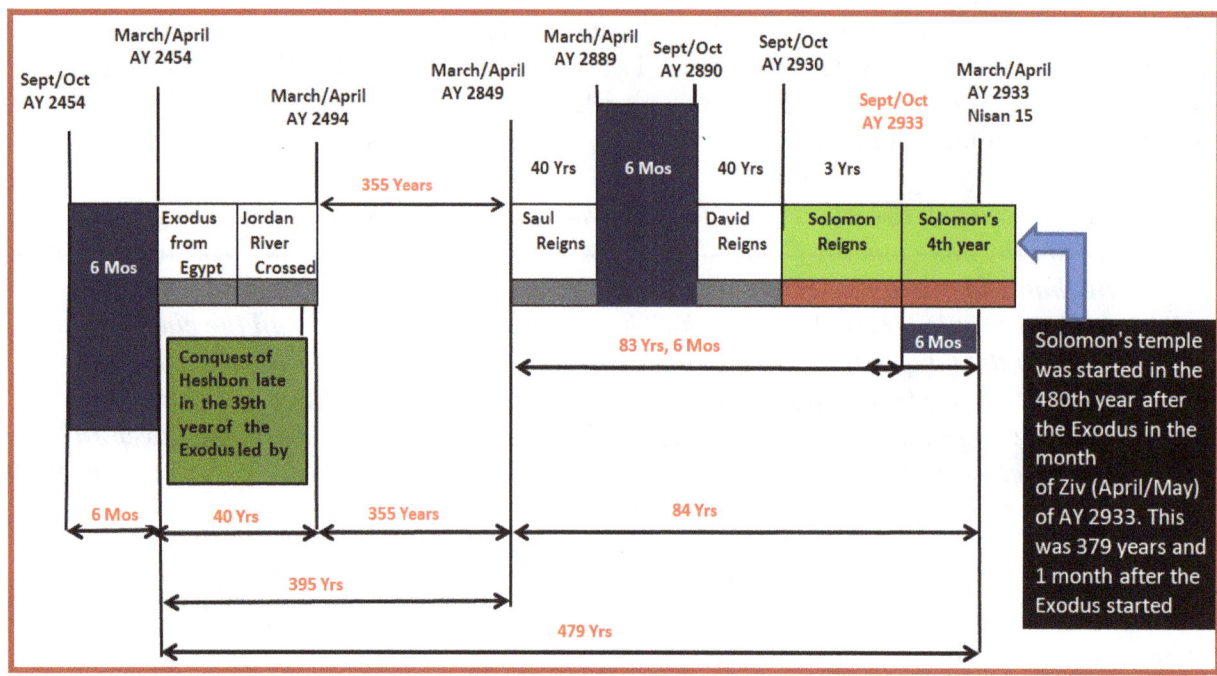

It is *important to note* from this graphic that in mapping the years that are associated with the exodus, the reign of Josua, the time of the elders, the time of the Judges and the reign of Saul, David and Solomon into the 480th year of I Kings 6:1 is initiated on Nisan 15 at the exodus from Egypt, and continues unbroken into the 4th year of King Solomon's reign. This period of time is *entirely contained* within a 480 year set of Tishri 1-Tishri 1 years initiated in AY 2454 and terminating at the end of AY 2933. Refering to the above graphic, 479 full Nisan-Nisan (March/April-March/April) years will elapse until the middle of the 4th year of King Solomon's reign, which begins on Tishri 1 of AY 2933 and continued until Tishri 1 of AY 2934. The temple was started in April/May of King Solomon's 4th year of reign no more than 6 months and 2 weeks after AY 2933 began. The elapsed time from when the children of Israel left Egypt until the temple was started (Nisan 15, AY 2494 *to* Nisan 15, AY 2933) is exactly 479 Religious calendar years, plus 2 weeks in the month of Nisan, plus 4 weeks or less in the month of Ziv. To the knowledge of this author, this is the first time that such a detailed chronology has ever been published. It completely solves the apparent conflict between II Samuel 5:4 and II Samuel 5:6.

Summary & Conclusions: We have shown that the 480 years of I Kings 6:1 refer to Nisan 1-Nisan 1 religious calendar years. The 479 Nisan 1, AY 2454 to the beginning of Nisan 1, AY 2933 years are framed within the ancient Tishri 1, AY 2454 - Tishri 1, AY 2933 Civil Calendar years. The exodus began on Nisan 15 in March/April of AY 2454. The 480th year after the exodus fell in the 4th year of King Solomon's reign, and started on Nisan 15 (March/April) of AY 2933 and ended in March/April of AY 2934. Solomon's temple was started no more than 45 days into the 480th Nisan 1-Nisan 1 exodus year. Between when the exodus began and the end of the 479th Nisan 1-Nisan 1 year we have identified 123 years. This leaves a period of 356 years which must be resolved between when Joshua took over as commander and chief and King Saul began to reign. Note these are all Nisan 15 - Nisan 15 years, and are contained within the Tishri 1-Tishri 1 AY years. We will now begin to reduce these 355 years to zero. We will first address the time that Joshua was Commander-and Chief and the time of the elders.

Joshua as Commander-in-Chief and Rule of the Elders

Moses died when he was 120 years old (Deut 31:2, 34:7-8). He died on the first day of the 11th month in the 40th year after leading the children of Israel out of Egypt. He was mourned for 30 days befitting a man of his stature, and then Joshua assumed leadership. Joshua remained the commander and chief of all Israel until his death at the age of 110 years old. At this point, we note that the biblical records are silent as to how old Joshua was when he replaced Moses. However, we are fairly certain that Joshua must have been about 30-50 years of age when the exodus occurred. To determine the history of Joshua, we need to look beyond the Holy Bible. Be sure that this author has no problem obtaining information from non-biblical sources as long as those sources do not create a conflict with the biblical KJV records. A source often used is the Works of Flavius Josephus, a renowned Jewish historian who compiled a massive history of the Jewish nation. His most important works were *The Jewish Wars* (circa 75 AD) and *Antiquities of the Jews* (circa 94 AD). Josephus has been praised as a competent historian, but he has also been widely criticized for his chronological statements. Josephus clearly used a wide variety of written and oral sources for his narratives, and it is not uncommon for him to contradict himself. Nevertheless, his works have stood the test of time as a magnificent and detailed historical record. As with any other non-biblical source, including archeological findings, dates and data need to be examined with scrutiny and compared to the Holy Writ to establish their validity. Josephus makes the statement that Joshua served for 25 years as commander and chief after Moses died, and that he died at the age of 110 (Antiq. 5:1:29). Since Moses died one month shy of a 40-year exodus journey, we can say that Joshua was 45 years old at the exodus and was born circa AY 2468 when Moses was age 35. This is consistent with what we have conjectured about Joshua. In the absence of biblical records, we will accept this information from Josephus. This narrows the 480-year period of time to 415 years. It is now important to break the 25 years of Joshua's leadership down into two parts: (1) the first is how long it took to conquer the land, and (2) the second is when the children of Israel were sent home to their inheritance, and how long Joshua lived after the land was divided.

27

Dividing the Land

We are now ready to prove that under the leadership of Joshua, the land was conquered in just over 6 years. To prove this, we need to do a little *detective work.*

It is amazing how many different time periods (years) have been proposed for Joshua and the army of God to conquer the various nations and kings in the land of Canaan. Of course, the land was never fully conquered, and after the initial period of conquest, the children of Israel became complacent and failed to fully fulfill their destiny. The author has seen estimates ranging from five years to more than 40 years required to conquer the land, divide the land among the 11 tribes (the Levites got no land inheritance), and the subsequent settling and working of the land. If carefully studied, the biblical record is quite clear on how long this actually took. Looking at the previous chronology of the exodus, we can trace the main events of the exodus from Egypt. The time period required to conquer the land of Canaan can also be determined with scriptural help. Moses led the nation of Israel out of Egyptian bondage starting shortly after midnight (Exodus 12:29-30) on Nisan 15, a Thursday in AY 2454. This was the first day of the *Feast of Unleavened Bread* (Ex 12:17). They crossed the Red Sea seven days later and emerged a new, free nation (a type of rebirth which was a shadow and type of our Lord's resurrection). On the 47th day after they left Egypt, they arrived at Mt. Sinai and on the 50th day (Exodus 19:1) God gave them the law (a shadow and type of when the New Covenant was ratified as the Holy Spirit fell on the day of *Pentecost*). The tabernacle was finished on the 20th day of the second month in the second year after the exodus, and on that day Moses and the children of Israel departed for the Promised Land. They arrived at Kadesh-barnea one year, two months and 15 days after leaving Egypt (Num 10:11). The journey from Mt. Sinai took 40 days, including a seven-day delay for Miriam to be cleansed (Num 12:15). Moses immediately sent 12 men to spy the land (Lev 13:2-3), and after 40 more days they returned. Upon their return, 10 of the spies gave a bad report, and only Joshua and Caleb gave a good report (Num 13:25-33). In one of the most tragic events in biblical history, the 10 spies who gave the bad report were killed by a plague, the Lord sentenced the nation of Israel to wander 38 more years in the wilderness (Deut 2:7), and none of the generation that rebelled were allowed to see the Promised Land (Num 26:64-65). Only Joshua and Caleb were declared worthy to enter Canaan of all those who were at Kadesh-barnea (Num 14:22-24, 30, 37-38, Deut 1:1-38). This is a stark testimony to anyone who refuses to trust in the Lord and not respond to a sacred calling. Moses stayed at Kadesh-barnea for about eight months and five days (Deut 2:14). He finally departed on or near the first day of the third year after leaving Egypt (Deut. 2:13). He then led the nation of Israel through the wilderness for 38 more years. In the 40th year, on the first day of the 12th month, Moses gathered all the people to him. He reviewed all of the events that had transpired since they had left Egypt, and he read all of the Law. Moses was 120 years old on that very day (Deut 31:1-2). Having been instructed by God, he inaugurated Joshua as the new commander-in-chief (Deut 31:23), recorded the law in a *book* (Deut 31:24), and was then taken to Mt. Nebo by God before Israel ever entered the Promised Land (Deut 32: 48-50). The entire nation of Israel wept for 30 days (Deut 34:8) and on Nisan 1; exactly 39 years 11 months and 15 days after leaving Egypt, they broke camp and prepared to cross the River Jordan. They crossed the River Jordan, Joshua circumcised every male, and then they pitched camp at Gilgal on Nisan 14. This was exactly 40 years after leaving Egypt (Josh 5:1-12). Manna ceased the next day (Nisan 15) and a short time later Joshua began the conquest of Canaan at Jericho (Josh 5:12-15, Josh 6).

It was necessary to examine in detail the exodus journey to establish how long it would take Joshua and his army to conquer the land. The duration of the conquest, which terminated in a division of the Promised Land, is determined as follows.

Joshua, Caleb and 10 other men were sent to spy on the enemy one year two months and 15 days after leaving Egypt. They were gone for 40 days, and returned one year three months and 25 days after leaving Egypt. Most chronologists stumble on this point, but after God passed judgment on the nation of Israel, Moses remained at Kadesh-barnea for eight months and five days. At this point, Moses broke camp and began 38 additional years wandering in the wilderness. When Caleb was sent to spy the land, he was 40 years old. Caleb said:

> ***"I was 40 years old when Moses the servant of the Lord sent me from Kadesh-barnea to spy out the land."*** Josh 14:7.

We now move forward to the division of Canaan by Joshua.

> ***"So Joshua conquered all the land: the mountain country and the lowland and the wilderness slopes, and all their kings, he left none remaining, but utterly destroyed all that breathed, as the Lord of Israel had commanded. Then Joshua returned, and all Israel with him, to the camp at Gilgal (Josh 10:43). So Joshua took the whole land, according to all that the Lord had said to Moses; and Joshua gave it as an inheritance to Israel, according to their divisions by tribes. Then the land rested from war."***
> Joshua 11:25

Note carefully that the tribes did not inherit the land until this point in time. In the book of Numbers, the Lord's instructions are given as to when the land was to be divided and inherited by the tribes of Israel.

> ***"Speak to the children of Israel, and say to them: When you have crossed the Jordan into the land of Canaan… you shall dispossess the inhabitants of the land and dwell in it…and (then) you shall divide the land by lot, as an inheritance among your families."***
> Num 33:51-54.

God gave these instructions for possessing the land just before Joshua crossed the River Jordan. Many chronographers have assumed, based upon this passage, that this first year in the land was a Jubilee or Sabbatical year. Nowhere is this implied in these instructions. The land was not to be inherited until (1) the land was conquered, and (2) the land was divided by lots. When was the land divided? Chapter 13 in the book of Joshua is dedicated to a detailed account of how the land was to be divided. At that time: ***"Joshua was old*** (91 or 92 years old), ***and advanced in years"*** (Josh 13:1). The narrative continues as the Lord admonishes Joshua for not fully completing the conquest (Josh 13:2-5). God then said: ***"I will drive (all of them) out before the children of Israel; only divide it by lot to Israel as I have commanded you"*** (Josh 13:6). Here is another great object lesson and the propitiation of grace. Even though we are weak and sometimes falter, when God has a plan he will bring it to completion. When the Lord calls, he will see you through. So Joshua divided the land as recorded in Joshua 13:8-33 and Joshua 14:1-5. But now something unusual happens. Caleb approaches Joshua and says:

"Then the children of Judah came unto Joshua in Gilgal: and Caleb the son of Jephunneh the Kenezite said unto him, Thou knowest the thing that the LORD said unto Moses the man of God concerning me and thee in Kadesh-barnea. Forty years old was I when Moses the servant of the LORD sent me from Kadesh-barnea to spy out the land; and I brought him word again as it was in mine heart. Nevertheless my brethren that went up with me made the heart of the people melt: but I wholly followed the LORD my God. And Moses sware on that day, saying, Surely the land whereon thy feet have trodden shall be thine inheritance, and thy children's for ever, because thou hast wholly followed the LORD my God.   Josh 14:6-10*

Can you just imagine this confrontation between Caleb and Joshua, who was the most powerful and respected man in all of Israel. Caleb is saying to Joshua, *Moses promised me a piece of this land and I want it now!* Caleb now provides the following justification.

"And now, behold, the Lord has kept me alive, as he said, these forty and five years, even since the LORD spake this word unto Moses, while the children of Israel wandered in the wilderness: and now, lo, I am this day fourscore and five years old."
Josh 14:10-11

There you have it! On that very day, Caleb is 85 years old. It is now time to do a little math.

➤ Caleb and Joshua were sent to spy on the land one year, three months, and 25 days after leaving Egypt.

➤ Caleb was 40 years old when he was sent to spy on the land

➤ It is 45 years later when Caleb has his confrontation with Joshua

➤ Caleb is *exactly* 85 years old when he confronts Joshua

➤ The time between when Caleb and Joshua were sent to spy the land to when the River Jordan was crossed is 38 years, eight months and five days.

➤ The children of Israel remained at Kadesh–barnea for eight months and five days before leaving on a 38-year wilderness journey   (Deut 2:14)

➤ Joshua and Caleb were the only people remaining alive to pass on eye-witness accounts of the miracles in Egypt, the manna which fell from heaven and the parting of the red sea

If Caleb had *just turned* 40 years old when he returned from spying the land, and was promised an inheritance by Moses, there were 45 years between this event and his confrontation with Joshua. This leaves six years, three months and 25 days that were spent conquering the land. If, in fact Caleb was 40 years old when he was sent to spy the land, but *one day later* he would be 41 years old, the conquest of the land would have taken five years, three months and 25 days. We do not know exactly how old Caleb was when he was sent to spy the land, but following these scriptural clues we can state with certainty that the *average time* to conquer the land can be determined as five years, nine months and 25 days. The exact number of years and months that it took Joshua and his armies to conquer the land to the point where it could be divided among the 11 tribes of Israel (The Levites received no land inheritance) will probably never be known with certainty. However, based upon careful examination of the Biblical records, we can assert with certainty that it took less than 7 years. The following graphic gives a snapshot of the years between the exodus and when the land was divided.

5 Yrs, 3 Months, 25 days ≤ Time to Conquer the Land ≤ 6 Yrs, 3 Months, 25 days

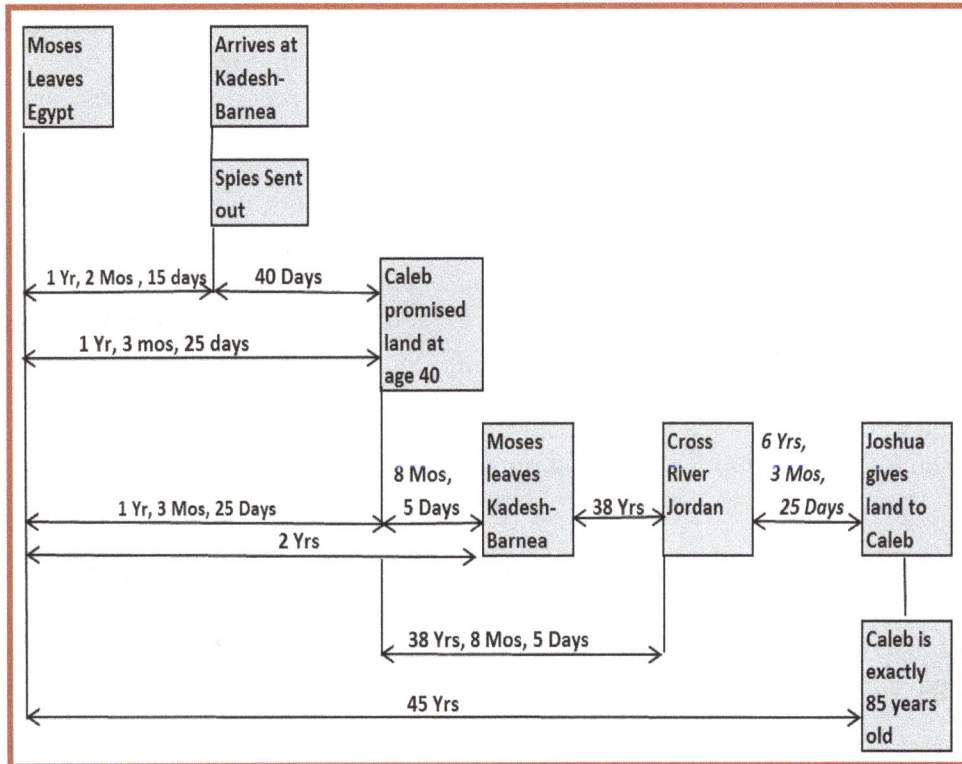

We will now show that it is likely that in the late spring or early summer of AY 2500 was the AY year in which the land was divided and inherited. The Jordan River was crossed in AY 2494 and the conquest of the land was started in the same year. We have shown that conquering the land took a minimum of about five years, three months, 25 days and a maximum of about six years, three months and 25 days. The shortest and longest time periods yield an average of about five years and nine months. It is my belief that the land took about six years to conquer after looking at all the facts. Six years from March/April of AY 2494 would bring us to March/April of AY 2500.

After Joshua gathered all of his armies to himself, he moved the ark to a permanent home which was constructed in Shiloh, and also built himself a house. Joshua also surveyed and mapped the Promised Land by sending out representatives from each tribe. The land was then divided by lots in late spring or early summer of AY 2500. At that point in time, the tribes would have finally inherited the land as God had promised; they would now return home and start to work (plant) the land. Of course, there was never an end to wars because of Israel's rebellion. But God's promise had been fulfilled under Joshua. It is now almost certain that the conquest and division of the land and the planting took just less than God's number of completeness - seven years. It was not the number of completeness, because the children of Israel never fully possessed all of the land that God gave to them. The following facts can be recovered from this investigation. Recall that all AY years start on Tishri 1 (September/October) but the land was conquered starting in the spring (Nisan 15, March/April). The following facts are now available.

- ➤ The exodus began on Nisan 15, AY 2454 (March/April of 1490 BC)
- ➤ One year, two months and 15 days later the children of Israel camped near the promised land at Kadesh barnea and Moses sent 12 men out to spy the land

- ➤ Because of disbelief that the Lord God would carry them to victory in the land of promise, God punished the nation of Israel by forcing them to wander in the wilderness for an additional 38 years after the spies delivered a bad report and Moses camped in Kadesh barnea another 8 months and 5 days

- ➤ The exodus lasted exactly 40 years, including 5 days across the Jordan river
  Nisan 15 (Mar/April: AY 2454 - Nisan 14(Mar/April): AY 2494

- ➤ Out of all the adults that left Egypt in AY 2454, only Joshua and Caleb were allowed to cross the River Jordan after a 40 year exile in the wilderness

- ➤ Conquest of the land took less than seven years: 5 years, 3 months and 25 days minimum ; 6 years, 3 months and 25 days maximum; and an average of 5 years, 9 months and 25 days. In all likelihood, it probably took just over 6 years.

- ➤ All of the tribes were called to Shiloh by Joshua: (1) The entire land of Canaan was visited, surveyed and assessed by a group of men chosen by Joshua, (2) A permanent tabernacle was constructed for the Ark of the Covenant, and (3) Joshua read all of the law and gave final instructions to the people.

- ➤ The land was divided in the late spring or early summer of AY 2500

- ➤ The tribes of Israel inherited the land and returned home. The land was prepared for cultivation and the first seed was sown. The first Sabbatical year count started on Sept/Oct of the first year back in the land, which was AY 2501

- ➤ The first Sabbatical year started 6 years later in AY 2507. The first Jubilee year was 50 years later in AY 2550

We are now confident that if Joshua did rule for 25 years after replacing Moses, that period of time was divided into six years and 19 years, narrowing the gap in time between when Joshua died to the first year of King Saul to 330 years. After Joshua, there was a period of time during which the Elders provided leadership. This period of time is not given in the Holy records, but again the ancient Book of Jasher and Josephus both state that the time of the elders was 20 years.

There is no way to validate this period of time, but it is not at all unbelievable. Subtracting the 20 years of elders narrows the gap to 310 years. The following diagram shows what has been determined and how it relates to the 480-year prophecy of I Kings 6:1.

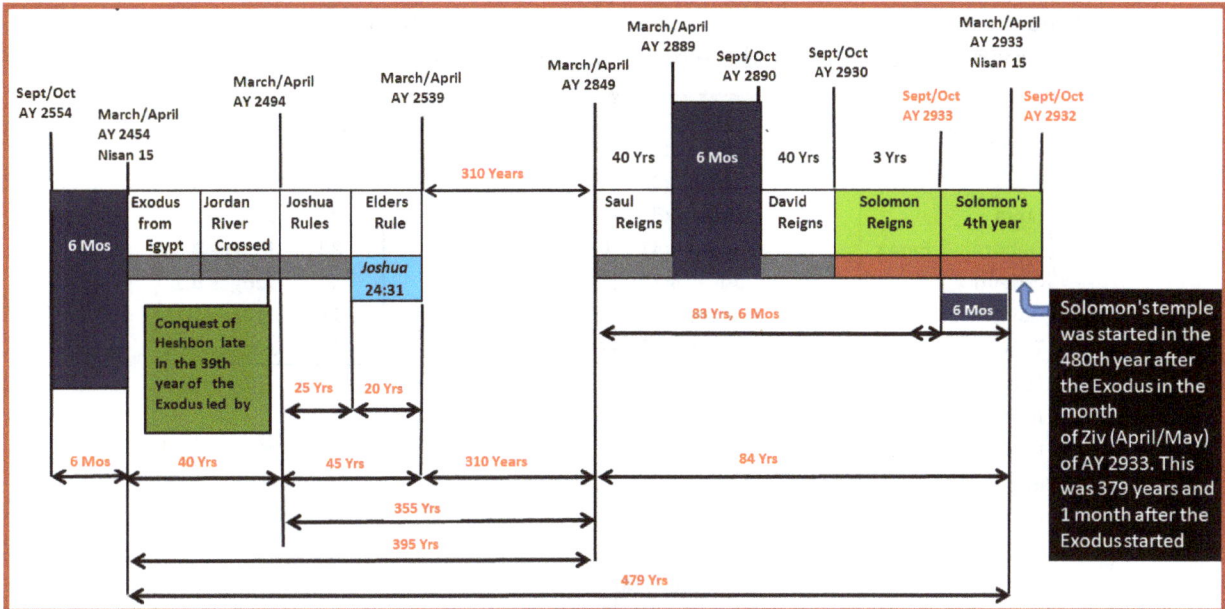

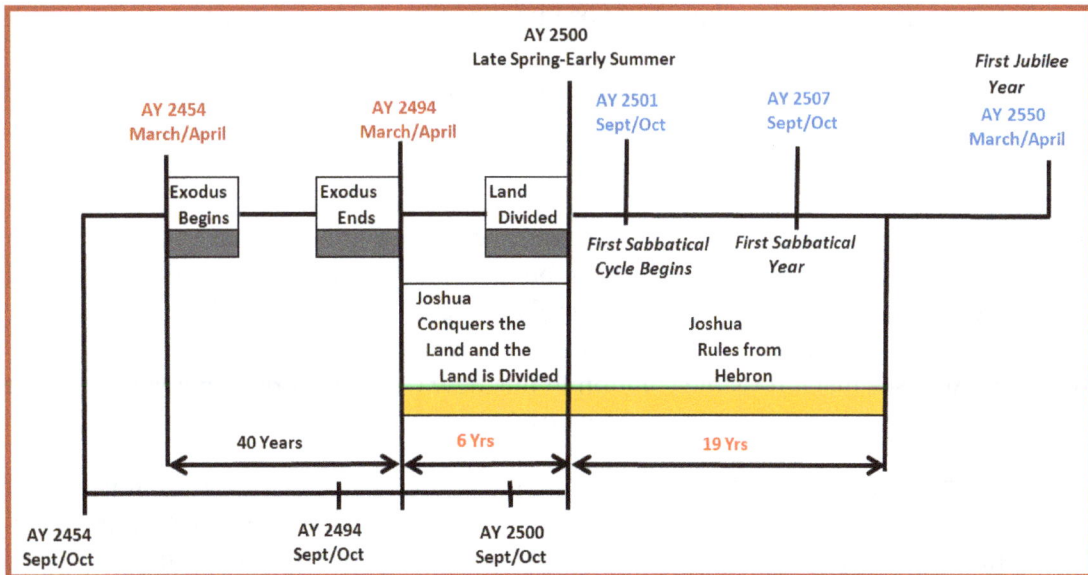

At this point in time, the nation of Israel was given Judges by God. However, the period of the Judges has proved to be a quagmire for everyone who has tried to map it out. We will now demonstrate how the period of the judges fits into the 310 remaining years.

The Period of the Judges

The period of the judges took place following rule of the elders and ended with Samuel during the reign of King Saul. The Judges must fit into a 310 year time period as previously shown. These 310 years consist entirely of the period of time during which the Judges served, and periods of time during which Israel was oppressed by other nations or tribes. The following table provides a summary of the Judges and the periods of oppression.

Judges	Years		Oppressions	Years	
Othniel	40	Judges 3:11	Mesopotamia-Cushan	8	Judges 3:8
Ehud	80	Judges 3:30	Moabites-Eglon	18	Judges 3:14
Jabin	20	Judges 4:3	Philistines	??	Judges 3:31
Deborah & Barak	40	Judges 5:31	Canaanites-Jabin	20	Judges 4:3
Gideon	40	Judges 8:28	Midianites	7	Judges 6:1
Abimelech	3	Judges 9:22	Philistines-Ammon	18	Judges 10:8
Tola	23	Judges 10:2	Philistines	40	Judges 13:1
Jair	22	Judges 10:3	*Total Years:*	111	
Jephthah	6	Judges 12:7			
Ibzan	7	Judges 12:9			
Elon	10	Judges 12:11			
Abdon	8	Judges 12:14			
Samson	20	Judges 15:20			
Eli	40	I Samuel 4:18			
Samuel	20	I Samuel 7:2			
Total Years:	379				

The biblical record records 379 years that the judges reigned, and at least 111 years that the nation of Israel was under foreign oppression. The problem with the recorded lengths of kings and oppressions is obvious; the remaining gap in time is only 310 years but the total years recorded is 490. At this point, most non-literal biblical scholars simply throw in the towel and declare that there are multiple scribal errors or that the Bible is simply wrong.

The most common line of biblical compromise is to: (1) assume that the 80-year reign of Ehud is in error and should be only eight years, and/or (2) Postulate that the 111 years of oppression overlap and run in parallel with the rule of one or more judges. The first compromise is rejected because this study begins with the assumption that durations of time given in the Holy Scripture of the King James Bible are without error. The second compromise can have merit if by carefully studying the scriptures such an assumption can be justified. For those who believe that the Holy Bible is without error, this type of dilemma simply presents itself as something that can only be solved by carefully studying the inerrant word of God and seeking justifiable or verifiable solutions. We will see that a possible solution to this new *Gordian knot* is that some but not all of the oppressions occur in parallel with the reign of Judges.

By carefully reading Judges 3:7-8 and comparing these verses to Judges 3:9-10, it is clear that the eight-year period of oppression under Cushan and Mesopotamia took place in the latter years of the Elders' 20-year reign. We can therefore subtract these years from the total of 111 years of foreign oppression. In Judges 3:9-10, the Lord raised up a deliverer (Judge) called Othniel who defeated the Mesopotamians and ruled for 40 years. At this point, a series of Judges and oppressing nations is introduced between Judges 3:12 and Judges 12:6. Between these two biblical verses there are seven Judges and four periods of oppression. The Judges are Othniel (40 years), Ehud (80 years), Deborah (40 years), Gideon (40 years), Abimelech (three years), Tola (23 years), and Jair (22 years). This is a total of 248 years. The oppressions are the Moabites (18 years), the Canaanites (20 years), the Midianites (7 years), and the Philistines (18 years). This is a total of 63 years. This particular sequence of Judges and oppressors were not chosen arbitrarily. In Judges 11:1, we are told that immediately following the 18 years of Ammonite oppression (Judges 10:8) the people of Israel sought a deliverer. The deliverer is found in Judges 11:1-11, and the man was Jephthah of Gilead. The people approached Jephthah, and as recorded in Judges 11:6-11, he agreed to lead a rebellion and immediately sent messengers to the King of Ammon. Jephthah inquired: ***"Why have you come to fight against me in my land?"*** (Judges 11:12). The Ammonite oppressor replied: ***"Because Israel took away my land when they came up out of Egypt; from the Ammon to the Jabbok, and to the Jordan River"*** (Judges 11:13). Jephthah responded in an authoritative and remarkable way; he corrected the King of Ammon and said that Israel did *not* take away the land of Ammon or Moab (Judges 11:15). A careful study of the scriptures shows that Jephthah was correct. Israel did not war against anyone in the kingdom of the *Ammonite*s, but bypassed them and made war against the *Ammorites (*Judges 15-22*)*. Jephthah then made a remarkable statement.

> ***"While Israel dwelt in Heshbon*** *(Ammorite territory)* ***and its villages, in Aroer and its villages, and in all the cities along the banks of the Arnon*** *(River)*, ***for three hundred years, why did you not recover them within that time?"***   Judges 11:26

Jephthah said without any hesitation or ambiguity, that Israel had been in the land of *Ammon* for 300 years, and asked why they had not questioned their right to this land for these 300 years. We identify this remarkable statement as an *Assertion of Exactness*. The theological interpretation is one of certainty. Jephthah did not say *about 300 years* or for *almost 300 years*; he said …. *300 years*. Contrast this to an *Assertion of Inexactness* or ambiguity. In Dr. Luke's gospel, he said that Jesus Christ was baptized by John the Baptist at *about the age of 30* (Luke 3:23). This is an *Assertion of Inexactness*. Christ could have been 29 years or more nearing 30, or He could have been 30 years old moving toward age 31. Theologians have almost universally rejected the statement of Jephthah as not being an exact statement, and more than often they declare that he was simply wrong, or the 300 years was a scribal error. In fact, this very statement by the Assertion of Exactness is not only authoritative and correct but it provides the key to unlocking the period of the Judges. If Jephthah is correct, then the 490 years obtained by combining the Judges' time of rule and with the times of oppressions of Israel *demands* that there is an overlap between these epochs of recorded time. *First*, we note that the 300-year assertion of Jephthah begins shortly before Moses and the children of Israel crossed the River Jordan, and ends just before Jephthah advanced upon the Ammonites and defeated them (Judges 11:28-32), which was in the same year he was anointed a Judge (Judges 11:33-12:7). The total period of time recorded in the scriptures for every Judge from the first judge Othniel to Jephthah is 248 years. Othniel (40 years), Ehud (80 years), Deborah & Shagmar (40 years), Gideon (40 years), Abimilech (3 years), Tola (23 years), and Jair (22 years). To this we must add the 25 years that Joshua was commander-in-chief and the 20 years of the elders. This brings the total number of years to 293. In carefully analyzing the 64 years of foreign oppression over this same period of time, we can associate the eight years of Assyrian oppression, the 18 years of Moabite oppression and the 20 years of Canaanite oppression as occurring concurrently with the judges Othniel, Ehud and Deborah. Following the reign of Deborah, a seven-year oppression of the Midianites occurred before Gideon became a judge. Adding the seven years of Mideonite oppression to the 293 years of Judges previously identified, the total number of sequential years is 300 years!!

Having successfully confirmed that the 300 years of Jephthah (Judges 11: 26) can be mapped into a meaningful chronological sequence, a period of time equal to (300-45) = 255 years can now be subtracted from the previously undetermined time of 310 years. This leaves (310-255) = 55 years of time which must be filled by the Jephthah to the last judge, Samuel. The 55 years of time follows the judgeship of Jair, and is between when Jephthah began his six-year period as a judge, and when Samson ended his 20-year reign as a judge. The 55 years is shown below.

36

Jephthah, Ibzan, Elon, Abdon and Sampson

The Holy Writ leaves us little choice but to sequentially link the period of Jephthah (six years), Ibzan (seven years), Elon (10 years), Abdon (eight years), and Sampson (20 years). This period of time totals 51 years. The real problem is the 40 years of Philistine oppression (Judges 13:1, 15:20, 16:31): However, these 40 years can be located as follows. During the 20-year judgeship of Samson, he began to slide further and further into a womanizing hero. Samson married a Philistine (Judges 14:1-2, 15), then he gave her to one of his companions (Judges 15:6). He turned to a harlot (Samuel 14:1) and finally he fell in love with Delilah, another Philistine woman (Judges 16:4) who sold him out to the Philistines (Judges 16:18). The strength of Samson was in his hair (he was a Nazarite) and having revealed this to Delilah she told the Philistines and they cut off all of his hair (Judges 16:19), put his eyes out (Judges 16:21), and cast him into prison (Judges 16:21). In time, his hair grew out again (Judges 16:22). He was then taken to the Temple of Dagon to *perform* for his captors (Judges 16:25); however, Samson called upon God and found favor. He stationed himself between the two main pillars of the temple, and in a tremendous show of strength he pulled the entire temple down killing more people than he had previously killed in his entire life (Judges 16:29-30). Samson had served as a Judge for 20 years (Judges 16:31).

Clearly, the Philistine oppression was during the 40-year period when Samson reigned, but when did the oppression begin and end? We must carefully study all available clues to move on. The last act of Samson was to pull down the Temple of Dagon. This must have infuriated the Philistines, because it was recorded in I Samuel 4:1-11 that shortly after his death and the destruction of the Temple of Dagon, the Philistines were engaged in a battle with Israel and Israel was losing (I Samuel 4:1-3). So Israel sent for the Ark of the Covenant at Shiloh where it had been since Joshua placed it there just prior to the division of the land. However, God was not pleased because Israel had placed their faith in the ark and not in Him. Hence, the army of Israel was defeated, the Ark of the Covenant captured, and the two sons of Eli; Hophni and Phinehas were slain (I Sam 4:10-11). So here we can clearly determine that Eli was a Judge and a priest during the Philistine oppression. It is significant to note that every Judge but Eli was a warrior and was constantly in battle. Eli was never a warrior-Judge. In fact, it was never written that he went to battle. His primary station and duties were to minister to the people. Now, Samuel had a special relationship to Eli. There was a certain woman from the tribe of Ephraim (I Sam 1:1) who was anointed by God to bear a son called Samuel (I Sam 2:21). After his birth, she dedicated him to the Lord's service and gave him to Eli the priest at a young age (I Samuel 3:1). Eli raised Samuel as his own son (I Sam 3:16).

It is evident that when Samuel heard that the Philistines had slain Hophni and Phinehas, who for all practical purposes were like brothers to Samuel; when he was told that Eli had fallen over backward and died, it is not stretching the imagination to assume that he immediately went to avenge their death. The scriptural accounts seem to indicate that this is exactly what happened. He called the people together in Mizpah and gave an offering to the Lord (I Sam 7:6). Samuel found favor with the Lord, and ***"he pursued them and smote them: And the Philistines came no more against Israel all the days of Samuel"*** (I Sam 7:11-13). Following Samuel's crushing defeat of the Philistines, he became a Judge for 40 years (I Sam 7:17).

The Prophet Eli

The role of Eli in the period of the Judges needs to be discussed. It is clear that Elli emerged just prior to the judgeship of Samuel, who was the last of the judges. Eli was the High Priest of all Israel and lived in Shiloh. Shiloh is where Joshua divided the land among the tribes of Israel, and then built a tabernacle for the Ark of the Covenant where it remained until it was seized by the Philistines in battle. Eli lived there until his death. Recall that Eli was resting on a bench when he was told that his two sons had perished and the ark was taken in a devastating defeat by the Philistines at Eben-ezer. Upon hearing the news, he fell over backward…broke his neck… and he died. According to jewish tradition, Eli died on Iyar 10 (April/May). These events place the death of Eli just before the judgeship of Samuel and just after the death of Sampson in or around 1099-1098 BC (AY 2845-2846). He was 98 years old when he died and had served as high priest for 40 years (I Sam 5:15-18), which means he was 58 years old when he became high priest.

The problem is found in I Samuel 4:18 which says that he had *judged Israel* for 40 years. Recall that when Sampson pulled down the Temple of Dagon, the enraged Philistines attacked Israel…soundly defeated them..and captured the Ark of the Covenant. Eli died shortly after this battle. Samuel then retaliated and destroyed the Philistine army. Eli was not a warrior or a deliverer, but was the High Priest of Israel. Eli would naturally assist Ibzon, Elon, Abdon and Sampson during their period as judges. Of course, Sampson was a womanizer who seldom judged at all. I Sam 14:3 called Eli the *Lord's Priest.* His primary anointed role was as a Levitical High Priest, and he only functioned as a judge when necessary. Eli seldom if ever left Shiloh; hence the 40 years he served as a judge should not be counted sequentially with the anointed judges. Eli simply did not fulfill the description of a judge offered in Judges 2:16-18.

The purpose of this lengthy narrative is to firmly establish three facts: (1) Eli served as a judge for 40 years, but he was primarily a priest, (2) Eli served concurrently with the Philistine oppression, and (3) the Philistine oppression of 40 years ended when Samuel immediately arose after the death of Eli and defeated the Philistines. Since this ended the Philistine oppression, the inescapable fact is that the beginning of the Philistine oppression occurred 40 years before the anointing of Samuel as judge, placing the birth of Eli 98 years earlier. Hence, we can safely superimpose the 40 years of Eli's priesthood and judgeship over the reign of Samson, Abdon, Elon, Ibzan, Jephthah, Jair and Tola. We will therefore not sequentially insert the last 40 years of his life as a judge chosen by God, but rather in parallel with full time judges.

We now need to identify a period of time which has been almost universally ignored in previous studies. Immediately after Samson died, the nation of Israel seemed to be in a state of disbelief and political disarray. Three times (Judges 18:1, 19:1, and 21:25) it was noted that **"*In those days there was no king in Israel: Every man did that which was right in his own eyes.*"** The phrase *in those days* has the force of a relatively short period of time. We do not know how long this period of apostasy without a Judge lasted, but we would be wrong to simply ignore this period of time that was mentioned in three different verses. We have already established that Samuel defeated the Philistines and became a Judge shortly after the death of Levi which followed the death of Samson and seizure of the Ark by the Philistines. It is not likely that the period of time in which there was no ruler over Israel exceeded one year, and this period of time will be added to the timeline immediately preceding the destruction of the Philistines by Samuel and his anointing as a Judge. The diagram on the next page summarizes these findings up until the first year of Samuel's reign. The undetermined period of time remaining is now only (55-52) = 3 years.

March/April AY 2800	March/April AY 2807	March/April AY 2817	March/April AY 2825	March/April AY 2845	March/April AY 2846		
6 Yrs	7 Yrs	10 Yrs	8 Yrs	20 Yrs	1 Yr		40 Year Reign of Saul
Jephthah	Ibzan	Elon	Abdon	Samson	No King in Israel		
Judges 12:7	Judges 12:9	Judges 12:11	Judges 12:14	Judges 16:31	Judges 18:1, 19:1		
			Philistine Opression…. 40 Years Judges 13:1,15:20,16:31				
52 Years						3 Years	40 Years

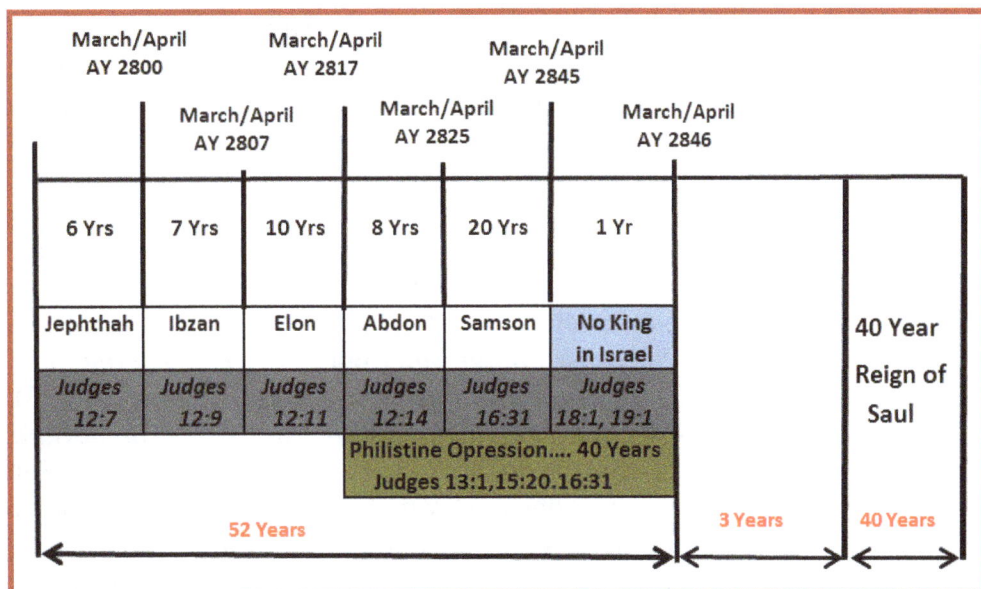

We are now ready to complete a chronology of the 479, Nisan 15-Nisan 15 years that elapsed between the exodus and the end of King Solomon's 3rd year of reign. A formidable *Gordian knot* now appears. The gap in time remaining is only 3 years, and the last remaining judge is Samuel who reigned 30 years. An impossible situation has arisen… or has it?

Samuel to the Fourth Year of King Solomon

At first glance, the fact that there is only 3 years left to allocate to Samuel when Samuel served as a Judge for 30 years appears to create an impossible situation; another *Gordian knot*. However, when the Judgeship of Samuel is carefully investigated, certain facts emerge that can be used to sever that knot. First, if the Holy record is read between when Samuel began to function as a Judge (I Samuel 7:1-14) until he died (I Samuel 25:1), it is crystal clear that the 40-year Judgeship of Samuel overlapped much of King Saul's 40-year reign. First, like his godfather Eli, Samuel was never really interested as serving as a warrior-Judge even though he vanquished the Philistines to avenge the deaths of Hophni and Phinehas, who were like brothers to Samuel. I Samuel 7:15-16 records that Samuel ***"judged Israel all the days of his (remaining) life, and he went from year to year in circuit to Bethel, and Gilgal, and Mizpeh."*** Samuel was what we called in the old western years of the United States a *circuit Judge*. Samuel was already growing old when he became a judge, and ***"when Samuel was old he made his (two) sons judges over Israel"*** (I Samuel 8:1). However, his two sons were wicked (I Samuel 8:3) and the elders of the 12 tribes came to Samuel and bitterly complained (I Samuel 8:3-5). It is interesting that Samuel was only displeased; perhaps he did not want to admit that his two sons had rejected the Lord (I Samuel 8:6). The elders approached Samuel and said: ***"Give us a King"*** (I Samuel 8:6). The Lord told Samuel to listen to the people. The people had rejected God's will, but He instructed Samuel to tell the people exactly what would happen to them (I Samuel 8:7-18) if they wanted a king. Even after the people were told the bad things that would happen to them under a king instead of a theocracy, they said ***"Nay, but we will have a King over us"*** (I Samuel 8:19).

The period of time that the two sons of Samuel functioned as Judges are not even recorded in the Holy Scriptures, and even if we knew how long they served as judges it was a short period of time and was parallel to the Judgeship of Samuel. It is sad that the Lord instructed Samuel to give the people a king if that is what they wanted (I Samuel 8:22), even though Joshua prophesied that it would end in disaster (I Sam 8:10-19). Here is a great object lesson to the churches of today. Religious beliefs and the hearts of people have given way to *itching ears*. Churches are springing up today that give the people what they want; and not what God wants for His people. If the people of God today do not turn away from man-made religion and return to God's laws, the United States of America will perish just as the Northern and Southern Kingdoms which followed King Solomon perished. But we digress. The Lord told Samuel to choose Saul as the first king of Israel (I Samuel 9:1-27). Due to pride, Saul rebelled against the Lord and Samuel later prophesied: ***"because though you (Saul) have rejected the word of the Lord, He (the Lord) hath also rejected you (Saul) from being King"*** (I Samuel 15:23). In a curious and interesting statement, the Lord said (He) ***"regretted that He had made Saul King over Israel"*** (I Samuel 15:35). And so the mantle of the Lord passed from Saul, and Samuel looked elsewhere for a new king. He found one in David, the shepherd boy. ***"And Samuel took the horn of oil, and anointed him (David) in the midst of his brethren: and the spirit of the Lord came upon David from that day forward"*** (I Samuel 16:13). For reasons unknown, Saul was allowed to rule as king for possibly 4-5 years after David was prophesied to be king. During that time there were periods of both friendship and enmity between Saul and David (I Samuel 16:14 - I Samuel 30:31). During the reign of King Saul, we are told that David was protected for an unknown period of time by Samuel (I Samuel 19:18-24), and later by the Philistines (I Sam 27:1) After 40 years as king of Israel, Saul perished in a battle with his old enemy the Philistines; David then became King over Judah (I Samuel 31:1-6).

The purpose of this long narrative is to point out that Samuel served as a Judge parallel with King Saul for a number of years, and Samuel was still judge when David was being pursued by King Saul during the latter years of Saul's reign (I Samuel 21-23). This provides authority for us to stitch together the Judgeship of Samuel primarily within the reign of King Saul. In time Samuel died (I Sam 25:1), and it was not long before the death of Saul: Unfortunately, the Holy Bible does not give a specific month or year. We do know that David fled to the land of the Philistines to avoid an encounter with King Saul, and we do know that David remained in hiding for one year and four months just before Samuel died (I Samuel 27:7; 28:3). In a remarkable incident, a woman prophetess from Endor met with Saul and called the spirit of Samuel forth from the grave to give advice to Saul (I Samuel 28:3-28) as to how to fight the growing Philistine army. The prophetess informed King Saul that ***"the kingdom would be given to David"*** (I Samuel 28:17) but that Saul would be given the hand of God to defeat the Philistines (I Samuel 28:19). Shortly after this, David was run out of the Philistine camp where he had been in hiding (I Samuel 29:1-11). From there, he went to battle and defeated the Amalekites who were oppressing southern Israel (I Samuel 30:1-31). In close proximity to this point in time, King Saul advanced on the Philistine armies in the north and he was killed in battle (I Samuel 31:1-6). Shortly after the death of Saul, David became king of Israel (II Samuel 1:1-27). For some unknown reason, David reigned as king of Israel for seven years and six months in Hebron (II Samuel 2:11); he then moved to Jerusalem where he reigned for 33 years. He began to reign at age 30 and reigned 40 years until his death (II Samuel 5:1-5). It might be noted that while the scriptures seem to hint that David might have co-reigned with Saul, it does not seem likely because Saul and David were enemies for several years before Saul died. Saul would never elevate David to co-regency during the same period of time he was seeking to destroy him.

The hatred between the Northern tribes and King David might explain why David remained in Hebron for several years before moving to Jerusalem. Of course, we do know that both the tribe of Judah and King David were both anointed by Christ, and a covenant was made between David and God that the house of David would reign forever; so the outcome was in hindsight divinely ordained. The House of David will once again rule over Israel during the future 1000-year millennial kingdom. Our conclusion is that Samuel was a sovereign Judge and leader of Israel only 3 years before he anointed Saul as the first king of Israel. He then became a *circuit judge* for 38 more years before his death, with all of these 38 years within the rule of King Saul. After the death of Samuel, Saul only reigned for 2 more years as sovereign King of Israel. The biblical logic of this conclusion rests in comparing I Sam 25:1 with I Sam 27:7. These verses confirm that Samuel died at least 1 year and 4 months before the death of King Saul. It is our conclusion that Samuel died no more than 2 years before Saul was killed in battle at Mt. Gilboa. To the best of our knowledge, this chronological solution has not been previously proposed in the biblical literature.

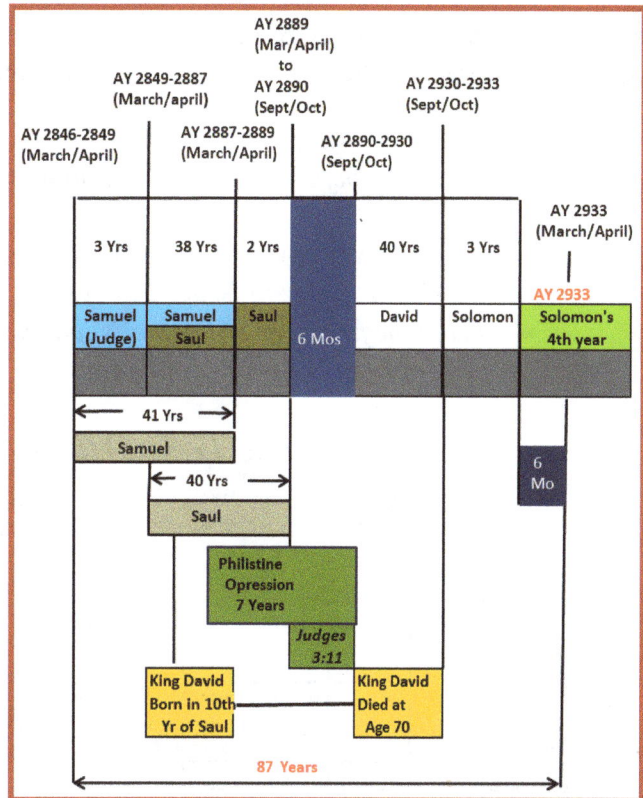

To sum up this lengthy discussion, we conclude that Samuel was the only judge in Judah and Israel for the remaining three years in our chronology. Following that period of time, God told him to give the people a king if that is what they wanted. Here we see another supernatural act of God superimposed upon the role of Samuel choosing Saul. Samuel gathered all of the tribes before him at Mizpeh, and he cast lots to choose the tribe from which the King would be chosen. The lot fell upon the tribe of Benjamin (I Sam 10:20). Samuel then gathered all of the families of Benjamin to him and the family of Matri was chosen by lot. Finally, Saul was chosen by the same process from the family of Matri. The process of choosing by lot was undoubtedly executed by using the Urim and Thummin.

The 4th Year of King Solomon

King Solomon was the third king of Israel following Saul (40 years) and David (40 years). The construction of Solomon's Temple was started *in the 480th year* after the exodus occurred, in the Month of Ziv (April/May), in the 4th year of King Solomon's reign. This was in AY 2933. David was born in the fourth year of Samuel's Judgeship. The following diagram shows the reigns of Samuel, Saul, David, the first three years of King Solomon, and Solomon's fourth year.

41

The time between the start of Samuel's reign and the end of the third year of King Solomon's reign is 86.5 years. Since King Solomon and the Kingdom of Judah followed a Tishri 1-Tishri 1 regnal year system, the 4th year of Solomon's reign did not start until 6 months into AY 2933. The temple was started less than two weeks later in the month of Ziv (April/May).

We are now ready to synthesize the four periods of time which span the 480 years between the exodus from Egypt and the fourth year of King Solomon. The sequence of time periods is:

- *Exodus Journey.... 40 years*
- *From just before the River Jordan was crossed to Jephthah's first year as a Judge ... 300 years*
- *Jephthah's first year of reign to the last year of Samson's reign .... 51 years*
- *No king or judge in Israel ... 1 year*
- *From the first year of Samuel's judgeship to Nisan 15 (March/April) in the 4th year of King Solomon ... 87 years*

Total Time Duration: 479 years

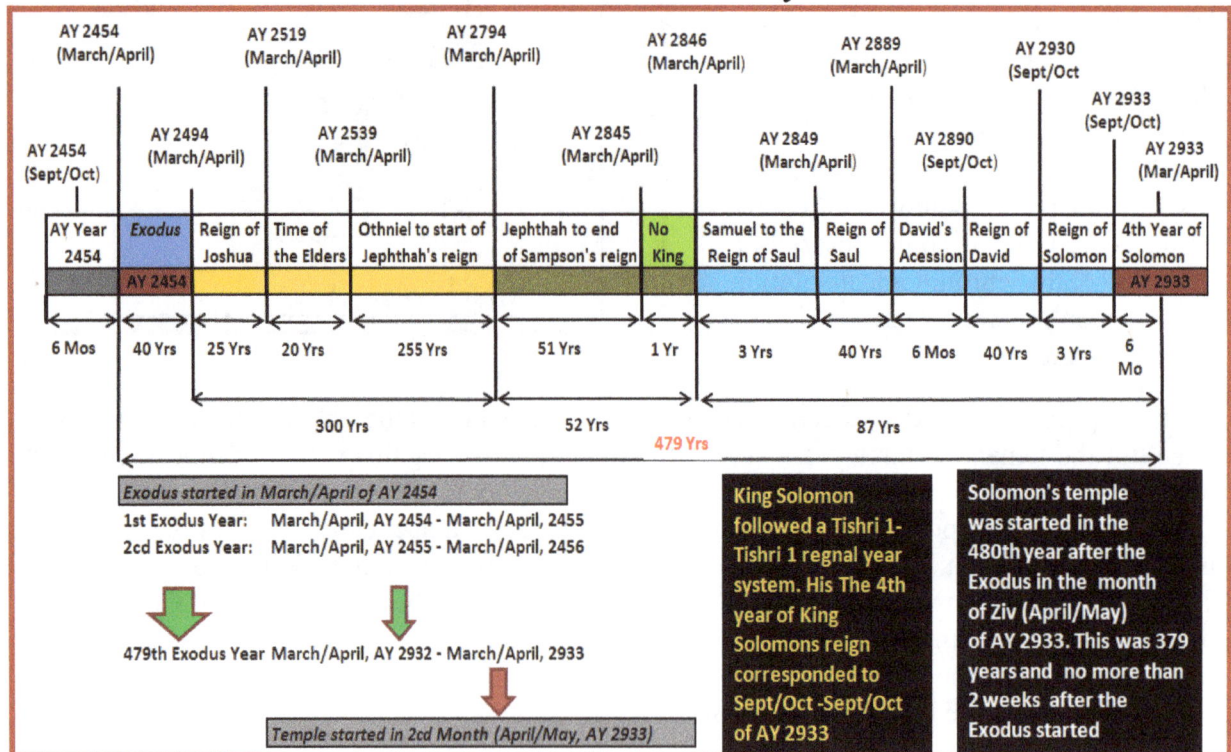

The 480th year after the Exodus from Egypt began in March/April of AY 2933. Solomon's temple was begun in the month of Ziv (April/May) in AY 2933. King Solomon's 4th year of reign was September/October of AY 2933. His first year of reign was therefore in AY 2930, and his last and 40th year of reign was in AY 2969. The total time that actually passed from when the exodus from Egypt started … Nisan 15 (March/April) of AY 2454 until construction on the temple was started in the 4th year of King Solomon's reign ….was no more than 479 years and 6 weeks duration. The temple was started in the 480th year after the exodus from Egypt. Hence, the Holy Record is absolutely correct and without error. The previous graphic summarize these findings.

" And it came to pass in the 480th year after the children of Israel were come out of the land of Egypt, in the fourth year of reign of Solomon's reign over Israel, in the month of Ziv, which is the second month, that he began to build the house of the Lord ".   I Kings 6:1

I Kings 6:1 is proven correct.

Finally, we are in a position to address a highly-controversial statement made by the Apostle Paul in Acts 13:20. Paul was addressing born again Jews in Antioch. On the Sabbath day (Saturday) he arose in the synagogue and said:

> *"Men of Israel, and ye that fear God, give audience. The God of this people of Israel chose our fathers, and exalted the people when they dwelt as strangers in the land of Egypt, and with an high arm brought he them out of it. And about the time of forty years suffered he their manners in the wilderness. And when he had destroyed seven nations in the land of Canaan, he divided their land to them by lot. And after that he gave unto them judges about the space of four hundred and fifty years, until Samuel the prophet."*   Acts 13:15-20

The difficulty is that Paul referred to a period of 490 years which appears to start from the time that the children of Israel dwelt in the land of Egypt until Samuel the prophet. The children of Israel spent 215 years in Egypt; the exodus was 40 years in duration; the land was conquered and divided in about six years; Samuel died 19 years later; the elders ruled for 20 years; and the time of the judges from Othniel to Samuel was 277 years. This totals 577 years. Was Paul wrong? The answer lies in the way the facts seem to be stated and what Paul actually said. Quoting from John Gill's exposition of the bible:

*"The Alexandrian copy and the Vulgate Latin version read this clause in connection with the preceding words, "he divided their land unto them, about the space of four hundred years, and after that he gave unto them judges"; agreeably hereunto the Ethiopic version renders it, "and after four hundred and fifty years, he set over them governors". So that this account respects not the time of the judges, or how long they were, but refers to all that goes before, and measures out the space of time from God's choice of the Jewish fathers, to the division of the land of Canaan: and reckoning from the birth of Isaac, when the choice took place, and in whom Abraham's seed was called, there was much about such a number of years; for from the birth of Isaac to the birth of Jacob, were sixty years; from thence to his going down into Egypt, an hundred and thirty years; and from thence to the Israelites coming out of Egypt, two hundred and ten years; and from thence to their entrance into the land of Canaan, forty years; and from that time to the division of the land, seven years, which in all make four hundred and forty seven years: so that, according to this account, there were three years wanting of the sum in the text; hence the apostle might with great propriety say, that it was about the space of so many years. It follows, **until Samuel the prophet**; the meaning of which, is not that there was such a space of time as before mentioned, from the distribution of the land of Canaan until the times of Samuel the prophet, during which space judges were given; but that after that term of time was expired, God gave them judges, or raised up one after another, until Samuel the prophet, who was the last of them."*

The chronology which has been determined between when Isaac was born to when Joshua conquered and divided the land fully supports the Gill interpretation of Acts 13: 15-20. Isaac was born the child of promise in AY 2049, and the land was divided in the late spring or early summer of AY 2500. The space of time between these two events is 451 years! Gill was not far off in his sequence of events and their total duration, and Paul was correct when he stated *about 450 years.* This is not proof that our derived chronology is correct, but by the testimony of two witnesses it is surely believable.

The following tables provide a tabular summary of the reign of the elders, judges and kings.

		Julian Year Dates			Duration		AY Years Sept/Oct	Sept/Oct
Exodus	April	1490	April	1489	40	Exodus	2454	2455
	1451			1450			2494	2495
Joshua	April	1450	April	1449	25	Joshua	2494	2495
	April	1426	April	1425			2519	2520
Elders	April	1425	April	1424	20	Elders	2519	2520
	April	1406	April	1405			2539	2540
Judges	April	1405	April	1404	40	Othiniel	2539	2540
	1386			1365			2579	2580
	April	1365	April	1364	80	Ehud	2579	2580
	1286			1285			2559	2560
	April	1285	April	1284	40	Deborah	2659	2660
	1246			1245			2699	2700
	April	1245	April	1244	7	Mideonite Opression	2699	2700
	1239			1238			2706	2707
	April	1238	April	1237	40	Gideon	2706	2707
	1199			1198			2746	2747
	April	1198	April	1197	3	Abimilech	2746	2747
	1196			1195			2749	2750
	April	1195	April	1194	23	Tola	2749	2750
	1173			1172			2772	2773
	April	1172	April	1171	22	Jair	2772	2773
	1151			1150			2794	2795

		Julian Year Dates			Duration		AY Years Sept/Oct	AY Years Sept/Oct
Judges	April	1150	April	1149	6	Jephthah	2794	2795
		1145		1144			2799	2800
	April	1144	April	1143	7	Ibzan	2800	2801
		1138		1137			2806	2807
	April	1137	April	1136	10	Elon	2807	2808
		1128		1127			2816	2817
	April	1127	April	1126	8	Abdon	2817	2818
		1120		1119			2824	2825
	April	1119	April	1118	20	Sampson	2825	2826
		1100		1099			2844	2845
	April	1099	April	1098	1	No King	2845	2846
	April	1098	April	1097	3	Samuel	2846	2847
		1096		1095			2848	2849
	April	1095	April	1094	38	Samuel &	2849	2850
		1058		1057		Saul	2886	2887
Kings	April	1057	April	1056	2	Saul	2887	2888
		1056		1055			2888	2889
	April	1055	Sept	1055		Transition 6 Months	2889	2890
	Sept	1055	Sept	1054	40	David	2890	
		1016		1015			2929	
	Sept	1015	Sept	1014	40	Solomon	2930	
		976		975			2969	
	Divided Kingdom........................ 975-974				AY 2970			

Exodus to Solomon's 4th Yr	479
Exodus to Solomon's 40th Yr	515

We are now ready to navigate the treacherous ground between the last year of King Solomon's reign and the destruction of the Divided Kingdom. We will now see that after the death of King Solomon, the united Nation of Israel which was ruled by Solomon was ripped into two pieces following a short power struggle over who should succeed Solomon.

Thoughts and
   Things………

Chapter 4
Epoch 3
The Fourth Year of Solomon's Reign to the End of the Divided Kingdom

During the 80-year combined reigns of King David and King Solomon, the kingdom of Israel reached its zenith. The kingdom flourished and grew strong. King David recovered the Ark of the Covenant which was captured by the Philistines, and King Solomon constructed Solomon's Temple in Jerusalem to centralize corporate worship. However, after a glorious beginning, King Solomon fell into apostasy. Solomon wed and loved many foreign women. He had 700 wives, many princesses and 300 concubines. He built an altar to Molech and *"did evil in the sight of the Lord"* (I Kings 11:1-7). Solomon had a son named Rehoboam who was Solomon's choice to succeed him as king: However, a man arose named Jeroboam, who was a son of Nathan an Ephraimite. He was anointed by the prophet Abijah to be king over 10 tribes of Israel (I Kings 11:28-32). Because of God's promise to David that his kingdom would be perpetuated, Abijah also prophesized that Judah would be given to Rehoboam, who was Solomon's son (I Kings 11:36, 12:27). In hearing this prophecy, Solomon sought to kill Jeroboam; but Jeroboam fled to safety in Egypt (I Kings 11:40). Shortly thereafter, King Solomon died. A power struggle ensued, and the prophecy of Abijah came to pass. The tribe of Judah and the Levites went with Rehoboam to Jerusalem, and the other 10 tribes went with Jeroboam to Shechem in the mountains of Ephraim (I Kings 12:25). This began a period in the history of corporate Israel called *The Divided Kingdom*. The two kingdoms were called the *Northern Kingdom* and the *Southern Kingdom*. The Southern Kingdom was also called the *Kingdom of Judah* and the Northern Kingdom was called *Israel*.

In the Books of I Kings, II Kings, I Chronicles and II Chronicles the Holy Bible records the name of each king that ruled in both kingdoms. Each king in both the Northern and Southern Kingdoms is cross-referenced to a king in the other kingdom. The following information is usually given:

- Name of the king that just died,
- The years of reign credited to the king that just died,
- Name of the deceased King's successor,
- The duration of the new King's reign,
- The name of the reigning king in the other kingdom,
- The regnal year of the king in the other kingdom during which the new king comes to the throne.

Hence, the year in which each new king in the Northern/Southern Kingdom comes to the throne is crossed-referenced to the regnal year of the king currently ruling in the other kingdom. For example, Nadab was the second king of the Northern Kingdom and Asa was the third king of the Southern Kingdom. The scriptures record

> **"So *Asa rested with his fathers, and was buried with his fathers in the City of David his father* (Jerusalem). *Then Jehosephat his son reigned in his place. Now, Nadab the son of Jeroboam became king over Israel* (the Northern Kingdom) *in the second year of Asa king of Judah* (the Southern Kingdom), *and he reigned over Israel two years*"**
> I Kings 15:24-25

With this much information, it would seem to be an easy task to sequentially determine when each king in either kingdom came to the throne, and when he died, by cross-referencing to the reigning king in the other kingdom. However, this has proven to be a daunting task that has confounded many biblical researchers. There are two things which determine when any one king might legally assume the throne, and how many calendar years were actually spent on the throne. The first issue depends upon when the regnal years of each king actually began. In ancient times, different kingdoms began regnal years in different calendar months. In fact, we will see that the Southern Kingdom began its regnal years on Tishri 1 (September/October), and the Northern Kingdom on Nisan 1 (March/April). The second confounding factor is how were partial years counted? In the biblical record, all years of reign were recorded as whole years. If a king happened to die early in a regnal year, and was immediately succeeded, who gets credit for the rest of the regnal year? We will see that in some cases, both the preceding and the succeeding king both claimed a full year's credit for the same partial year! These two issues can greatly influence the passage of actual calendar time through a serial sequence of regnal years recorded for separate kings. Before we can begin to address an acceptable chronology which spans the existence of both the Northern and Southern Kingdoms, and when each King reigned, these two questions must be settled.

The Beginning of Regnal Years

Each ancient kingdom had their own calendar system which was used to mark the beginning of a king's reign. Each ancient kingdom employed a slightly different calendar, but most had learned that the length of a solar year was determined by the sun, which we now know is exactly 365.2422 days. A year was composed of 12 months (13 in a leap year), and a week of seven, 24-hour days. The number of days in each month varied from kingdom to kingdom, as did the actual number of months in each year. The length of a month in ancient times was usually set at either 29 or 30 days. This is because the actual length of a lunar month is determined by the rotation of the moon, and is 29.53059 days. Calendars are designed to mark time by the passage of months, with the number and initiation of each month designed over time such that the number of days in a series of 12 or 13 months would coincide with the solar year. However, there is no combination of 29- and 30-day months that can equate to a solar year on a yearly basis. There were two common solutions to the problem: the first was to add days at the end of each year; the second is to periodically add an extra (13th) month to the normal 12-month year. For example, the Egyptians used a simple 12-month calendar consisting of 12 months of 30 days per year. This would total to 360 days per year. They then added five days at the end of the 12th month, so that their year was 365 days. This was close to the actual solar year, but fell short about 0.2422 days per year. Hence, the calendar *drifted backward* about one day every four years. After about 1460 years, the Egyptian year would move back in sync with a true solar year. For example, if today was Christmas using this calendar, in about 730 years Christmas would be in July! The calendar used by the nation of Israel was designed to be a *lunar-solar* calendar. It consisted of 12 alternating 29 and 30 day months. Simple math shows that a Hebrew year was only 354 days, which is about 11.25 days short of a solar year. About every three years, the calendar would drift back approximately 33.75 days. To keep the lunar-based 12-month year in sync with the solar year, it was discovered that by adding seven extra months over a 19-year period of time, 19 lunar calendar years of 12 (13) months would almost exactly equal the solar calendar over the same period of time. This 19-year period of time with seven inter-calculated months is called a *Metonic cycle*. With some minor adjustments to prevent back-to-back Sabbaths and other anomalies, the same calendar is in use today. The Babylonians seem to be the first to have discovered the *Metonic cycle* and put it into formal use. However, it must be stressed that since the Seven Feasts of Israel were ordained by God, and were to be observed every year following agricultural cycles, the Hebrews after the exodus also had to keep their 12-month lunar calendar in sync with the solar year. Whether this was done by a formal method such as the one just described or done by observation of crop maturity is unknown. However, after the Babylonian exile the Hebrews almost surely adopted and used a Metonic cycle. Each civilization had its own names for each month of the year, but after the 70-year Babylonian exile, the Hebrews adopted the Babylonian calendar names with only slight variations. The calendar we use today is called the *Gregorian calendar*. It was derived from the old *Julian calendar*. The Gregorian calendar is very accurate, as is the modern Jewish calendar over a 19 year period of time. The modern Jewish calendar was first implemented by the Patriarch Hillel II in 358 AD. The following table is a summary of the Julian, Gregorian, Babylonian and Hebrew calendars.

	Julian	Gregorian	Hebrew	(Civil)	Babylonian	
Month	Name	Name	Name	Months	Name	Months
1	Januarius	Jan	Tishri	Sept/Oct	Nisanu	Mar/Apr
2	Februarius	Feb	Heshvan	Oct/Nov	Aiaru	Apr/May
3	Martius	Mar	Chislev	Non/Dec	Simanu	May/Jun
4	Aprilus	April	Tebeth	Dec/Jan	Duzu	Jun/July
5	Maius	May	Shevat	Jan/Feb	Abu	July/Aug
6	Junius	June	Adar	Feb/Mar	Ululu	Aug/Sept
7	Julius	July	Nisan	Mar/Apr	Tashritu	Sept/Oct
8	Augustus	Aug	Iyyar	Apr/May	Arahsamnu	Oct/Nov
9	Septembris	Sept	Sivan	May/Jun	Kislimu	Non/Dec
10	Octobris	Oct	Tammuz	Jun/July	Tebetu	Dec/Jan
11	Novembris	Nov	Ab/Av	July/Aug	Shabatu	Jan/Feb
12	Decembris	Dec	Elul	Aug/Sept	Addaru	Feb/Mar

Ancient Calendar Years

*The Hebrew Civil year was used from antiquity to the Exodus. Month 1 was always Tishri. After the Exodus, God ordained that the Religious year would begin in Nisan. All festivals and "Month 1" in the scriptures always referred to the month of Nisan. Before the Exodus in scripture, all "Month 1" references referred to Tishri.

**Egyptian years always began on Thoth 1. The Julian date of Thoth 1 has to be calculated using modern computers. It "drifts" back across Julian months at a rate of about 1 day every 4 years.

After Persia and Cyrus the Great overthrew the Babylonian Empire in 538 or 539 BC, it appears that the Persian Empire also adopted the Babylonian calendar for their own use. The Babylonians, Israelis, Egyptians and Persians did not use a common method for determining when a king came to reign. The Babylonians and the Persians used Nisan 1 (March/April), the Egyptians used Thoth 1(August) and the Hebrew Southern Kingdom of Judah used Tishri 1 (Sept/Oct) until the Babylonian destruction and exile in 586 BC: The Northern Kingdom of Israel used a Nisan 1 (March/April) - Nisan 1 (March/April) regnal year start date until it fell to the Assyrian empire in 721 BC. This was discovered and published by Edwin Thiele, and is now widely accepted. To summarize, we will follow the work of Thiele and use Tishri 1 (Sept/Oct) as the beginning of Southern Kingdom regnal years and Nisan 1 (March/April) as the beginning of Northern Kingdom regnal years. In fact, it is difficult if not impossible to synchronize the reign of both Northern and Southern Kingdom kings without invoking this convention.

The Beginning of Regnal Years: Accession vs. Non-Accession System

A critical issue in formulating an accurate reconstruction of the Divided Kingdom is to properly define the way in which the regnal years of both the Northern and Southern Kingdom kings were determined. There were two methods that were primarily used during the Divided Kingdom. The *first* is called the *Accession Method*; the *second* is called the *Non-Accession Method*. The first biblical scholar to properly identify that these two methods were used during the divided kingdom was again Edwin Thiele. His contributions to this era cannot be underestimated.

An *accession-year system* operates in the following manner: suppose that a king from the Southern Kingdom is in his 20th year of reign in the month of November, 950 BC and he dies. Assume that his 20th year of reign started on Tishri 1 in September of 950 BC. Further assume that one of the king's sons ascended to the throne shortly after his death, say on December 1, 950 BC. By the a*ccession-year system*, the king who just died would be credited with a full year of reign (his 20th) between September (Tishri 1) of 950 BC and September/October (Tishri 1) of 949 BC, even though he died in November of 950 BC. The son who succeeded him would not begin his first official year of reign until September/October of 949 BC, even though he actually became king nine months earlier. Imagine the confusion that this might create in the kingly records. Suppose that the new king immediately won a decisive and historical battle in the spring of 949 BC. How would this battle be recorded, during the 20th year of the dead king or in the first year of the new king? Neither would be correct under this accounting system!

A *non- accession-year system* would operate as follows. When the reigning king in our previous example died, he would be credited with a full 20th year of reign between Tishri 1, 950-Tishri 1, 949 BC as in the accession-year system; but his successor would also claim that same full year starting on the previous Tishri 1 (Sept/Oct) as his first official year of reign! Again, imagine the confusion in recording a decisive battle in October of 950 BC. One scribe might record this as during the 20th year of the dead king and honor him with the victory, while a second scribe might identify the victory as occurring in the first year of the successor king's reign

Under a non-accession year system, the old king is given full credit for the last year of reign, and the new king is also given credit for that same full year as his first year of reign; even if the previous king died on Tishri 2! This is sometimes called *antedating*. Clearly, if antedating is used, the last year of a king's reign is counted twice; both the old and the new king are given credit for the same year. It must be noted that when historical records are found which list the lengths of successive kings in the accession-year system, if the regnal years of multiple sequential kings are totaled from a common start date, the sum of the regnal years will coincide with calendar years. However, if a non-accession system is used, one year must be subtracted from the reign of *each* king to have the sum of regnal years match the sum of calendar years. It is obvious that the problems associated with proper and accurate synchronization of the regnal years of both Northern and Southern Kingdom kings require great care and careful interpretation of scriptural facts.

From Chapter 3, we know that the first regnal year of King Solomon was AY 2930 (Sept/Oct-Sept/Oct). Solomon's last (40th) year was AY 2969 (Sept/Oct-Sept/Oct). Solomon claimed the entire year AY 2969 as his last year of reign. The Nation of Israel ruptured in late spring or early summer of AY 2969, and the first year of the divided kingdom was AY 2970. This is shown in the graphic on the right.

In this chapter, we will show that AY 3358 is equivalent to Tishri 1 of 587 BC to Tishri 1 of 586 BC. From this synchronization, every other *previous* and *subsequent* AY date can be cross referenced to a Julian calendar date. In establishing this *anchor date*, it will be convenient to show both AY years and Julian calendar years throughout this chapter. It is widely accepted that the final fall of Jerusalem to the Babylonian empire was on July 18, 586 BC. The table on the next page shows AY and Julian calendar dates from the first year of the Divided Kingdom (AY 2970) to the year that the Southern Kingdom and Jerusalem fell to the Babylonian empire (AY 3358). Note from these dates that the Southern kingdom of Judah lasted 389 years AY 2970 to end of AY 3358. We will show that King Solomon likely died in late spring or early summer of 975 BC. If the disruption is reckoned from that point in time, the count is 389.5 Julian calendar years. This table should be marked for future reference throughout this chapter.

Solomon		
Sept/Oct AY Year		
2930	Solomon Year 1	
2970	Solomon Year 2	
•	•	•
•	•	•
2969	Solomon Year 40	
2970	**Divided Kingdom**	

Let us now discuss another key assumption (Thiele and Finnegan). Throughout the 389 year duration of the Southern Kingdom of Judah, the reign of every king of Judah followed an accession-year system and a Tishri 1 (Sept/Oct) to Tishri 1(Sept/Oct) regnal year system (non inclusive for convenience). The following simple graphic depicts the 389 year period of time that Southern (Judah) kings actually reigned.

AY 2970	Sept/Oct, 975 BC – Sept/Oct, 974 BC
	389 Years
AY 3358	Sept/Oct, 587 BC – Sept/Oct, 586 BC

Block 61

61	1			2			3			4			5			6			7		
1	2941	1004	1003	2942	1003	1002	2943	1002	1001	2944	1001	1000	2945	1000	999	2946	999	998	2947	998	997
2	2948	997	996	2949	996	995	2950	995	994	2951	994	993	2952	993	992	2953	992	991	2954	991	990
3	2955	990	989	2956	989	988	2957	988	987	2958	987	986	2959	986	985	2960	985	984	2961	984	983
4	2962	983	982	2963	982	981	2964	981	980	2965	980	979	2966	979	978	2967	978	977	2968	977	976
5	2969	976	975	2970	975	974	2971	974	973	2972	973	972	2973	972	971	2974	971	970	2975	970	969
6	2976	969	968	2977	968	967	2978	967	966	2979	966	965	2980	965	964	2981	964	963	2982	963	962
7	2983	962	961	2984	961	960	2985	960	959	2986	959	958	2987	958	957	2988	957	956	2989	956	955

Block 62

62	1			2			3			4			5			6			7		
1	2990	955	954	2991	954	953	2992	953	952	2993	952	951	2994	951	950	2995	950	949	2996	949	948
2	2997	948	947	2998	947	946	2999	946	945	3000	945	944	3001	944	943	3002	943	942	3003	942	941
3	3004	941	940	3005	940	939	3006	939	938	3007	938	937	3008	937	936	3009	936	935	3010	935	934
4	3011	934	933	3012	933	932	3013	932	931	3014	931	930	3015	930	929	3016	929	928	3017	928	927
5	3018	927	926	3019	926	925	3020	925	924	3021	924	923	3022	923	922	3023	922	921	3024	921	920
6	3025	920	919	3026	919	918	3027	918	917	3028	917	916	3029	916	915	3030	915	914	3031	914	913
7	3032	913	912	3033	912	911	3034	911	910	3035	910	909	3036	909	908	3037	908	907	3038	907	906

Block 68

68	1			2			3			4			5			6			7		
1	3284	661	660	3285	660	659	3286	659	658	3287	658	657	3288	657	656	3289	656	655	3290	655	654
2	3291	654	653	3292	653	652	3293	652	651	3294	651	650	3295	650	649	3296	649	648	3297	648	647
3	3298	647	646	3299	646	645	3300	645	644	3301	644	643	3302	643	642	3303	642	641	3304	641	640
4	3305	640	639	3306	639	638	3307	638	637	3308	637	636	3309	636	635	3310	635	634	3311	634	633
5	3312	633	632	3313	632	631	3314	631	630	3315	630	629	3316	629	628	3317	628	627	3318	627	626
6	3319	626	625	3320	625	624	3321	624	623	3322	623	622	3323	622	621	3324	621	620	3325	620	619
7	3326	619	618	3327	618	617	3328	617	616	3329	616	615	3330	615	614	3331	614	613	3332	613	612

Block 69

69	1			2			3			4			5			6			7		
1	3333	612	611	3334	611	610	3335	610	609	3336	609	608	3337	608	607	3338	607	606	3339	606	605
2	3340	605	604	3341	604	603	3342	603	602	3343	602	601	3344	601	600	3345	600	599	3346	599	598
3	3347	598	597	3348	597	596	3349	596	595	3350	595	594	3351	594	593	3352	593	592	3353	592	591
4	3354	591	590	3355	590	589	3356	589	588	3357	588	587	3358	587	586	3359	586	585	3360	585	584
5	3361	584	583	3362	583	582	3363	582	581	3364	581	580	3365	580	579	3366	579	578	3367	578	577
6	3368	577	576	3369	576	575	3370	575	574	3371	574	573	3372	573	572	3373	572	571	3374	571	570
7	3375	570	569	3376	569	568	3377	568	567	3378	567	566	3379	566	565	3380	565	564	3381	564	563

Table of AY years and Julian Calendar Years
Grey Columns: AY Years
White Columns: Julian Years
All AY years span two Julian Years (Sept/Oct)-(Sept/Oct)

The Northern Kingdom of Israel always followed a Nisan 1 (March/April) to Nisan 1 (March/April) regnal year (non inclusive for convenience); but we will subsequently show that not every Northern Kingdom king used a non-accession-year system. We will also show that the only way to synchronize the biblical records is to use a non-accession-year system in the Northern Kingdom from the reign of Jeroboam I in AY 2970 (March/April, 975 BC) through the reign of Jehu (Israel); which ended in AY 3087 (March/April, 857 BC). Following the reign of Joram, Jehu began to reign by conquest and murder in 884 BC. The last year of Jehu was March/April 858-March/April 857 BC. For some unknown reason, his successor Jehoahaz switched to an accession year system. This system was then used by every other king in the Northern Kingdom until it was destroyed in the summer of 721 BC. Recognizing that different regnal-year systems were in use at different times, involving different kings is the key to reconstructing a chronology of the divided kingdom. A partial table of AY years with the corresponding Julian calendar years for the divided kingdom is shown on the next page.

Ahaz	12	Sept	731	730			
			730	730	April		10
	13	Sept	730	729			
			729	729	April	Hoshea	1
	14	Sept	729	728		Sole-Rex	
			728	728	April		2
	15	Sept	728	727			
			727	727	April		3
	16	Sept	727	726			
			726	726	April		4
Hezikiah	1	Sept	726	725			
			725	725	April		5
	2	Sept	725	724			
			724	724	April		6
	3	Sept	724	723			
			723	723	April		7
	4	Sept	723	722			
			722	722	April		8
	5	Sept	722	721			
			721	721	April		9
	6	Sept	721	720			
				720			

This color coded table shows a clear example of why it is necessary to understand how regnal years are determined. This table assumes a Tishri 1-Tishri 1 regnal year for Hezekiah, and a Nisan 1-Nisan 1 regnal year for Hoshea. II Kings 17 and 18 provide five distinct references to the reign of Hoshea (Israel) and all must be satisfied.

> ***"in the third year of Hoshea son of Elah king of Israel, that Hezekiah the son of Ahaz king of Judah began to reign.***
> II Kings 18:1

> ***"And it came to pass in the fourth year of king Hezekiah, which was the seventh year of Hoshea son of Elah king of Israel, that Shalmaneser king of Assyria came up against Samaria, and besieged it."***
> II Kings 18:9

> ***"And at the end of three years they took it: even in the sixth year of Hezekiah, that is the ninth year of Hoshea king of Israel, Samaria was taken."***
> II Kings 18:10

> ***"In the twelfth year of Ahaz king of Judah began Hoshea the son of Elah to reign in Samaria over Israel nine years."***
> II Kings 17:1

> ***"Then the king of Assyria came up throughout all the land, and went up to Samaria, and besieged it three years. In the ninth year of Hoshea the king of Assyria took Samaria, and carried Israel away into Assyria"***
> II Kings 17: 5-6

It *appears* that the record of II Kings 18:1 is in error, since it demands that Hezekiah began to reign in the 3rd year of Hoshea. The first year of Hezekiah is shown as Sept 726–Sept 725 BC, but the third year of Hoshea is clearly April 727 - April 726 BC and there is no intersection of these two epochs of time. Immediately a cry goes up from a biblical non literalist, there is a scribal error or that the bible is in error. Of course, neither is true! One must remember that using the non-accession year system, Hezekiah actually became king between Sept 727–Sept 726 BC upon the death of Ahaz. In fact, the Holy record indicates that Hezekiah started functioning as a king between Sept 727 and April 726 BC. The scribe is cross referencing the *actual* first year of Hezekiah's reign to the 3rd year of Hoshea and not his official first year. Note that this synchronization also demands an accession-year system for the Southern Kingdom at this time.

II Kings 18:10 demands that the 6th year of Hezekiah is the 9th year of Hoshea, and II Kings 18:9 demands that Hezekiah's 4th year corresponds to the 7th year of Hoshea. Using the color coded graphic, both assertions are true. Finally, II Kings 17:1 asserts that the 1st year of Hoshea correspond to the 12th year of Ahaz. This appears to be in error. Hoshea, using the accession year system instituted after Jehu, claimed April-729-April 728 BC as his first credited year of reign. However, he started to function as a sovereign king sometime between April-Sept of 730 BC. Hence, not only are the records of II Kings 18:1, 18:9, 17:1, 17:6 and 18:10 correct; the biblical records attest to the absolute accuracy of the Holy Record.

As we unravel the corresponding reigns of both the Northern and Southern Kingdom kings, we will discover that these sort of *cross references* are woven into the fabric of the biblical records. In spending many hours trying to verify and validate all cross references to the kings in both kingdoms, it was discovered that the only way to resolve *all* apparent discrepancies was to place each year in the reign of every king in the proper Tishri-Tishri or Nisan-Nisan setting, and further consider which king was using an accession system and which king was using a non-accession-year system. *All cross references* can only be confirmed by careful scrutiny and interpretation of the Holy Scriptures. It is also critical to recognize that every king in the *Southern Kingdom of Judah* actually *began* to reign sometime during the year *preceding* his/her first credited year of reign, but the first official year of reign would not commence until the first Tishri 1 (Sept/Oct) following the preceding king's death.

Although this is all very confusing, this type of accounting *DOES* occur in the Holy Bible, and to the reader that has not been exposed to these anomalies the result is to declare the Holy Writ in error and untrustworthy. To the biblical literalist who recognizes the Holy Bible as divinely inspired, any apparent difficulties in resolving conflicting regnal year references simply represent a normal occurrence because of the different systems in use at the time regnal records were recorded. It is now important to repeat previous statements which were made pertaining to the way in which the Northern and Southern Kingdoms recorded regnal years.

> **The *Southern Kingdom* during the Era of the Divided Kingdom always used an *Accession-year System*. The Southern Kingdom always used a Tishri 1-Tishri 1 (September/October) regnal year.**

> **The Northern Kingdom of Israel during the Era of the Divided Kingdom started with a Non-Accession year system, which continued from Jeroboam to Jehu. From that point on, the Northern Kingdom used an Accession-year system. The Northern Kingdom always used a Nisan 1-Nisan 1 (March/April) regnal year.**

We should again recognize that the use of these two systems for the Northern and Southern Kingdoms were first proposed and used by Edwin Thiele in his landmark book, *The Mysterious Numbers of the Hebrew Kings*. Thiele used these two systems in establishing a chronology from the death of King Solomon to the final destruction of the Jewish Nation by the Babylonian Empire, which initiated a 70-year exile in Babylon. Thiele proposed a chronology which will be discussed later, but unfortunately his chronological conclusions cannot be accepted if biblical records are to be used without significant violation. A repudiation of his derived chronology is given in Appendix A. Nevertheless, two important things emerged from the work of Thiele which we accept as true: (1) The definition of accession and non-accession year systems and which one was used by the Northern and Southern Kingdoms, and that (2) the Southern Kingdom of Judah *always* used Tishri 1- Tishri 1 (Sept/Oct) regnal year accounting; and the Northern Kingdom of Israel initially used a Nisan 1-Nisan1 (March/April) regnal year accounting system, but beginning with Jehoahaz they switched to an accession year system.

Finally, we will decisively show that the AY year in which the Northern Kingdom fell to Assyria and was carried into exile can be determined from the biblical records; but the calendar year, month and day was not recorded for any major event. However, using recently-discovered historical records the exact date that Jerusalem and the Southern Kingdom of Judah fell to the Babylonian Empire was determined to be July 18, 586 BC (Jack Finnegan, Floyd Nolan Jones, Thiele and others). The date of July 18, 586 BC is now widely accepted and enormously important to this study. That date provides the anchor point which can be equated to the specific AY date in which the Southern Kingdom fell; which was AY 3358, in the 29th year of Hezekiah's reign. Once that has been accomplished, *any* AY date in our offered chronology can be equated to a *Proleptic* Julian calendar year. The task ahead is to develop a biblically sound chronology of both the Northern and Southern Kingdoms between the disruption which occurred upon the death of King Solomon in AY 2969 and the final fall of Jerusalem and Judah in AY 3358. We will present evidence that King Solomon likely died in the summer of 975 BC, and the final fall of Jerusalem and the Southern Kingdom was in AY 3358 on July 18, 586 BC.

The Chronology of the Divided Kingdom
We have previously established a chronology that started with the year that Adam and Eve were driven from the Garden of Eden (AY 1) to the fourth year of King Solomon's reign in AY 2933. This would place the last year of King Solomon's reign in AY 2969 and the first year of his reign in AY 2930. The schism occurred in late AY 2969. We will show that the Northern Kingdom of Israel ceased to exist in the summer of AY 3225 (720 BC), and that the Southern Kingdom of Judah survived until AY 3358 (April 18, 586 BC). The elapsed period of time that the Southern Kingdom existed was 389 years (It will also be clearly established that AY 3358 corresponds to Tishri 1, Sept/Oct), 587 BC – Tishri 1, Sept/Oct, 586 BC). The table on the next page *a'priori* shows how both the AY years and Proleptic Julian calendar years for key events between AY 1 and AY 3358 can be easily calculated assuming that the final fall of the Southern Kingdom of Judah occurred on July 18, 586 BC in AY 3358.

AY 3358 corresponds to Sept, 587 BC-Sept, 586 BC. Proving this fact will allow us to calculate the Proleptic Julian year dates which correspond to all other previous AY years. In the investigations which follow, it will be much easier to understand regnal synchronizations by referring to both AY and Julian years. The following table will be referenced frequently.

AY Year		Julian Year
1	Year Adam Left Eden	Sept, 3944-Sept, 3933
		2454 years
2454	Year of the Exodus	Sept, 1491-Sept, 1490
2454	Year of the Exodus	Sept, 1491-Sept, 1490
		480 years
2933	Solomon's 4th Year	Sept, 1012-Sept, 1011
2930	Solomons 1st Year	Sept, 1015-Sept, 1014
		4 years
2933	Solomon's 4th Year	Sept, 1012-Sept, 1011
2930	Solomons 1st Year	Sept, 1015-Sept, 1014
		40 years
2969	Solomon's 40th Year	Sept, 976-Sept, 975
2970	Divided Kingdom	Sept, 975-Sept, 974
		389 years
3358	Final Fall of Judah	Sept, 587-Sept, 586

Once again, note that the AY years we are using to increment time are Tishri 1-Tishri 1 Hebrew Civil calendar years, which correspond to the Southern Kingdom regnal years. We will now show that all regnal years for the Southern Kingdom of Judah and the Northern Kingdom of Israel are documented in the Holy Bible, and that the reign of every king from both the Northern and Southern Kingdom can be *perfectly* matched and synchronized, satisfying more than 50 biblical cross references. Recall that upon King Solomon's death, the 12 tribes split into the Southern Kingdom (Judah, Levites and parts of Ephraim and Manasseh), and the Northern Kingdom (the other tribes plus parts of Ephraim and Manasseh). The tribe of Levi remained in the Southern Kingdom to minister priestly duties in Solomon's Temple. In the biblical record, the Southern Kingdom is called *Judah*. The Northern Kingdom is called *Israel*. Finally, note once again that the Southern Kingdom always used an *accession-year* system when transitioning from one king to the succeeding king. The Southern Kingdom initially used a *non-accession-year* system and later switched to an *accession-year* system. The Southern Kingdom always used a Tishri 1-Tishri 1 regnal year system, and the Northern Kingdom *always* used a Nisan 1-Nisan 1 regnal year system. Finally, note that each Nisan 1- Nisan 1 year crossed into *two* consecutive AY years.

From the previous table, the 40th year of King Solomon was AY 2969. It started on Tishri 1 (September/October) of 976 BC and ended on Tishri 1 (September/October) of 975 BC. The last day of any AY year is actually the last day of the month Elul, but we use Tishri 1-Tishri 1 for convenience; similarly Nisan 1-Nisan 1 is used to designate regnal years in the Northern Kingdom. King Solomon died sometime in AY 2969. We will subsequently show that it was likely in the month of July. The first southern king was Rehoboam, the son of King David. He began a 17-year reign on Tishri 1, beginning in AY 2970. Recall that Jeroboam was divinely appointed by God to reign as king over the Northern Kingdom. He had fled to Egypt to escape being assassinated by King Solomon. Upon returning from Egypt, for reasons unknown, he adopted a Nisan 1-Nisan 1, non-accession-year system. Both Rehoboam and Jeroboam came to their respective thrones shortly after King Solomon died, likely in the late spring or early summer of AY 2969. Using a non-accession system, Jeroboam began a 22-year reign on Nisan 1

(March/April) of AY 2770. Starting with this information, we will now trace the reign of both Northern and Southern kings from when the United Kingdom of King Solomon divided until the end of the Southern Kingdom of Judah in AY 3358. Here we will also note that the Northern Kingdom was destroyed after about 255 years in 721 BC by the Assyrian Empire. This will be shown true in the chronological development to follow. It was approximately 134 more years until the Southern Kingdom fell to the Babylonian Empire. Hence, If the end came in 586 BC (July 8, 586 BC... Finnegan), and if King Solomon died in the summer of 975 BC, the 389 credited regnal years of Judah kings plus the 6 month accession period of Rehoboam probably totaled 389.5 years. The first regnal year of King Rehoboam (Judah) is determined to be Tishri 1, 975 BC-Tishri 1, 974 BC, initiating an accession-year system for the Southern Kingdom. The first regnal year of King Jeroboam would be Nisan 1, 975 BC to Nisan 1, 974 BC, initiating a non-accession year system. The following table shows the regnal years for every king of Judah and the scriptural confirmation.

Southern Kingdom Kings			
Name of King	Duration of Reign		
Rehoboam	17	Years	I Kings 14:21
Abijah	3	Years	I Kings 15:1-2
Asa	41	Years	I Kings 15:9-10
Jehosephat	25	Years	I Kings 22:41-42
Jehoram	8	Years	II Kings 8:16-17
Ahaziah	1	Years	II Kings 8:25-26
Athaliah	6	Years	II Kings 11:1-21
Joash	40	Years	II Kings 11:17-20, II Kings 18:1
Amaziah	29	Years	II Kings 14:1-2
Uzziah	52	Years	II Kings 15:1-2
Jotham	16	Years	II Kings 15:32-33
Ahaz	16	Years	II Kings 16:1-2
Hezikiah	29	Years	II Kings 18:1-2
Manasseh	55	Years	II Kings 21:1
Amon	2	Years	II Kings 21:19
Josiah	31	Years	II Kings 22:1
Jehoahaz	1	3 Months	II Kings 23:31
Jehoakim	11	Years	II Kings 23:34
Jehoiachin		3 Months, 10 Da	II Kings 24:8
Zedekiah	11	Years	II Kings 25:17-18
Total Years: 394 Years, 3 Months, 10 Days			

It can be verified that the total regnal years of all Southern Kingdom monarchs total 394 years, three months and 10 days. This is four years, three months and 10 days longer than the stated 389 years. However, we now need to note that in II Kings 8:16-17 the following historical record is given.

> *"Now in the 5th year of Joram (Northern Kingdom) the son of Ahab, King of Israel (Northern Kingdom), Jehosephat having been King of Judah, Jehoram the son of Jehosephat (Southern Kingdom) began to reign as King of Judah... and he reigned for eight years in Jerusalem."* II Kings 8:16-17

We will later show that without a doubt Jehoram co-reigned with his father Jehosephat for four years. This co-regency reduces the total time period to 390 years, 3 months and 10 days. Note also that both Jehoahaz and Jehoiachin were recognized as ruling for less than one year, and

57

normally both would receive no regnal year credits. However, the short reign of Jehoahaz (3 months) crossed Tishri 1, and at that time he formally became a recognized king. Even though he likely formally reigned as king for less than six weeks, he was credited for a full year of reign. His successor Jehoakim actually ruled on the throne for almost 12 years, but using the accession-year system he was only credited with 11 years since his 1st year of reign began after Tishri 1. Jehoiakim died in his 11th year of reign, and Jehoiachin took his place. Jehoiakin was on the throne for 3 months and 10 days, but using the accession year system, his short reign fell entirely between when Jehoiakim died and the following Tishri 1. Hence, he was not credited with any formal regnal years. This has been confirmed by Finnegan. After only 3 months, Nebuchadnezzar came to Jerusalem, took him prisoner and removed him to Babylon (II Kings 24: 8-12). Nebuchadnezzar then placed Mattaniah (an uncle of Jehoiachin) on the throne and changed his name to Zedekiah (II Kings 24:17).

Finally, a strange and convoluted sequence of events resulted in both Joram (Judah) and Amaziah (Judah) both receiving credit for the same regnal (AY) year... AY 3059, Sept 886- Sept 885. We will provide details of this assertion later in this chapter. So, by an unusual set of circumstances, the total number of credited regnal years summed to 389. Since the Southern Kingdom of Judah never abandoned the Tishri 1-Tishri 1 accession year system, the number of Julian calendar years also summed to 389.

We will now show that the written records of the Holy Bible over the 389 year regnal period of time that the southern kings of Judah actually reigned are both reliable and accurate. It will be advantageous to make extensive use of color-coded time charts with Julian regnal years to clearly portray the interactions between the kings in both kingdoms. The Southern Kingdom kings are shown on the left side, and the Northern Kingdom kings on the right side. The regnal calendar years and a corresponding regnal year count for each king is also given. Narratives are sometimes given in the left or right margins.

The synchronization of each king in the Southern Kingdom of Judah to each King in the Northern Kingdom of Israel was a very difficult task involving multiple EXCEL spreadsheets. As previously stated, there are over 50 cross-references from the Holy Scriptures which must be satisfied. In developing a chronology of the Divided Kingdom, there is one thing that must be observed without compromise. The Holy records which cross reference the beginning year of a king's reign in one kingdom to a corresponding king and regnal year in the other kingdom must not be compromised.

It will be easier for the reader to confirm these synchronizations by using (1) the AY year designation, (2) the Julian year designation and (3) the elapsed number of calendar years from when the united kingdom of Israel disrupted into the Northern and Southern kingdoms upon the death of King Solomon. We have previously shown that King Solomon died in AY 2969. We will subsequently show that the last king of Judah was Zedekiah who was taken to Babylon when Jerusalem finally fell on the Julian year date of July 18, 586 BC. Once AY 2969 is matched to the last regnal year of Zedekiah (Sept 587-Sept 586 BC) then every other AY year can be absolutely matched to corresponding Julian years. The tables shown on the following two pages will be extremely helpful in understanding the difficult divided kingdom.

The Divided Kingdom: *The Southern Kingdom of Judah*

King	Years Reigned	AY Years	Julian Years	Year Count
		(BC)		
Rehoboam	17	2970-2986	975-958	1-17
Abijah	3	2987-2989	958-955	18-20
Asa	41	2990-3030	955-914	21-61
Jehosephat	25	3031-3055	914-889	62-86
Jehosephat co-ruled with his son Jehoram for the last 4 years of his reign This is very clear from II Kings 8:16				
Joram/Jehoram	8	3052-3059	893-885	83-90
Ahaziah	1	3059	886-885	90-91
Athaliah	6	3060-3065	885-879	91-96
Joash/Jehoash	40	3066-3105	879-839	97-136
Amaziah/Ahaziah	29	3106-3134	839-810	137-165
Uzziah/Azariah	52	3135-3186	810-758	166-217
Jotham	16	3187-3202	758-742	218-233
Ahaz	16	3203-3218	742-726	234-249
Hezekiah	29	3219-3247	726-697	250-278
Manasseh	55	3248-3302	697-642	279-333
Amon	2	3303-3304	642-640	334-335
Josiah	31	3305-3335	640-609	336-366
Jehoahaz	3 mo.	3336	609-608	367
Jehoiakim	11	3337-3347	608-597	368-378
Jehoiakin	3mo,10 days	3347	597	378
Zedekiah	11	3348-3358	597-586	379-389

The Divided Kingdom: *The Northern Kingdom of Judah*

King	Years Reigned	AY Years	Julian Years	Year Count
			(April/April)	
Jeroboam	22	2969/2970 - 2990/2991	975/974 - 954/953	1-22
Nadab	2	2990/2991 - 2991/2992	954/953 - 953/952	22-23
Baasha	24	2991/2992 - 3014/3015	953/952 - 930/929	23-46
Elah	2	3014/3015 - 3015/3016	930/929 - 929/928	46-47
Zimri	7 days			
Omri	12	3015/3016 - 3026/3027	929/928 - 918/917	47-58
Ahab	22	3026/3027 - 3047/3048	918/917 - 897/896	58-79
Ahaziah	2	3047/3048 - 3048/3049	897/896 - 896/895	79-80
Joram/Jehoram	12	3048/3049 - 3059/3060	896/895 - 885/884	80-91
Jehu	28	3059/3060 - 3086/3087	885/884 - 858/857	91-118
Jehu was a warrier-King who usurped the throne. He started an accession year system				
Jehoahaz	17	3087/3088 - 3103/3104	857/856 - 841/840	119-135
Jehoash	16	3104/3105 - 3119/3120	840/839 - 825/824	136-151
Jeroboam	41	3120/3121 - 3160/3161	824/823 - 784/783	152-192
Interregum… or more likely, an unrecorded reign of 12 years				
	12	3161/3162 - 3172/3173	783/782 - 772/771	193-204
During year 12 , Zachariah attempted to become king and was killed after 6 months by Shallum Enraged and infuriated, Menahem pursued Shallum and killed him after only 1 month.				

Zachariah	6 months	3172/3173	772/771	204
Shallum	1 month	3172/3173	772/771	204
Menahem	10	3173/3174 - 3182/3183	771/770 - 762/761	205-214
Pekahiah	2	3183/3184 - 3184/3185	761/760 - 760/759	215-216
Pekah	20	3185/3186 - 3204/3205	759/758 - 740/739	217-236
Hoshea killed Pekah in the 20th year of his reign; he was subjugated to Ahaz (Judah) as a puppet king for 10 years.... A pro-rex ruler				
Hoshea	10	3205/3206 - 3214/3215	739/738 - 730/729	237-246
Ahaz	10	3205/3206 - 3214/3215	739/738 - 730/729	237-246
Hoshea was finally able to gain the throne in 739 BC and break the yoke of Ahaz				
Hoshea	9	3215/3216 - 3223/3224	729/728 - 721/720	247-255
The Northern Kingdom of Israel fell to the Assyrians in the summer of 721 BC. They vanished as a unified kingdom forever... known as the *lost 10 tribes* .				

Building the Chronology of the Divided Kingdom

Rehoboam was the first king of the Southern Kingdom of Judah, and he reigned 17 years beginning in Sept, 975 BC. He began to reign on Tishri 1 (Sept/Oct) of 975 BC using the non-accession year system started with King David. Jeroboam was the first king of the Northern Kingdom of Israel and he reigned 22 years. He immediately instituted the accession year system in the Northern kingdom and began his first regnal year in March/April of 975 BC.

We will now discuss the death of Rehoboam (Judah) and the transition to Abijah.

> *"Now, in the 18th year of King Jeroboam, the son of Nebat, reigned Abijam (Abijah) over Judah".*   I Kings 15:1

Abijah used the *accession-year* system. Note that Tishri 1 could begin in either September or October. For convenience only, we will graphically show September as the beginning of each regnal year for each king in the Southern Kingdom. Similarly, the Northern Kingdom used a Nisan 1 regnal year as the start date, which could be in either March or April. For convenience only, we will show April. Since Rehoboam could have died anytime between September, 959

BC and September, 958 BC, his successor (Abijah) could have become *de'facto* king any time between those two points in time.

Rehoboam	16	Sept	960		959		Jeroboam	17		
			959	959	959	April				
	17	Sept	959		958			18	3 yrs	Abijah: 18th year of Jeroboam
			958	958	958	April				(I King 15:1)
Abijah	1	Sept	958		957			19		
			957	957	957	April				
	2	Sept	957		956			20		
			956	956	956	April				

Abijah would have ascended to the throne immediately following the death of Rehoboam. However, his first official regnal year would not begin until September of 958 BC. We are also able to verify that Abijah started to reign between April 1, 958 BC and Sept 1, 1958 by synchronizing I Kings 15:1. Hence, Rehoboam died between Passover (March/April), 958 BC, and the Feast of Trumpets (Sept/Oct) in 958 BC. To the best of our knowledge, this level of detail has not previously been presented There are over 50 similar cross references in the biblical records, and all must be shown true. In developing the chronology of the Divided Kingdom, not one can be disregarded or called a *scribal error*. So, with that in mind, let us continue our journey through time and scriptures. We will now address the reign of Asa (Judah).

Abijah	1	Sept	958		957					
			957	957	957	April		19		
	2	Sept	957		956					
			956	956	956	April		20	41 yrs	Asa: 20th year of Jeroboam
	3	Sept	956		955					(I King 15:9)
			955	955	955	April		21		
Asa	1	Sept	955		954					
			954	954	954	April	Jeroboam	22		

Asa succeeded Abijah. Asa's first year of credited reign was Sept of 955 – Sept 954 BC. In I Kings 15:9, we are told that *Asa became king in the 20th year of Jeroboam*. The 20th year of Jeroboam was between April, 956 BC and April, 955 BC. Clearly, there is no common period of time in this reference. However, note that Abijah died sometime between September, 956 BC and September, 955 BC and Asa assumed the throne immediately following the death of Abijah. It is clear that the holy scribe is referencing the 20th year of Jeroboam to the *accession year* of Asa which was Sept 956-Sept 955 BC. Certainly Asa was reigning as a full king during his accession period of time. Comparing cross reference, Asa became the ruler of Judah between September of 955 and April of 954 BC. This happens frequently in the records of the Kings. It undoubtedly reflected the viewpoint of the scribe who recorded the event. We will now address the reign of Jeroboam, the first King of Israel and his successor Nadab..

Jeroboam died in his 22th year of reign, which was April, 954 BC-April, 953 BC. He was succeeded by Nadab sometime in this same year, and Nadab ruled for two years, both following

Asa	1	Sept	955		954					
			954	954	April	Jeroboam	22	Nadab	1	Nadab: 2cd year of Asa
	2	Sept	954		953			Baasha		
			953	953	April		2		1	
	3	Sept	953		952					
			952	952	April		2			
	4	Sept	952		951			24 yrs		Baasha killed Nadab in the 3rd year of Asa
			951	951	April		3			and in the 3rd year of Asa and immediately
	5	Sept	951		950					assumed the throne(I King 15:28)
			950	950	April		4			

a non-accession-year system. In I Kings 15:25 we are told that *Nadab became king in the second year of Asa*. Hence, Nadab became king sometime between September, 954 BC and April, 953 BC. Baasha assassinated Nadab and became king of Israel in the third year of Asa sometime between Sept 954 BC–April 953 BC. Baasha claimed April, 954 BC-April, 953 BC as his first official regnal year using the non-accession-year system.

We are now ready to move on to the strange events concerning Elah, Zimri and Omri. The following graphic show the years that Elah, Omri, Baasha and Zimri reigned.

Asa	25	Sept	931		930						
			930	930	April	Baasha	24	Elah	1		2 yrs — Elah: 26th year of Asa (I Kings 16:6-23)
	26	Sept	930		929						
			929	929	April	Omri	1	Zimri...7 day	2		7 days — Zimri killed Elah in the 27th year of Asa...Zimri was burned to death in his palace 7 days later by Omri, who immediately assumes throne(I King 16:15)
	27	Sept	929		928						
			928	928	April	2	2				During a short period of time , Elah (died) Zimri was(killed) and Omri (new King) assumed the throne of the Northern Kingdom (Israel)
	28	Sept	928		927						
			927	927	April	3	3	Omri is in			Omri claimed 12 years as King. The first 4 years were in fact in turmoil between him and
	29	Sept	927		926			Tibni 4 yrs			His first official year as soverign monarch was
			926	926	April	4	4	while half			in April of 924 BC -April, 923 BC , in the
	30	Sept	926		925			follow			31st year of Asa (II Kings 16:23)
			925	925	April	5	1	Tibni and			Omri was in Tibney for 6 years... Then he reigned for 6 years in Jerusalem.
	31	Sept	925		924			half follow			This is concluded from careful study of I Kings 16:23
			924	924	April	6	2	Omri			and I Kings 16:29. The 12 years of I Kings 16:23
	32	Sept	924		923						were from the assasination of Zimri to the reign
			923	923	April	7	3	Omri			of Ahab. Omri obviosly honored the Non-acession
	33	Sept	923		922			prevails			year system, counting April 929-April 928 as his first
			922	922	April	8	4	and is King			year of reign.
	34	Sept	922		921			for 8 years			
			921	921	April	9	5	in			
	35	Sept	921		920			Jerusalem			
			920	920	April	10	6				
	36	Sept	920		919						
			919	919	April	11	7				
Asa	37	Sept	919		918						

Baasha reigned until the 26th year of Asa (I Kings 16:8) and he died sometime between Sept 930 BC and April 929 BC. He was succeeded by Elah. Elah was credited with his first year of reign in April of 930 BC, using the same non-accession system as Baasha did before him. One of his servants named Zimri got drunk and killed Elah in the 26th year of Asa (I Kings 16:9-10). Omri immediately pursued Zimri who fled to Tirzah. Seeing he was doomed, Zimri burned his house down and perished in the fire only seven days after killing Elah. Because Zimri was only a defacto king for 7 days and did not cross over Nisan 1, he was not credited with any regnal year (I Kings 16:16-20).

We will now address Ahab (Israel) and Jehosephat (Judah). Ahab became king of the Northern Kingdom in the 38th year of Asa, and reigned for 22 years (I Kings 16:29). Asa reigned for a long 41 years in the Southern Kingdom. Toward the end of his reign, he was *diseased in his feet* (I Kings 16:23). What his disease was or how it affected his reign is not recorded. In II Chronicles 17:12, we are told that he became diseased *in the 39th year of his reign*, and that *his malady was very severe.* It is likely that his son Jehosephat helped him reign over the last 2.5 years, and so we conjecture that Jehosephat was *pro-rex* for this period of time.

											Notes
					919	919	April	11	7		
	Asa	37	Sept	919		918					
		38	Sept	918	918	918	April	12 / Omri	8	Ahab 1	Ahab: 38th year of Asa (I King 16:29)
						917					
		39	Sept	917	917	917	April		2		Asa was diseased in his feet
						916					
Jehosephat		40	Sept	916	916	916	April		3		Asa diseased in his feet
Pro Rex						915					in his 39th year. Possibly
		41	Sept	915	915	915	April	Ahab	4		sugar diabetes (II Chron 16:12)
Pro Rex	Asa					914				25 yrs	Jehosephat: 4th year of Ahab
	Jehosephat	1	Sept	914	914	914	April		5		(II King 22:41-42)
	Sole Rex				913	913	April		6		

The terms "Pro-rex", "co-rex" and "sole-rex" need to be explained.
A *sole-rex* is a sovereign King. A *co-rex* is someone who is reigning with full authority and power beside a reigning king. Co-rex year(s) are usually counted as reigning years by both monarchs. A *pro-rex* is someone who is acting as a King under the direction and authority of the official king. Pro-rex years are not counted as regnal years.

When Asa died Jehosephat assumed the throne in the fourth year of Ahab (I Kings 22:41). Note that this biblical cross-reference refers to the *actual* year that Jehosephat assumed the throne, and not his first *official* year of reign. This is to be expected, because for some time prior to the death of Asa, Jehosephat was probably assuming visible and full authority because of Asa's severe illness. This identifies the death of Asa as between Sept, 915 BC and April of 914 BC. Asa ruled over the Southern Kingdom of Judah for 25 years in Jerusalem (II Chron 20:31) and Ahab reigned for 22 years over the Northern Kingdom of Israel in Tibney. We now need to address the reigns of Ahaziah and Jehoram/Joram, both Kings of Israel.

Judah (note / king)	Judah yr		Sept	Judah yr	Israel yr	April	Israel king	Israel yr	Israel king 2	yr	Note
Joram must have assumed the role of pro-rex in year 17 to satisfy II Kings 1:17.	Joram /Jehoram Pro-Rex		17	Sept 898	897						
					897	897	April	Ahab	22	Ahaziah	1 (2 yrs)
			18	Sept 897	896						
					896	896	April		2	Joram / Jehoram	1
			19	Sept 896	895						
					895	895	April		2		
	Jehosephat		20	Sept 895	894						
					894	894	April		3		
			21	Sept 894	893						
					893	893	April	Joram	4		
Joram / Jehoram	1		22	Sept 893	892						
Co-Rex	2				892	892	April		5		
			23	Sept 892	891						
					891	891	April		6		
	3		24	Sept 891	890						
					890	890	April		7		
Joram / Jehoram	4		25	Sept 890	889						
					889	889	April		8		
			5	Sept 889	888						
During his last two years he had an incureable disease in his bowels. (II Chronicles 21: 18-19)					888	888	April		9		
			6	Sept 888	887						
					887	887	April	Joram	10		
			7	Sept 887	886						

Right-side annotations:

Ahaziah: 17th year of Jehosephat (I Kings 22:51) (I King 22:51)
Ahaziah: 2cd year of Joram: (II King 1:17)

12 yrs Joram: 18th year of Jehosephat (II Kings 3:1)...Joram(Israel) in 18th year of Jehosephat(Judah)

8 yrs Joram(Judah) began reign in the 5th year of Joram (Israel) (II Kings 8: 16-17)

Joram is the only King that is specifically identified as a Co-Rex (II Kings 8:16, 1:17)

As previously stated, Ahab (Israel) ruled for 22 years. Toward the end of his 22nd year, he and King Jehosephat (Judah) met and joined forces to go against the king of Syria to liberate Gilead. Ahab was killed by an arrow in the ensuing battle. Ahaziah assumed sole rule in Ahab's last credited year of reign and ruled as king until he fell through the lattice work of his room and died shortly thereafter. Both claimed April, 897 BC-April, 896 BC as a regnal year by the non-accession system.

A source of much confusion is the period of time between 897 BC and 885 BC, during which the kings of Judah and Israel had exactly the same name of Joram/Jehoram. When developing a correct chronology, proper identification of the referenced king is critical. By II Kings 8:16-17, Joram (Judah) and Joram (Israel) simultaneously served as kings. It is also specifically stated that Joram (Judah) became ruler in the fifth year of Joram (Israel). We are faced with the decision to have Joram (Judah) serve as co-rex with his father, Jehosephat, for either three years or four years. We will shortly establish that four years is the correct choice. For now, note that if Joram (Judah) reigned as co-rex for four years his first year of reign would be Sept, 893 BC-Sept, 892 BC. The fifth year of Joram (Israel) is determined to be April, 892 BC-April, 891 BC. Joram (Judah) did not follow the normal accession-year system; he became king while his father Jehosephat was still alive. By matching biblical records, we know that Joram (Judah) must have become co-rex between April, 893 BC and Sept, 892 BC. This is the source of a statement made previously that Joram (Judah) was a co-rex with Jehosephat (Judah) for four years.

A **Gordian knot** is formed by II Kings 1:17 which states that Joram (Israel) *came to the throne in the second year of Jehoram (Judah)*. But II Kings 3:1 states that Joram (Israel) *came to the throne in the 18th year of Jehosephat (Judah)*. How can this be true? The year that Joram (Israel) became sole monarch of the Northern Kingdom is clearly between April, 896 BC-Sept, 895 BC in the 18th year of Jehosephat (Judah)(II Kings 3:1). So how could II Kings 1:17 reference the second year of Joram (Judah) to the first year of Joram (Israel), when Joram of Judah did not become co-rex until Sept, 893 BC and sovereign king until September of 889 BC? The *Gordian knot* is severed by recognizing that somewhere around the 17th or 18th regnal year of Jehosephat; he embarked on a campaign to repel an Assyrian threat to the city of Ramoth-Gilead which lay on the western border of Judah. The forces against Jehosephat were strong, so Jehosephat entreated Ahab, who was his father-in-law and king of the Northern Kingdom, to join him in liberating Ramoth-Gilead. Ahab accepted the invitation (II Chronicles 18:3). This was in the 18th year of Jehosephat. We know this to be true because by divine proclamation Ahab was killed in the ensuing battle (II Chronicles 18:4-19). In the face of great danger, it is likely that before Jehosephat departed for this battle he appointed Joram his son to reign in his absence as a pro-rex. Jehoram probably knew by prophecy that Ahab was destined to be killed, and he no doubt feared that he might also be killed. The holy scribe related this event to the first year of reign of Ahaziah (I Kings 22:51). Using a non-accession-year system, Ahaziah claimed two year's reign but likely lived only a short time over one calendar year as sovereign king of Israel (II Kings 1:17). He fell through the *lattice of his upper room in Samaria* (II Kings 1:2) and was seriously injured. Elijah the prophet was told by the Lord that Ahaziah would soon die, and so he did shortly thereafter (II Kings 13-17). He was succeeded by Joram/Jerhoram (Israel) sometime between April, 896 BC and Sept, 896 BC. But this was in the second year since Joram (Judah) had been named co-rex by his father Jehosephat (Israel). So, the *Gordian knot* is severed.

We now come to a time at which several interesting and disruptive events occurred within a very short period of time. We are now ready to examine the sequence of strange events which surrounded the rise of Jehu in the Northern Kingdom. According to II Kings 8:18, Joram (Judah) married the daughter of wicked King Ahab in the Kingdom of Israel. He then "walked in the ways of the kings of Israel". Joram (king of Judah) died in the eighth year of his reign (II Kings 8:17). He had reigned four years as co-rex, and four years as sole-rex. He died a painful death: his bowels fell out (II Chronicles 21:18-20), and his son Ahaziah began to reign over Judah in the 12th year of Joram (Israel). Ahaziah, probably due to the influence and personal relationship with the Kingdom of Israel immediately claimed Sept 886-Sept 885 BC as his first year of reign. Both kingdoms had fallen into adultery and turned away from God, so Elisha the prophet called for one of his sons (II Kings 9:1) and sent him to persuade Jehu the son of Jehosephat to be the deliverer (II Kings 9:1-6). Jehu agreed and was anointed to kill both the King of Judah (Ahaziah), the King of Israel (Joram), and also Jezebel who had introduced adultery into the House of Israel (II Kings 9:10). In the early spring of 885 BC, King Joram (Israel) was severely wounded in a battle with the Assyrians (II Kings 9:15) and he retreated to Jezreel to recover from his wounds (II Kings 9:15). At that time King Ahaziah (Judah) went down to Jezreel to visit Joram (II Kings 8:29, 9:16). Jehu, seeing that both kings were together, conspired against Joram and Ahaziah, and went to Jezreel to kill both kings (II Kings 9:14). When Joram saw Jehu and his army approaching, both he and Ahaziah went forth to meet Jehu (II Kings 9:21). Jehu drew his bow and shot Joram in the heart (II Kings 9:24).

Ahaziah was also wounded by an arrow (II Kings 9:27) and he retreated to Meggido where he died shortly thereafter (II Kings 9:27). Jehu followed Ahaziah to Meggido. Upon arriving there, he found that Ahaziah had perished and that Jezebel was in the palace of the King (II Kings 9:30). At Jehu's command, several of her servants threw her from a high window, and *her blood splattered everywhere* (II Kings 9:33). It is interesting that Jezebel was left on the ground, while

During his last two years he					888	888	April		9	1 yr		Ahaziah reigned in 11th yr of
had an incureable disease			6	Sept	888	887						Joram (Israel) II Kings 9:29
in his bowels.					887	887	April	Joram	10			Ahaziah reigned in 12th yr of
(II Chronicles 21: 18-19)			7	Sept	887	886						Joram(Israel) II Kings 8:25
					886	886	April		11			
Ahaziah	1		8	Sept	886	885						
(Jehoahaz)	0				885	885	April		12	Jehu	1	Jehu killed Joram, Ahaziah and
Age of Joash	1	Athaliah	1	Sept	885	884						all in kingly line but baby Joash
					884	884	April		2			II Kings 10:36 just says Jehu
	2		2	Sept	884	883						reigned 28 years
					883	883	April		3			
	3		3	Sept	883	882						Jehu Kills Ahaziah and then Joram(Israel)
					882	882	April		4			between Sept, 885 and April, 884
	4		4	Sept	882	881						There is now now King in either the
					881	881	April		5			Northern or Southern Kingdoms.
	5		5	Sept	881	880						Athaliah moves to killl all of her sons and
					880	880	April		6			assumes the throne immediately....but
	6		6	Sept	880	879						little Joash, her youngest son, is
					879	879	April		7			hidden and saved. Jehu continues to war....
	7	Joash/Jehoash	1	Sept	879	878						also killing Jezebel. He declares himself
					878	878	April		8			King of Israel in 885.
			2	Sept	878	877			9			In 7th year of Jehu, Joash began
Jeoash was annointed					877	877	April					to reign..(II King 12:1, II Chron 12:1)
as King at age 7, at			3	Sept	877	876						Joash took throne between April-Sept of 878 BC
the beginning of					876	876	April		10			Josepus recorded that Joash was less than 1 year
Athaliah's 7th year			4	Sept	876	875						old when hidden by Jehosheba (Ahaziah's sister
in the 7th year of					875	875	April		11			and wife of High Priest Jehodia (Antiq 9:7:1)
Jehu (Israel)			5	Sept	875	874						

Jehu drank wine in the palace. After a great celebration, Jehu commanded that she be buried, but when they sought her body, there was nothing there but her skull, her feet and the palms of her hands (II Kings 9:35). So it was that a previous, curious prophecy by Elisha the prophet came true, that *"In Jezreel dogs would eat the flesh of Jezebel"* (I Kings 21:23). At this point, there was no king in either Israel or Judah; both reigning kings had been killed in a short period of time by Jehu. The proper synchronization of all these events which follows the biblical descriptions is interesting and unique. The following graphic illustrates the unusual sequence of events which took place between April of 886 BC and April of 884 BC.

II Kings 9:29 states that Ahaziah came to be King in the 11th year of Joram (Israel). But II Kings 8:25 specifically states that Ahaziah became king in the 12th year of Joram (Israel). Here is another clear case of how the accession-year system of Judah and the regnal years of Israel uniquely

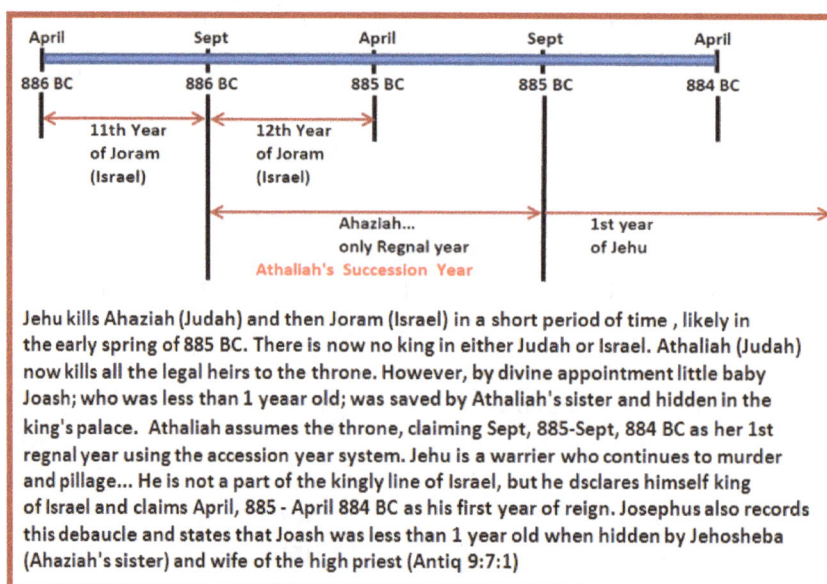

Jehu kills Ahaziah (Judah) and then Joram (Israel) in a short period of time , likely in the early spring of 885 BC. There is now no king in either Judah or Israel. Athaliah (Judah) now kills all the legal heirs to the throne. However, by divine appointment little baby Joash; who was less than 1 yeaar old; was saved by Athaliah's sister and hidden in the king's palace. Athaliah assumes the throne, claiming Sept, 885-Sept, 884 BC as her 1st regnal year using the accession year system. Jehu is a warrier who continues to murder and pillage... He is not a part of the kingly line of Israel, but he dsclares himself king of Israel and claims April, 885 - April 884 BC as his first year of reign. Josephus also records this debaucle and states that Joash was less than 1 year old when hidden by Jehosheba (Ahaziah's sister) and wife of the high priest (Antiq 9:7:1)

synchronize. Joram (Judah) died sometime between Sept 886 BC and Sept 885 BC. The accession year of Ahaziah started at the death of Joram (Judah) in his eighth year of reign, which lasted until September, 886 BC. The 11th regnal year of Joram (Israel) was April, 886 BC-April, 885 BC, so Ahaziah began operating in the king's capacity during the 11th regnal year of Joram (Israel). Ahaziah started his first official regnal year on Tishri 1 (Sept/Oct) of 886 BC, which fell in the 12th regnal year of Joram (Israel). So, II Kings 9:29 and II Kings 9:25 are both correct: one refers to when Ahaziah actually *assumed* the throne, and the other refers to when his first *official year of reign* actually started. This attests to the absolute accuracy of the King James biblical records.

Jehu killed both Ahaziah (Judah) and Joram (Israel) during a short period of time between Sept, 886 BC and April, 885 BC. Since both kingdoms were without a king in the same year, the accumulated regnal years in both kingdoms should be the same. The following table tabulates the regnal years in each kingdom.

Southern Kingdom Kings			Northern Kingdom Kings		
Name of King	Recorded Reign	Independent Years	Name of King	Duration of Reign	Independent Years
Rehoboam	17 Years	17	Jeroboam II	22 Years	22
Abijah	3 Years	3	Nadab	2 Years	1
Asa	41 Years	41	Baasha	24 Years	23
Jehosephat	25 Years	25	Elah	2 Years	1
Jehoram	8 Years	5	Zimri	7 Days	0
			Omri	12 Years	11
Total Years:	94 Years	91	Ahab	22 Years	21
			Ahaziah	2 Years	1
			Joram	12 Years	11
			Total Years:	98 Years	91 Years

Note that the regnal years credited to the southern kings of Judah add up to 94 years. In the Northern Kingdom of Israel, the credited regnal years add to 98 years. Clearly, there seems to be something wrong. However, recall that every king of Judah ascended to the throne using the *accession-year system* with the exception of Jehoram, who co-reigned with Jehosephat for four years. The actual number of sequential calendar years from Rehoboam through the reign of Joram/Jehoram is therefore *90 years.* In the Northern Kingdom, every King from Jeroboam to Joram used a *non-accession system.* Hence, the total regnal years of all the Northern Kingdom kings would be one year longer *for each king* than those of the Southern Kingdom kings. This would result in (98-8) = 90 sequential years (Zimri received no regnal years credit).

Hence, the *conundrum* is solved. This analysis proves three important things: (1) The chronology from the death of King Solomon to the last year of Jehoram/Joram (Judah) and Joram (Israel) is correct using the biblical records for each kingdom, (2) The assumption that the Southern Kingdom used an accession system and that the Northern Kingdom used a non-accession system to this point in time is correct, and (3) the assumption that the Southern Kingdom used a Tishri 1-Tishri 1 Regnal year and the Northern Kingdom used a Nisan 1-Nisan 1 regnal year uniquely provides an exact match to the biblical records up to this point in time. In continuing further, the Southern Kingdom will never abandon the accession-year system, but we will show that starting with the reign of Jehu, the Northern Kingdom will abandon the non-accession-year system for some unknown reason. We are now ready to further address the confusing reigns of Athaliah, the child-king Joash/Jehoash , and the reign of Jehu.

Judah	Age of Joash	Ruler	Ruler yr	Month	Year	Year	Israel	Jehu/Joram yr	Note	Description
				April	887	887	Joram	10	1 yr	Ahaziah reigned in 11th yr of
			7	Sept	887	886				Joram (Israel) II Kings 9:29
				April	886	886		11		Ahaziah reigned in 12th yr of
Joram		Joram	8	Sept	886	885				Joram(Israel) II Kings 8:25
				April	885	885		12	Jehu 1	Jehu killed Joram, Ahaziah and
Ahaziah	0-1	Athaliah	1	Sept	885	884				all in kingly line but baby Joash
(Jehoahaz)				April	884	884		2		II Kings 10:36 just says Jehu
			2	Sept	884	883				reigned 28 years
	1-2			April	883	883		3	6 yrs	Athaliah siezed the throne when
			3	Sept	883	882				when her son Ahaziah was slain
	2-3			April	882	882		4		by Jehu, sometime between
			4	Sept	882	881				Oct 886-March 885.
	3-4			April	881	881		5		Jehu Kills Ahaziah and then Joram(Israel)
			5	Sept	881	880				between Oct, 886 and Mar, 885
	4-5			April	880	880		6		There is now no King in either the
			6	Sept	880	879				Northern or Southern Kingdoms.
	5-6			April	879	879		7		Athaliah moves to kill all of her sons and
Age of Joash	6-7	Joash/Jehoash	1	Sept	879	878				assumes the throne immediately....but
				April	878	878		8		little Joash, her infant son, is hidden
			2	Sept	878	877				and saved.
				April	877	877		9		Jehu continues to war....
			3	Sept	877	876				also killing Jezebel. He declares himself
				April	876	876		10		King of Israel in winter of 884 BC.
			4	Sept	876	875				
				April	875	875		11		In 7th year of Jehu, Joash began
			5	Sept	875	874				to reign..(II King 12:1, II Chron 12:1)
				April	874	874		12		Joash took throne after he turned 7 in 878 BC
			6	Sept	874	873				Josepus recorded that Joash was less than 1 year
				April	873	873		13		old when hidden by Jehosheba (Ahaziah's sister
			7	Sept	873	872				and wife of High Priest Jehodia (Antiq 9:7:1)

Jeoash was annointed as King at age 7, at the beginning of Athaliah's 7th year in the 7th year of Jehu (Israel)

Jehu evidently continued to rampage for at least one more year. He killed 70 sons of Ahab (II Kings 10:1, 7) and 42 brothers of Ahaziah! (II Kings 10:2-14. Meanwhile, Athaliah *arose and destroyed all the royal heirs to the (*her*) throne* (II Kings 11:1) to insure that there would be no male heir left alive to become king of Judah. But the daughter of the slain King Joram (Judah), and the sister of Ahaziah, took Jehoash who was the infant son of deceased king, Ahaziah (Judah), and hid him in *the house of the Lord* for six years (II Kings 11:2-3). At the time he was hidden, Jehoash was not yet one year old (II Kings 11:2, 4, 21). Athaliah reigned as sole rex over the land for six years (II Kings 11:3). In the seventh year of her reign, the high priest Jehoiada revealed little Jehoash/Joash as the true king to the other priests. The people then yelled: *Long Live the King* !

The people then killed Athaliah, and made Jehoash king of Judah at age seven (II Kings 11:21). Athaliah was credited with six years of reign (II Kings 11:3), claiming Sept 880-Sept 879 BC as her last year. The correctness of this sequence of events is confirmed in II Kings 12:1 in which we are told that Jehoash became king in *the seventh year of Jehu.* This is graphically shown in the above table. This sequence of events is attested to by both the Holy Scribe and by Josephus, the Jewish historian. Josephus recorded that Jehoash was less than one year old when he was hidden by Ahaziah's sister, Jehosheba, and he was seven years old when he became boy-king of Judah (Antiq 9:7:1). The Holy Scriptures simply say that Jehu reigned as king of Israel in Samaria for 28 years (II Kings 10:36). Jehoash reigned for 40 years in Jerusalem (II Kings 12:1). We now turn our attention to Jehoahaz (Israel).

	21	Sept	859	858					
			858	858	858	April	Jehu	28	
Joash / Jehoash	22	Sept	858		857				
			857	857	857	April	Jehoahaz	1	17 yrs — Jehoahaz: 23rd year of Joash (II Kings 13:1)
	23	Sept	857		856				
				856	856	April		2	*Jehoahaz suddenly switched to an acession year system*
	24	Sept	856		855				
			855	855		April		3	
	25	Sept	855		854				

The initial year of the reign of Jehoahaz is clearly given in II Kings 13.

> **"In the 23rd year of Joash, the son of Ahaziah King of Judah, Jehoahaz the son of Jehu became King over Israel in Samaria, and reigned 17 years."** II Kings 13:1

Jehoahaz chose to use the accession-year system introduced by Jehu, and this system was then used by every remaining king in the Northern Kingdom. Jehoahaz was succeeded by his son Jehoash. We will now discuss the reign of Jehoash and his unusual correlation to the reign of Amaziah, also known as Ahaziah, in the Southern Kingdom of Judah.

> **"In the 37th year of Joash King of Judah, Jehoash the son of Jehoahaz became King of Israel in Samaria, and reigned 16 years"** II Kings 13:10

Both Amaziah and Jehoash used the accession-year system, so their first year of reign would

	35	Sept	845		844					
			844	844	844	April	Jehoahaz	14		
Joash / Jehoash	36	Sept	844		843			15		
			843	843		April				
	37	Sept	843		842					
			842	842		April		16	Jehoash Pro Rex	1
	38	Sept	842		841				Pro Rex	2
			841	841		April		17		
	39	Sept	841		840					
			840	840		April	Jehoash Sole Rex	1		
	40	Sept	840		839			16		
			839	839		April		2		
Amaziah/ Ahaziah	1	Sept	839		838					
			838	838		April		3		
	2	Sept	838		837					
			837	837		April		4		
	3	Sept	837		836			29		
			836	836		April		5		
	4	Sept	836		835					

Jehoash (Israel) began to reign as Pro Rex with his father Jehoahaz in the 37th year of Jehahaz' reign. He became sole ruler after two years. Synchronization with all the other Kings of Judah and Israel demand this interpretation.

In 2cd year of Joash/Jehoash (Israel) Amaziah began reign He reigned 29 years in Jerusalem (II Kings 13:10)

actually begin in the immediately-preceding year, following the death of their fathers. Their first official regnal year would begin on the first day of Tishri (Amaziah) or on Nisan 1 (Jehoash).This is exactly as shown in the above graphic. This chronology is confirmed in II Kings 14.

> *"In the second year of Joash (Jehoash) the son of Jehoahaz, Amaziah (Ahaziah) the son of Joash, King of Judah, became king. He was 25 years old when he became King, and he reigned 29 years in Jerusalem."*   II Kings 14:1-2

A new *Gordian knot* is uncovered by the record of II Kings 13.

> *"In the 37th year of Joash King of Judah, Jehoash the son of Jehoahaz became King of Israel in Samaria and he reigned 16 years in Jerusalem."*   II Kings 13:10

			844	844	April	Jehoahaz	14			
Joash / Jehoash	36	Sept	844	843						
			843	843	April		15			
	37	Sept	843	842						
			842	842	April		16	Jehoash		Jehoash (Israel) began to reign as
	38	Sept	842	841				Pro Rex		Pro Rexwith his father Jehoahaz
			841	841	April		17	Pro Rex		in the 37th year of Jehoash' reign.
	39	Sept	841	840						
			840	840	April	Jehoash	1			
	40	Sept	840	839		Sole Rex			16	He became sole ruler
			839	839	April		2			after two years. Synchronization with all the other
Amaziah/	1	Sept	839	838						Kings of Judah and Israel demand this interpretation.
Ahaziah			838	838	April		3			
	2	Sept	838	837					29	In 2cd year of Joash/Jehoash (Israel) Amaziah began
			837	837	April		4			reign. He reigned 29 years in Jerusalem
	3	Sept	837	836						(II Kings 13:10)

Examining the previous graphical record, the 37th year of Joash (Judah) was September, 843 BC-September, 842 BC. This places the first year of Jehoash (Israel) beginning no earlier than shortly after Nisan 1, 843 BC and no later than before Nisan 1, 842 BC This also demands that the first official regnal year of reign for Jehoash (Israel) was 1-2 years before the death of his father, Jehoahaz, sometime before Nisan 1, 840 BC. This can only be true if Jehoahaz (Israel) was placed into a recognized position of reign well before his father, Jehoahaz, died. The only way that this could happen is if Jehoash (Israel) reigned as pro-rex with Jehoahaz until his death, probably between January and April of 840 BC. The second year of Jehoash (Israel) is locked into April, 839 BC-April, 838 by synchronization with Amaziah (Judah), and is subsequently demanded in order to synchronize the Northern and Southern Kingdom kings which follow.

The two-year pro-rex reign of Jehoash with Jehoahaz was probably motivated by the following turn of events. The last years of Jehoahaz's reign were spent under Syrian oppression (II Kings 13:2-4). Several cities of Judah were captured (II Kings 13:25) and the armies of Jehoahaz decimated (II Kings 13:7). Due to public unrest and private humiliation, Jehoahaz likely retreated from public reign and named his son, Jehoash/Joash, as a pro-rex during the 16th year of his reign. Upon the death of Jehoahaz, Jehoash/Joash assumed the throne and subsequently claimed his first year of reign about two years later starting in April of 840 BC. At the time, both the people and Jehoash might have simply assumed that he had already been co-rex king for two years, an assumption obviously corrected by the official scribe in the now lost *Book of the Chronicles/ Kings* which is strangely now mentioned in II Kings 13:8 and quoted in II Kings 13:10 and 14:1-2. The seemingly conflicting statements of II Kings 13:1 and II Kings 14:1-2 were evidently left in the Canon of the II Book of Kings. So, another *Gordian knot* is severed.

Amaziah/								
			826	826	April		15	
Amaziah/	14	Sept	826	825				
			825	825	April	Jehoash	16	
	15	Sept	825	824				
			824	824	April	Jeroboam II	1	41 yrs
	16	Sept	824	823				
			823	823	April		2	
	17	Sept	823	822				
			822	822	April		3	
	18	Sept	822	821				
			821	821	April		4	
	19	Sept	821	820				

Jeroboam II: 15th year of Amaziah
  (II King 14:23)
Amaziah year 15: Sept, 825-Sept, 824
Amaziah lived 15 years after the death of Joash
  (II Chron 25:25)
Joash must have died early in his 16th (last) year

Jehoash reigned for 16 years, and he was succeeded by his son, Jeroboam II. The first year of reign for Jeroboam II was April 824 BC-April, 823 BC, and this is synchronized to the 15th year of Amaziah (Judah) by II Kings 14:23. A second witness that this chronological sequence is correct is given in II Chronicles 25:25. Here we are again told that Amaziah lived for 15 years after the death of Jehoash/Joash (Israel).

		Amaziah/	14	Sept	826	825			
					825	825	April	Jehoash	16
Amaziah lived 15 years after the death of Joash II Chronicles 25:25	1		15	Sept	825	824			
					824	824	April	Jeroboam II	1	41 yrs
	2		16	Sept	824	823			
					823	823	April		2
	3		17	Sept	823	822			
					822	822	April		3
	4		18	Sept	822	821			
					821	821	April		4
	5		19	Sept	821	820			
					820	820	April		5
	6		20	Sept	820	819			
					819	819	April		6
	7		21	Sept	819	818			
					818	818	April		7
	8		22	Sept	818	817			
					817	817	April		8
	9		23	Sept	817	816			
					816	816	April		9
	10		24	Sept	816	815			
					815	815	April		10
	11		25	Sept	815	814			
					814	814	April		11
	12		26	Sept	814	813			
					813	813	April		12
	13		27	Sept	813	812			
					812	812	April		13
	14		28	Sept	812	811			
					811	811	April		14
	15		29	Sept	811	810			
					810	810	April	Jeroboam II	15

Since Jeroboam II used an accession-year system, his father Jehoash must have died between April, 825 BC and April, 824 BC. If Jehoash died early in the spring or summer of 825 BC, this statement is correct (see the numbered years of Ahaziah starting in 825 BC as follows). This brings us to King Uzziah of the Southern Kingdom of Judah.

Age of Uzziah	King	Amaziah Yr	Month	Year BC	Year BC	April	Jeroboam II	Jeroboam Yr	52 yrs	Notes
15	Amaziah	29	Sept	811	810					
				810	810	April	Jeroboam II	15		
Age of Uzziah	Uzziah / Azariah	1	Sept	810	809			16	52 yrs	Uzziah…In 15th year of Jeroboam II
6				809	809	April		16		Uzziah was annointed King at age 6.
		2	Sept	809	808					Uncapable of reigning untill he matured,
7				808	808	April		17		Uzziah did not become sole monarch until
		3	Sept	808	807					he was age 18 in the 27th year of Jeroboam II
8				807	807	April		18		(II Kings 15:1-2, II Kings 14: 1-2, 23,27)
		4	Sept	807	806					
9				806	806	April		19		
		5	Sept	806	805					
10				805	805	April		20		
		6	Sept	805	804					
11				804	804	April		21		
		7	Sept	804	803					
12				803	803	April		22		
		8	Sept	803	802					
13				802	802	April		23		
		9	Sept	802	801					
14				801	801	April		24		
		10	Sept	801	800					
15				800	800	April		25		
		11	Sept	800	799					
16				799	799	April		26		
		12	Sept	799	798					
17				798	798	April	Jeroboam II	27		
	Uzziah/ Azariah	13	Sept	798	797					
18				797	797	April		28		

* * * * * * * *
* * * * * * * *
* * * * * * * *

King	Uzziah Yr	Month	Year BC	Year BC	April	Jeroboam II	Jeroboam Yr
			787	787	April		38
	24	Sept	787	786			
			786	786	April		39
	25	Sept	786	785			
			785	785	April		40
Uzziah/ Azariah	26	Sept	785	784			
			784	784	April	Jeroboam II	41
	27	Sept	784	783			

Amaziah was the father of Uzziah who was also called Azariah. As shown previously, Jeroboam II became king of Israel in the 15th year of Amaziah, and he reigned for 41 years (II Kings 14:23). As previously noted, the reigns of Amaziah and Jeroboam II are synchronized by II Kings 14:17, which state that Amaziah lived 15 years after the death of Jehoash in the summer of 825 BC. Amaziah ruled for 29 years (II Kings 14:1-2). Here we encounter another difficult *Gordian knot*. We are told that Uzziah began his reign in the *15th year of Jeroboam II* (II Kings 14:1-2, 23, 47 and II Kings 15:1-2). There is no reason whatsoever to doubt that Uzziah would immediately assume the role of king of Judah following the death of his father, Amaziah, as did all the kings before him. A *Gordian knot* is created when we read in II Kings 15:1-2 that Uzziah began to reign over the Southern Kingdom in the *27th regnal year of Jeroboam II* (Israel). The conflict is obvious: *how can Uzziah begin his reign in both the 27th year of Jeroboam and in the 15th year of Jeroboam?*

To answer that question, we need to look at all the available facts. Uzziah inherited the kingdom of Judah from his father Amaziah during a period of wars and conflict. Amaziah had previously faced King Jehoash of Israel in open battle where he (Amaziah) was soundly defeated. Jehoash took Amaziah captive to the southern capital of Jerusalem, effectively ending his power as king when he was captured and humiliated (II Kings 14:8-14, II Chronicles 25:17-24). King Jehoash attacked Jerusalem while Amaziah was captive and tore a 200-foot gap in the wall which surrounded Jerusalem. He then plundered Solomon's temple, took all of the gold and silver, and returned to the northern capital of Samaria with prisoners. At this point, although Amaziah was still officially king of Judah, his power had been removed, and Jerusalem was for all practical purposes reduced to a vassal city/state controlled by King Jehoash of Israel. King Amaziah died shortly thereafter, leaving little or nothing to his heir apparent, Uzziah. Taken in context, it is reasonable to assume that Uzziah inherited a throne and kingship in name only. It can therefore be conjectured that it took Uzziah 12 more years to strengthen the Southern Kingdom and gain enough power to establish himself as a sole monarch, finally breaking the yoke of domination under King Jeroboam of Israel. This conjecture gains plausibility by understanding that Uzziah inherited the throne from Amaziah at the age of 16 (II Kings 15:1-2). While a young man of 16 years certainly could wield leadership and power (King David was about that age when he slew Goliath, but he was dominated by Saul for many years), there was much to do to restore the kingdom of Judah to power. It can be conjectured that the restoration of Judah and Jerusalem took 12 years, and in his 13th year of reign, in the 27th year of Jeroboam (Israel), he established himself as a powerful King (II Chronicles 26:14-16). This is a believable and most-likely explanation of the kingship of Uzziah. The reign of Jeroboam II (Northern Kingdom) ended after 41 years in the 26th year of Uzziah's reign (II Kings 14:23-29). Jeroboam II died somewhere between April and September of 784 BC in his 41st year of reign.

This brings us to what we will call the *Mysterious Zachariah Dilemma*. According to the Holy Scriptures, Zachariah (Israel) *reigned for six months* and was then assassinated by Shallum in the 38th year of King Uzziah's reign (II Kings 15:13). The graphic on the next page shows these events.

The *Zachariah Dilemma* evolves by noticing that if Jeroboam died in the 26th year of Uzziah, and Zachariah reigned six months in the 38th year of Uzziah, a *gap in regnal years for the Northern Kingdom* of 11-12 years is created. This period without any king is called an *interregnum*. An interregnum is not an uncommon occurrence for other nations in ancient times, but it is never mentioned in the biblical records for either the Northern or Southern Kingdoms; suggesting that this period of time as a possible interregnum is not unique to this study. It has been encountered by practically every other chronologist and a definitive solution to this dilemma has never been found. It is *commonly assumed* that an interregnum *did occur*, interrupting the kingly reign of the Northern Kingdom; however, two other plausible solutions can be suggested. The *first* is to simply assume that the biblical records fail to record a total reign of 11 years and six months for Zachariah, and that he actually began to reign following the death of Jeroboam II in 783 BC. But, the biblical records are

Judah King	Judah Yr	Sept Year	Israel Year (April)	Israel King	Reign	Extra
			785		40	
Uzziah/ Azariah	26	Sept 785	784	Jeroboam II	41	
	27	Sept 784	783		1	
	28	Sept 783	782		2	
	29	Sept 782	781		3	
	30	Sept 781	780		4	
	31	Sept 780	779		5	
	32	Sept 779	778		6	
	33	Sept 778	777		7	
	34	Sept 777	776		8	
	35	Sept 776	775		9	
	36	Sept 775	774		10	
	37	Sept 774	773		11	
	38	Sept 773	772	Zachariah	6 Months	6 mos
	39	Sept 772	771	Shallum	1 Month	1 mo
			771	Menahem	1	
	40	Sept 771	770		2	
	41	Sept 770	769		3	10
	42	Sept 769	768		4	
	43	Sept 768	767		5	

Most chonologists record a 10-12 year interregum here, but it is more likely that Zachariah had an unrecorded reign of 11-12 years.

The Holy Scriptues simply state that "Zachariah reigned 6 months in the 37th year of Uzziah"

Zachariah reigned 6 months in the 38th year of Uzziah (II King 15:8)

Shallum killed Zachariah: reigned 1 month in the 39th year of Uzziah (II King 15:13)

In 39th year of Uzziah: Menahem killed Shallum and assumed the throne after the assassination (II King 15: 17). Menahem claimed the full year of Spring 771-Spring of 770 using Acession year logic

The Assyrian King PUL came aginst Menahem early in his reign. (II King 15:19)

complete and descriptive as to when every other king began his reign. Why would Zachariah be overlooked? The record of II Kings 14:29 seem to indicate that the reign of Azariah started immediately following the death of Jeroboam.

> *"And Jeroboam slept with his fathers, even with the Kings of Israel: and Zachariah his son reigned in his stead."* II Kings 14:29

There is certainly no indication that there was an 11-12 year gap in time between the death of Jeroboam and the rule of Zachariah in II Kings 14:29. In every other case, there are often parallel and identical accounts of regnal ascensions in I Kings, II Kings, I Chronicles or II Chronicles. A possible explanation is that this period of time and the king who reigned is omitted in the biblical records. Although complete omission seems unlikely, it must be considered.

A *second* explanation has been proposed by Dolen and later supported by Jones. The explanation revolves around the following record.

> *"In the thirty and eighth year of Azariah King of Judah did Zachariah the son of Jeroboam reign over Israel for 6 months."* II Kings 15:8

Dolen noticed that this passage simply states that Zachariah *reigned over Israel for six months* in the 38th year of Azariah. It does not say he *started to reign* at that time, only that he reigned for six months. Dolen also noted that the phrase *began to reign* or more specifically the word *began* was used for almost all of his predecessors. The conclusion by Dolan is that there is no specific reference to Zachariah beginning his reign 11-12 years earlier, but only a reference to the fact that he died in his 12th year of reign after six months. This *linguistic fo-pah* is appealing, but seems to be stretching the point a bit; however, it is certainly possible. We may never know the real explanation. However, synchronization of the biblical records from this point forward demand that Zachariah died somewhere in the late spring of 772 BC by assassination.

Continuing the chronology, we know with certainty that Zachariah reigned for six months in the 38th year of Uzziah (II Kings 15:8) After six months reign, Shallum *"conspired against him (Zachariah), killed him in front of the people, and reigned in his place"* (II Kings 15:10-13). This was in the 39th year of Uzziah (II Kings 15:13). After only one month, *"Menahem the son of Gadi went up from Tirzah into Samaria and killed him (Shallum)"* (II Kings 15:14). Menahem then assumed the throne *in the 39th year of Uzziah King of Judah, and reigned for ten years* (II Kings 15:17).

Upon his death, Menahem was succeeded by his son Pekahiah. He reigned for two years, at which time Hoshea the son of Elah led a conspiracy against him; so Hoshea *"struck and killed him"* (II Kings 15:30). Pekah assumed the throne in the 52nd year of Uzziah (Judah), and he reigned for 20 years (II Kings 15:27). Uzziah and his son Jotham had an interesting relationship. King Uzziah reigned for a total of 52 years. He was a good king, but became arrogant in his old age.

In II Chronicles 26:16 we are told that he entered the Temple of God to burn incense upon the Altar of Incense in the Holy Place. This undoubtedly happened on the Feast of Yom Kippur, when the High Priest was to burn incense before the Lord, and then enter into the Holy of Holies to plead the sins of the people before God. It was unlawful for anyone other than the priesthood to burn incense in the Holy Place. The high priest and eighty Levites went in after him, but Uzziah became furious and continued to approach the Alter of Incense with a Holy Censor full of incense. As he approached the Holy Altar, God struck him down with leprosy (II Kings 15:5),II Chronicles 26:19-23). King Uzziah was a leper until the day of his death, and he lived in an *isolated house* (II Chronicles 26:21). *"Then Jotham his son was over the king's house, judging the people of the land"* (II Chronicles 26:21).

Jotham served as a judge and a pro-rex for 6 years before Uzziah died; he then became the King of Judah (II Chronicles 26:18-23). This is demanded since the Holy Scriptures record that *Jotham began to reign as a sovereign king in the second year of Pekah* (II Kings 15: 32-33). The graphic on the following page show how these sequence of events fit together, and how all scriptural references are fully synchronized

			46	Sept	765	764				
					764	764	April		8	
Jotham Pro Rex	1		47	Sept	764	763				
					763	763	April		9	
Served as a	2		48	Sept	763	762				
					762	762	April	Menahem	10	
Judge	3		49	Sept	762	761				
for 6 years						761	761	April	Pekahiah	1	2 yrs
	4		50	Sept	761	760				
					760	760	April		2	
	5	Uzziah	51	Sept	760	759				
					759	759	April	Pekah	1	20 yrs
	6		52	Sept	759	758				
					758	758	April		2	
		Jotham	1	Sept	758	757				16 yrs
					757	757	April		3	
			2	Sept	757	756				
					756	756	April		4	

Jotham (Judah) reigned for 16 years starting sometime between Sept 759-Sept 758 BC. His first official year of reign was Sept 758-Sept 757 BC. We are now ready to look at the reign of King Ahaz (Judah). Ahaz began to reign in the 17th year of Pekah (Israel),

				744	744	April	Pekah	16
	15	Sept	744	743				
				743	743	April		17
Jotham	16	Sept	743	742				
				742	742	April		18
Ahaz	1	Sept	742	741				
				741	741	April		19
	2	Sept	741	740				

Ahaz reigned for 16 years. The first official year of Ahaz, King of Judah was Sept/Oct, 742-Sept/Oct, 741, but he became king between Sept 743 and April 742 BC (II Kings 16:1-2).

Ahaz was a wicked king who turned away from God: He walked in the ways of the kings of Israel, and instituted Baal worship in Judah. We will now see that this close alignment with Israel and their pagan practices will result in Ahab serving as a King of Israel for several years. We have now come to the last king of the Northern Kingdom, who was Hoshea son of Elah. Hoshea succeeded Pekah using an accession-year system. The reign of Hoshea has long presented significant problems to determining the final year of the Northern Kingdom. The following graphic will now be used to discuss the problems associated with when Hoshea began his reign.

	48	Sept	763	762					
			762	762	April	Menahem	10		
	49	Sept	762	761					
			761	761	April	Pekahiah	1	2 yrs	Pekahia began to reign in Uzziah's 50th year II Kings 15:23)
	50	Sept	761	760					
			760	760	April		2		
Uzziah	51	Sept	760	759					
			759	759	April	Pekah	1	20 yrs	Pekah began to reign in the 52cd year of Uzziah II Kings 15:27
	52	Sept	759	758					
			758	758	April		2		
Jotham	1	Sept	758	757				16 yrs	Jotham began to reign in 2cd year of Pekah II Kings 15:32-33
			757	757	April		3		
	2	Sept	757	756					
			756	756	April		4		

The reign of Hoshea presents the most difficult chronological problems of any king before him. The difficulties are that multiple records appear to exist in conflict of one another.

					743	743	April		17
Jotham	16	Sept	743			742	April		18
			742	742		741	April		19
Ahaz	1	Sept	742	741	741	740	April		19
	2	Sept	741	740	740	740	April	Pekah	20
	3	Sept	740	739	739	739	April	Hoshea Pro-Rex	1
Ahaz	4	Sept	739	738	738	738	April		2
	5	Sept	738	737					

16 yrs — Ahaz: 17th year of Pekah (II Kings 16:1)

> **"Then *Hoshea the son of Elah led a conspiracy against Pekah the son of Remaliah, and struck and killed him; so he reigned in his place in the 20th year of Jotham the son of Uzziah"***   II Kings 15:30

Looking at the previous graphic, Pekah was assassinated by Hoshea sometime between April 740 BC and April 739 BC. Hoshea would have begun to reign immediately, but his first official regnal year using an accession-year system is shown as starting in April 739 BC. This creates a *Gordian knot* formed by the witness of II Kings 17:1.

> **"In the 12th year of Ahaz king of Judah, Hoshea the son of Elah became king of Israel in Samaria, and he reigned 9 years."**   II Kings 17:1

The difficulty is in the record of II Kings 15:30, which states that *Pekah was killed in the 20th year of Jotham the son of Uzziah.* But Jotham only reigned 16 years, and his last year of reign was Sept/Oct, 743 BC–Sept/Oct, 742 BC. So how could Hoshea kill Pekah in the 20th year of Jotham? The answer can be found by observing that the reference to the 20th year of Jotham is clearly not to the 20th year of his reign, but to *the 20th year since Jotham began to reign as king.* The 20th year since Jotham began to reign is Sept 739 BC-Sept 738 BC, which corresponds to the year following the death of Pekah at the hand of Hoshea, April 739 BC-April 738 BC. The year that Hoshea killed Pekah and usurped the throne would be in April 739 BC–April 738 BC.

Having solved this problem, we now note another (apparent) serious problem in the reign of Hoshea. Hoshea only reigned nine years (II King 17:1), and as we will see in the next section, several years in the reign of Hoshea are cross-referenced to King Hezekiah in the kingdom of Judah, who had not even begun to reign until 13-14 years after the death of Pekah, the predecessor of Hoshea! This conundrum is exacerbated by the biblical record that without controversy cross-references the third year of Hoshea's reign to the first year of Hezekiah's reign, who became king of Judah following the death of King Ahab in his 16th year of reign.

"Now it came to pass in the third year of Hoshea the son of Elah, King of Israel, that Zedekiah the son of Ahaz, King of Judah, began to reign." II Kings 18:1

The *Gordian knot* is now tightened by the obvious fact that the third year of Hoshea's reign is also locked into the first year of Hezekiah's reign by II Kings 18:1. Hezekiah became king of Judah in September of 726 BC, and his first year of reign ended in September, 725 BC. The third year of Hoshea would therefore start in either Mar/April of 727 BC or Mar/April of 726 BC. The correct choice is discovered by looking at the following additional biblical record.

"Now it came to pass in the 4th year of King Hezekiah, which was the 7th year of Hoshea the son of Elah, king of Israel, that Shalmaneser king of Assyria came up against Samaria and besieged it." II Kings 18:9

The invasion of Samaria by Shalmeneser in the seventh year of Hoshea continued to the complete destruction of the Northern Kingdom three years later (II Kings 18:10). This invasion is locked into the fourth year of Hezekiah, which was September, 723 BC-September, 722 BC. This invasion is locked into the fourth year of Hezekiah, which was September, 723 BC-September, 722 BC. Since Hoshea followed a Nisan 1 (Mar/April) to a Nisan 1 regnal year (Mar/April-Mar/April), the seventh year of Hoshea *had* to be Mar/April, 723 BC-Mar/April, 722 BC. This in turn locks the first year of Hoshea to April, 729 BC-April, 728 BC.; but, what about the statement of II Kings 17:1 which states that *"in the 12th year of Ahaz Hoshea became King of Israel?"* The match of every biblical cross reference to this point except for II Kings 17:1 leaves a gap of 10 years between Mar/April, 739 BC and Mar/April, 729 BC.

This gap has caused many a chronographer to simply give up and declare that since Hoshea only reigned for nine years, there is a biblical error. The answer to this new *Gordian knot* is surprising; it is found in II Chronicles 28: 9-27. Ahaz, king of Judah, was closely associated with the kingdom of Israel. He *"walked in the ways of the kings of Israel"* (II Chronicles 28:2), and he *"sacrificed to idols and burned incense in high places"* (II Chronicles 28:4).

The king of Syria defeated Ahaz and delivered him and a great multitude to Pekah, king of Israel (II Chronicles 28:5). In a divine act of mercy, a prophet named Oded intervened and saved Ahaz and his people, and they returned to Jericho (II Chronicles 28: 6-15). After that, Ahaz became increasingly defiant and departed from the Lord: He shut up the Temple, made altars to foreign gods, and *"provoked God to anger"* (II Chronicles 28:25). In examining the acts of Ahaz over his last years of reign, we come across a curious set of information. In II Chronicles 28:19 we read that *"the Lord brought Judah low because of Ahaz, King of Israel"*. But Ahaz was the king of *Judah*: surely this is a scribal error... or, is it? In II Chronicles 28:26 we read that when Ahaz died, *"the rest of his acts and all his ways, from first to last, indeed they are written in the book of the kings of Judah and Israel"*.

The chronicler records that *"Ahaz rested with his fathers, and they buried him in the city, in Jerusalem; but they did not bring him into the tombs of the Kings of Israel"* (II Chronicles 28:27). Putting all of this together, it certainly seems that Ahaz abandoned the Lord and adopted the sinful practices of Israel (II Kings 16:1). He was then recognized as king of both Judah and Israel from the death of Pekah in 740 BC-739 BC until 729 BC, when Hoshea evidently gained enough strength and political power to become the sole ruler of Israel. It is concluded that Hoshea was recognized as a pro-rex king with Ahaz between the fourth year of King Ahaz's reign (739 -738 BC) and his 12th year of reign (731 BC-730 BC). He became a pro-rex (sovereign king) in 729 BC. If all of this is true, then another *Gordian knot* is severed.

We now turn our attention to other biblical data which when considered, virtually assures that the chronology shown here for the reigns of Hoshea (Israel) and Hezikiah (Judah) cannot be offered in any other way. Consider the following chronological record.

	King	Yr		Year	Year		Hoshea	Yr
	Ahaz	12	Sept	731	730			
				730	730	April		10
		13	Sept	730	729			
				729	729	April	Hoshea Sole-Rex	1
		14	Sept	729	728			
				728	728	April		2
Hezikiah began reign April-Sept,726 which is in 3rd year of Hoshea. Using the Acession year system, Hezikiahs first regnal year is Sept, 726 BC to Sept, 725 BC.....		15	Sept	728	727			
				727	727	April		3
		16	Sept	727	726			
				726	726	April		4
	Hezikiah	1	Sept	726	725			
				725	725	April		5
		2	Sept	725	724			
				724	724	April		6
II Kings 18:1 Hezikiah's 1st year was in 3rd year of Hoshea		3	Sept	724	723			
				723	723	April		7
II Kings 18:9...Hezikiah's 4th year was in 7th year of Hoshea		4	Sept	723	722			
				722	722	April		8
II Kings 18:10 Hezikiah's 6th year was in 9th year of Hoshea		5	Sept	722	721			
				721	721	April		9
II Kings 17:1 Hoshea began reign in 12th year of Ahaz		6	Sept	721	720			
				720				
		7	Sept	720				
II Kings 17:6 Samaria fell in the				719				
9th year of Hoshea's reign		8	Sept	719				

Following the death of Ahaz, Hezekiah became King of Judah in the third year of Hoshea, king of Israel, using the normal accession-year system (II Kings 18:1). As we have just shown, synchronizing II Kings 18:1 with II Kings 18:9 locks into place the first year of Hoshea's nine-year reign as April, 729 BC-April, 728 BC. This also determines that the ninth and final year of Hoshea was April, 721 BC-April, 720 BC, which synchronizes to II Kings 18:9 in which the seventh year of Hoshea's reign is equated to the fourth year of Hezekiah's reign. These multiple cross references render the chronology shown above both correct and unique to all biblical references. The reign of Hoshea ended at the destruction of the Northern Kingdom of Israel. We will now establish that the final destruction of Samaria was in the summer of 721 BC.

In the seventh year of King Hoshea, the king of Assyria uncovered a conspiracy against him and his kingdom (II Kings 17:4). Hoshea had evidently sought help from Egypt to overthrow the Assyrian oppression. Hearing of this, King Shalmaneser of Assyria *came up against him* (II Kings 17:3), and threw him into prison (II Kings 17:4). The Assyrian armies then laid siege to the capital city of Samaria. With Hoshea in captivity, a protracted siege began in the early fall of 723 BC in the seventh year of Hoshea. While the city was being assaulted, Shalmaneser became ill and retreated to his capital city of Nineveh in Assyria. Shalmaneser left his younger brother Sargon II in charge of the campaign. Shalmaneser died within the next six months, and Sargon declared himself king of Assyria. Sargon continued the siege and after another two years, in late spring or early summer of Hoshea's ninth year of official reign as King of Israel, Samaria fell. Almost all respected researchers have placed the fall of Israel between 723-721 BC. W.F. Albright and Floyd Nolan Jones also place the fall of Israel in 721 BC. Thiele placed it in 723 BC. According to Finnegan and Thiele, the Northern Kingdom fell in the summer of Hoshea's ninth and last year of reign. Hence, the ninth and final year shown here for Hoshea was credited to him between Mar/April 1, 721 BC and Mar/April 1, 720 BC. The northern tribes of Israel were all deported to Assyria and vanished into history. They are often called the *Lost 10 Tribes of Israel*. A few people from these tribes fled to the Southern Kingdom, but as a corporate entity with tribal identification they all vanished into oblivion. The Northern Kingdom had existed for about 255 years.

Following the deportation of the Northern Kingdom of Israel to Assyria, only the Southern Kingdom of Judah survived. This is exactly what was prophesied by the prophets (I Kings 11:29-36). The Northern Kingdom perished in the sixth year of King Hezekiah's reign (II Kings 17:6). Hezekiah continued to reign for another 23 years until he died a peaceful death. He was a good king who followed after the Lord all of his days. However, the biblical record of King Hezekiah's reign has been severely attacked and criticized. We have shown that difficult cross references between Hezekiah and Hoshea the Northern Kingdom can be resolved, but an ongoing and raging controversy concerning the last 15 years of Hezekiah's reign has developed over the past 400 years, fueled by archeological discoveries involving the ancient Assyrian Empire and parts of the Babylonian records (the Assyrian, Babylonian and Nabinitus Chronicles). Central to all the controversy is Edwin Thiele, who wrote three books on this subject, the last called *The Mysterious Numbers of the Hebrew Kings*. An assessment of Thiele's work and the problems he has created are contained in Appendix A. We will be primarily concerned with a correlation of events which transpired during the reign of King Hezekiah, and two kings of Babylon: Sargon II and Sennacherib. The focal point of ongoing theological investigations concerns events which transpired in the 14th year of King Hezekiah and the third year of Sennacherib's reign.

The Reign of Hezekiah

During the reign of King Hezekiah, some interesting and remarkable events occurred. Assyrian records show that after Sargon II conquered and deported the 10 tribes of the Northern Kingdom in 721 BC, he took many captives to the capital city of Nineveh. After successfully leading several military campaigns against his enemies, Sargon was killed in 705 BC in a battle against the Cimmerians. Sargon was succeeded by his son, Sennacherib, in that same year, and he reigned between 705–681 BC. Ancient Assyrian records have been found which record that in the third year of the reign of Sennacherib, he conducted a military campaign against Hezekiah. Using historical records for known eclipse dates in this period of time, Edwin Thiele firmly declared this to be identical to the 14th year of King Hezekiah and set the date of this invasion in 701 BC. His dogmatic belief was based upon the assumption that Sennacherib only invaded Jerusalem one time. Why he decided to use 701 BC instead of 703 BC or 702 BC for the third year of Sennacherib is unknown. 701 BC and the fourth year of Hezekiah was then his *anchor point* from which his chronological records could be referenced to determine the starting and ending year of every Northern and Southern Kingdom king. Note at this point that if the fall of the Northern Kingdom *did occur* as we have shown in 721 BC, and if Sennacherib invaded Jerusalem in 701 BC in the 14th year of Hezekiah as Edwin Thiel has proposed, these two events would occur at least 20 years apart and Hezekiah would not even be king at that time. However, the Holy Bible records in II Kings 18:9-10 record that the Northern Kingdom fell in the sixth year of Hezekiah, and that Sennacherib conducted a military campaign against Hezekiah in his 14th year. The Bible then places these two events only eight years apart. Hence, the chronology of Thiele violates the Holy Scriptures. But this is not the only problem that Thiele creates by equating the 14th year of King Hezekiah to 701 BC. It also violates the clear testimony of II Kings 17:1 and II Kings 18:1. However, the most blatant error in Thiele's work during the reign of Hezekiah is that his chronology places the ninth year of Hoshea (last king of Israel) and the corresponding fall of the Northern Kingdom *before* the first year of Hezekiah's reign over Judah. This is in clear opposition to the biblical record that places the fall of Samaria in the sixth year of Hezekiah (II Kings 17:6). At this juncture, we are faced with a choice of whether to accept the published and well-known chronology of Thiele and the Divided Kingdom as fact, or whether to accept the holy and divinely-inspired word of God. To this author, the choice is simple; the Chronology proposed by Thiele must be soundly rejected. It is not that Edwin Thiele failed to significantly contribute to what is now known about this period of time. His work will stand as a seminal point in understanding the divided kingdom. However, his chronology must be held in error. It is one thing to question and offer a logical interpretation of a difficult scriptural passage. It is quite another to accept a blatant and deliberate violation of Holy Scriptures.

It might be stated without strong controversy, that the dates and numbers produced by Thiele have almost universally and blindly been accepted by the academic biblical community. However, his work has certainly not remained unchallenged. Such notables as Faulstitch, W.F. Albright, Jack Finnegan, John Bright and others have recognized the conflict between known Assyrian archeological records, the biblical accounts and the Thiele chronology. More recently, logical and detailed assaults on the work of Thiele have surfaced from Jones and Larry Pierce (see Appendix A). Everyone recognizes that the Assyrian records are often fragmented and missing key information. This is not a condemnation but a known fact. It has unfortunately become the norm to assume that when there is a conflict between biblical and Assyrian records, or Egyptian and Babylonian archeological discoveries, the biblical records must yield to fragmented and incomplete archeological records. Traditionally, a cry has gone forth that there must be a *scribal error, or that the Holy records are in error.* These beliefs should be universally and dogmatically rejected by all biblical scholars that believe in the Holy Word. In fact, when there is a conflict, archeological records must yield to biblical truth. We will now present an analysis of the reign of Hezekiah which represents an educated, logical explanation of events during his reign. We may never know the exact truth unless additional ancient manuscripts are discovered which explain this mysterious period of history.

Hezekiah and the Assyrian Invasions of Sennacherib

The reign of King Hezekiah and the synchronization to Assyrian records which have been found have created enormous problems for those wishing to create a chronology of the divided kingdom. Every biblical scholar has noted that when the accounts in II Kings 18:13-20:21, II Chronicles 29:3-36, and II Chronicles 32-33 are compared to known Assyrian records, at least two invasions of Judah by Sennacherib seem to be indicated; but there is no clear correlation between the biblical records and Assyrian historical documents. This is not to say that the Assyrian records are in error, but it creates an opportunity to verify both the biblical accounts and the Assyrian records through some plausible common scenario. We will now offer a possible solution to this problem.

Although at least five or six different approaches to understanding the events which occurred during the reign of Hezekiah have been reported in the scholarly literature, there are fundamentally two lines of thought which have emerged. The first is the *single-invasion theory*. This theory associates an invasion of Judah and a siege against Jerusalem in the 14th year of King Hezekiah to be identical to an invasion and siege which is clearly described in the Assyrian records, which occurred in the third year of King Sennacherib. This community of scholars postulate that these two points in time are identical, and that only a single invasion of Judah by Sennacherib is described in the biblical accounts of II Kings 18:13-35, Isaiah 36-37 and II Chronicles 32:1-22. These biblical scholars almost universally follow after Edwin Thiele and his work. More recently, a second biblical interpretation has been proposed called the *two-invasion scenario*. The two-invasion proponents find enough differences in the biblical accounts and the Assyrian records to postulate that two invasions of Judah and Jerusalem must have occurred. It appears that the first scholar to introduce the two-invasion scenario was Rawlinson in 1858. The leading modern proponents of the two-invasion theory are Albright, Bright, Fullerton, Jones and Shea. Fundamentally, they assert that the biblical and Assyrian records recorded during the reign of Hezekiah (Judah), Sargon II (Assyria) and Sennacherib (Assyria) can only be harmonized by postulating that there were *two major invasions* of the Southern Kingdom by the Assyrians. The first was in the 14th year of Hezekiah, and the second was in the 26th year of Hezekiah. Both assaults seem to be recorded in the Assyrian historical records, and both were led by Sennacherib.

The justification for two invasions of the Southern Kingdom is complicated and involves, among other things, a detailed literary analysis of conflicts in the biblical accounts, and subsequent justification for how they can be resolved. In this section, we will only state with great conviction that a *single invasion* during the third year of Sennacherib, synchronized to the 14th year of Hezekiah, and subsequently equated to 701 BC, cannot be true without serious compromise and violation of the biblical records. For detailed analysis and arguments which support this conclusion, the interested reader is referred to the previous references of scholarly investigations and to Appendix A for a detailed analysis of Thiele's assumptions. In the chronology offered here, the two-invasion scenario by Sennacherib would play out as follows.

The first year of Hezekiah's 29-year reign would be Sept, 726 BC-Sept, 725 BC. Biblical records assert that the ninth and final year of reign for King Hoshea (Northern Kingdom) took place in the 6th year of King Hezekiah. Other synchronisms are shown in the following table.

Hezekiah Regnal Years	Hezekiah Regnal Dates	Hoshea Regnal Year	Hoshea Regnal Dates	Common Dates	Biblical Reference
Accession Year	Sept, 727 BC Sept 726, BC	Year 3	April, 727 BC April, 726 BC	Sept, 727 BC April, 726 BC	II Kings 18:1
Year 1	Sept, 726 BC Sept 725, BC	Year 4	April, 726 BC April, 725 BC	Sept, 726 BC April, 725 BC	II Kings 18:7
Year 6	Sept, 721 BC Sept 720, BC	Year 9	April, 721 BC April, 720 BC	Sept, 721 BC April, 720 BC	II Kings 17:6
Year 4	Sept, 723 BC Sept 722, BC	Year 7	April, 723 BC April, 722 BC	Sept, 723 BC April, 722 BC	II Kings 18:9

Clear and multiple biblical references point to somewhere between 720 BC-723 BC as the year that the Northern Kingdom fell. This chronology supports 721 BC. The first year of the Assyrian king Sennacherib is widely accepted as 705 BC by biblical and archeological scholars.

We will first show that it is not only possible to associate the first year of King Hezekiah with both the third and fourth year of Hoshea, but it attests to the accuracy of the biblical record. This synchronization can only be achieved by recognizing that Ahaz died as previously shown sometime in the 16th year of his reign, which was Sept, 727 BC-Sept, 726 BC.

Following an accession-year system, Hezekiah assumed the throne upon the death of Ahaz. II Kings 18:1 places this in the third year of Hoshea. We have shown that the accession-year of Hezekiah had to be sometime between April, 726 BC and Sept, 726 BC. In Sept 726 BC, Hezekiah started his first official year of reign. This occurred in the fourth year of Hoshea (II Kings 18:7). This synchronization of Hezekiah and Hoshea following the Holy Bible scriptural references can ONLY be realized if the Southern Kingdom used an accession-year system and started their regnal years on Tishri 1, along with the Northern Kingdom using a non-accession year system and a Nisan 1 regnal year start date. This shows that the 14th year of King Hezekiah's reign was Sept, 713 BC-Sept, 712 BC. We are now ready to address the strange events which occurred in the 14th year of Hezekiah's reign.

The 14th Year of King Hezekiah

The temple of God had fallen into decline and was in need of repair and restoration. In the first year of his reign, Hezekiah repaired and restored the temple. He then *"rebelled against the King of Assyria"* (II Kings 18:7) and sent word to all of the people in both the Northern and Southern Kingdoms to come to Jerusalem to observe the first Passover after he assumed the throne, which was six months later.

> ***"Hezekiah sent to all Israel and Judah…. That they should …. come to…Jerusalem and…keep the Passover."*** II Chronicles 30:1-5

It should be noted from II Chronicles 30:1-5 that there is not the slightest hint that the Northern Kingdom had ceased to exist at this time. The invitation to attend the Passover Feast in the fall of 727 BC was sent to *all Israel and Judah*. Further, we are told that while some scorned the invitation, many others came from all of the 12 tribes. This is impossible under the Thiele scenario, Thiele insists that the one and only invasion by Sennacherib occurred in the third year of Sennacherib's reign, in the 14th year of King Hezekiah, in 701 BC. This would place the great Passover celebration held by King Hezekiah in 714 BC.

Thiele dogmatically held to a synchronization which forces the 14th year of the reign of Hezekiah to 701 BC. Thiele is forced to ignore three biblical records to do this. According to the Bible:

1. *"Hezekiah started to reign in the third year of Hoshea"* (II Kings 18:1, 2).
2. *"In the sixth year of Hezekiah and the ninth year of Hoshea, the Northern Kingdom fell to Assyria"* (II Kings 18:10).
3. *"In the 12th year of Ahaz, Hoshea began to reign over Israel"* (II Kings 17:1).

Thiele claims these are late amendments to the biblical text, and is honest enough to admit he cannot make these verses fit his chronology. In forcing this synchronization, Thiele has the reign of Hezekiah and his son Manasseh co-reigning for at least 11 years. *There is no biblical evidence to support these conclusions.* It should be pointed out that the chronology offered in this book has no trouble accommodating these biblical records. We propose that the following events were what actually occurred in the 14th year of Hezekiah.

Either due to the fact that King Hezekiah had refused to honor Assyria, or due to his apparent success in unifying the entire remaining kingdom, King Sargon II mobilized his troops and sent Sennacherib, the *general* of his armies, to put Hezekiah in his place. This took place in Hezekiah's third year of reign, 724 BC-723 BC. Sennacherib first conquered several outlying Judean cities, and in a major campaign assaulted the stronghold of Lachish (II Kings 18:14). Hearing that Lachish was under siege and that the city was doomed to fall, Hezekiah evidently decided to buy off Assyrian destruction by offering a massive tribute. In II Kings 18:14-16, we are told that Sennacherib accepted 300 talents of silver and 30 talents of gold. Hezekiah had to strip the temple of all precious metals to assemble this prize. The reason that Sennacherib might have turned away just as he was on the brink of destroying the Southern Kingdom might be due to the fact that things were not going well in Babylon where an insurrection was brewing. At the same time, to his south, King Sargon received word that Egypt was growing stronger and might be planning a military campaign against Assyria. For whatever reason, Sargon directed Sennacherib to accept the tribute and turn away. Sennacherib evidently returned to Nineveh a hero.

It is well established that in 705 BC, Sargon II died in battle. He was succeeded by Sennacherib. According to verified Assyrian records, the third year of Sennacherib started in March/April of 703 BC, and it was later that year that he invaded Judah. It is impossible to honor the biblical records and equate a single invasion of Judah by Sennacherib in his third year of reign to the 14th year of King Hezekiah's reign. It is now apparent that Sargon II, and not Sennacherib, was King of Assyria in the 14th year of Hezekiah. It is well established that Sargon II died in 705 BC, and was succeeded by Sennacherib. This places Sennacherib's third year of reign in 703 BC. A single invasion theory cannot, therefore, be supported by both the biblical and Assyrian records.

Sennacherib's first regnal year was March/April, 705 BC-March/April, 704 BC. Assyrian records show that at this time, Sennacherib unified his kingdom, and shortly after marched on *Babylon* to put down an evolving insurrection and placed Babylon under his iron boot. The puppet king of Babylon, Merodach-baladan, was forced to flee into a nearby swamp and was never heard from again. Having solidified his northern borders and quelled a Babylonian insurrection, Sennacherib turned to threats in the south. A primary purpose of a southern campaign was to once and for all put King Hezekiah in his proper place.

In the third year of Sennacherib's reign, verifiable Assyrian documents called the *Assyrian Chronicles* record that Sennacherib mounted an assault on Jerusalem. If this was indeed in 703 BC, this would have occurred in the 23rd or 24th regnal year of Hezekiah. In 1968, Lukenbill translated and published a series of documents. One of his reports concerned what is now called the *Taylor Prism*. A partial account of the invasion of Judah and Jerusalem in the third year of Sennacherib is contained in the Taylor Prism; which is now housed in the British Museum of

Natural History (Luckenbill, ARAB, Vol. 2, P 120-121). Consider the following record from a translation by Luckenbill:

> *"The Taylor Prism proclaims that 46 walled cities and innumerable smaller settlements were conquered by the Assyrians, with 200,150 people, and livestock, being deported, and the conquered territory being dispersed among the three kings of the Philistines instead of being given back. Additionally, the Prism says that Sennacherib's siege resulted in Hezekiah being shut up in Jerusalem "like a caged bird". Earthworks were thrown up against the city, and anyone leaving its gates was turned back to misery. Hezekiah's mercenaries and 'Arabs' deserted him, and Hezekiah eventually bribed Sennacherib, having to give him antimony, jewels, ivory-inlaid furniture, his own daughters, harem, and musicians. In addition, Hezekiah was forced to pay a tribute of 30 talents of gold and 800 talents of silver"* (Luckenbill)

The similarities between the biblical accounts in II Kings 18:13-35, Isaiah 36-37 and II Chronicles 32:1-22 are as follows.

➤ The city under siege is Jerusalem
➤ Many northern cities were captured and taken before Jerusalem was assaulted
➤ The talents of gold offered as a tribute were 30
➤ In the biblical account of the siege which occurred in the 14th year of King Hezekiah, the Lord specifically revealed to King Hezekiah that he would be delivered

Here the similarities seem to vanish. There are significant differences between the Assyrian Chronicles, the record of the Taylor Prism, and the biblical accounts in II Kings 18:13-35, Isaiah 36-37 and II Chronicles 32:1-22. The following differences are summarized.

- In the Assyrian chronicles, Hezekiah is said to be *shut up like a caged bird*. In the biblical accounts, Hezekiah seems to not be under any severe confinement.
- In the Assyrian accounts, *earthworks were said to be thrown up against the city and the main gate*. In II Kings 19:32 the Lord himself said that a siege mound would not be built against the city.
- In the Assyrian Chronicles, it is recorded that Sennacherib took from Jerusalem all manner of valuable goods including chairs and couches. He also took away sons, daughters, musicians and livestock, even the King's harem. It is difficult to believe that Sennacherib would not have entered the city to supervise this deportation and bask in his glory. Yet, in II Kings 19:32-33 the Lord prophesied that *he shall not come into this city*.
- In the Assyrian Chronicles, Sennacherib records that he demanded and received 30 talents of gold and *800 talents of silver*. However, in II Kings 18:14 it is stated that Hezekiah paid 30 talents of gold, and *300 talents of silver*. It can easily be assumed that the amount of silver paid is simply different in the two accounts or is a scribal error, except for one important statement in the Assyrian Chronicles: Sennacherib says that: *I added to the former tribute*. This distinctly implies that 300 talents of silver were demanded at a *former* time and Sennacherib increased this to 800 talents at *some later date*. This would strongly suggest two invasions, not one.

- The Assyrian Chronicles state that Hezekiah was *overcome by his* (Sennacherib) *majesty*. In a description of the invading forces in II Kings 18:17, it is apparent that Sennacherib was not even at Jerusalem while the city was under siege. The entire assault was conducted by Sennacherib's generals (the Rabsaris and the Rabsakeh) while Sennacherib himself was engaged in an ongoing, intense battle at Lachish.
- The Assyrian Chronicles record that when Sennacherib first took his throne after the death of Sargon, his first incursion was against Merodach-baladan, his vassal king in Babylon who was mounting a revolt. As previously discussed, Sennacherib chased him out of the city (Babylon) into a swamp, and he was never heard from again. Yet, in II Kings 20:12 we read that the **same Babylonian king** sent an embassy to Jerusalem to present him tributes and inquire as to how he was miraculously saved by God. This account demands that the 14th year of Hezekiah's reign *precede* the third year of Sennacherib's reign if Sennacherib deposed Merodach-baladan in his first year as king.

We have carefully examined several important differences between the Assyrian Records of Sennacherib's reign and the biblical accounts which describe the reign of Hezekiah. It is true that these comparisons *prove* nothing. However, the two records do suggest that *it is possible* that there were two different invasions of Judah during the reign of Hezekiah. We propose that the first invasion was in the 14th year of Hezekiah's reign while *Sargon* was king of Assyria. We then propose that the second invasion was in the 24th year of Hezekiah in the third year of *Sennacherib's* reign. In fact, this scenario is *necessary* to support the chronology which is proposed by this author and to rationalize known archeological records.

As previously stated, in the biblical narrative of the Assyrian siege in the 14th year of Hezekiah, II Kings 18:13-37 has no record whatsoever of Sennacherib even being at Jerusalem! The narrative records that Sennacherib was in Lachish taking that city, and he sent "**the Tartan, the Rabsaris, and the Rabshakeh from Lachish with a great army to King Hezekiah at Jerusalem**" (II Kings 18:17). All of this again *seems* to indicate that there were two campaigns against King Hezekiah and Jerusalem, one in the 14th year of Hezekiah while Sennacherib, acting as general of the Assyrian army, was besieging the city of Lachish. The second invasion occurred sometime later conducted by Sennacherib after he had been named king following the reign of Sargon.

The 14th year of Hezekiah is determined in this chronology to be Sept, 713 BC-Sept, 712 BC. During this year, Hezekiah became extremely ill and feared that he might die (II Kings 20:10). In his bed, he humbled himself before God and called upon Him for mercy (II Kings 20:11). The Lord answered his prayer, and made him a promise that he (Hezekiah) would not die, but that he would in fact "*live for another 15 years*" (II Kings 20:6). Poor doubting Hezekiah asked for a "*sign*", and it was given to him; the shadow of a sundial went *backward* 10 degrees. God's covenant promise resulted in Hezekiah living for another 15 years and dying in the 29th year of his reign (14+15=29), which was sometime between Sept, 698 BC and Sept, 697 BC. The biblical records clearly and unambiguously record that during the 14th year of Hezekiah, Sennacherib "*came up against all the cities of Judah and took them*" (II Kings 18:3, Isaiah 36:1). How could this be true if he was engaged in a struggle at the city of Lachish? Further, Sennacherib was called "**King of Assyria**" in II Kings 18:13! We suggest and postulate that the second siege against Jerusalem occurred in 713 BC when *Sennacherib was King*, and the attack was led by Sennacherib himself. The result of this siege is one of the most remarkable events in the Old Testament. Hezekiah **tore his clothes and covered himself with sackcloth** (II Kings

19:1). The prophet Isaiah prophesied that the city and king would be delivered. That very night, an Angel of the Lord went forth to the camp of the Assyrians and killed 185,000 warriors; so

> *"Sennacherib King of Assyria departed and went away, returned home, and remained at Nineveh"* (II Kings 19:36).

In summary, we propose that the only way to rationalize and correlate the biblical accounts to known Assyrian records is to adopt a *two-invasion scenario*. This conjecture is further supported by the way in which the Lord came to the aid of Hezekiah. The first invasion came when Sargon II was King of Assyria in the 14th year of King Hezekiah's reign, between Sept, 713 BC and Sept, 712 BC. Sennachirib was general of the Persian armies. The second invasion of Jerusalem came during the third year of Sennacherib's reign, between 703 BC and 702 BC, in the 24th year of King Hezekiah. According to the biblical accounts, a very unusual promise was made to Hezekiah. The Lord promised Hezekiah that a *sign would be given.*

> *"And this shall be a sign unto thee, Ye shall eat this year such things as grow of themselves, and in the second year that which springeth of the same; and in the third year sow ye, and reap, and plant vineyards, and eat the fruits thereof."* II Kings 19:29

Contrast this sign with that obviously given previously, in which the sun moved backwards. The sign of II Kings 19:29 is Sabbath-year and Jubilee-year promises. We will show in the Chapter Five that 703 BC *was* a Sabbatical year but 702 was not a year of Jubilee. At first glance, this appears to be a fatal blow to this proposed scenario; but, is it? Consider the implications of the promise to Hezekiah. Suppose that 703 BC *was a Sabbatical year* and 702 BC *was a year of Jubilee.* If this were true, the promise from God would not have much import since these promises were given to Israel over 100 years ago! On the other hand, if God promised Hezekiah that He would provide food to him and the nation for not one year but two, and not in a combination Sabbatical and Jubilee year, now that would be a powerful sign! This is made more believable when we consider what happened when Herod's Temple fell to the Roman army of Titus in 70 AD. Josephus records that the final siege followed a Sabbatical year, but Titus had burned all of their crops in the field and the fall of the temple was not just due to military force. The Lord did not see fit to provide food to the Jewish forces in Herod's temple for a third year because of their rejection of Jesus Christ as their promised messiah for 40 years after 30 Ad (40 being the biblical period of trial and testing).Josephus further records that they were so weak from lack of food that they simply could not continue. This is exactly the same situation that Hezekiah would have experienced without divine intervention. This was a glorious deliverance and a sign of God's eternal grace! We, therefore, postulate and accept that two invasions of Jerusalem and King Hezekiah are highly possible if not likely, and that the year following 703 BC was an unscheduled year of plenty in which the land would provide food for Jerusalem.

Consider the following additional facts: Jerusalem had been in a period of isolation and great famine after a lengthy siege from King Sennacchirib of Assyria. (II Kings 18:13. Hezekiah had tried to buy off Sennacchirib with gold and all the treasures of his own house (II Kings 18:15-16) but to no avail (II Kings 19:1). Finally, Hezekiah turned to the prophet Isaiah who prayed to God to intervene. God honored the prayers of Isaiah with two supernatural signs: The first was to send an angel of death upon the Assyrians who killed 185,000 warriors in one night. The second *sign* was to provide food for the starving people. This sign was *not* a Sabbatical and Jubilee year sign but a miraculous event.

The Last 135 Years of the Southern Kingdom of Judah

Regardless of whether or not the *two-invasion theory* is true, it is a biblically-supported fact that Hezekiah ruled for 29 years (II Chronicles 29:1). Ignoring all the controversy surrounding the 14th year and 24th year of Hezekiah and the corresponding Assyrian records, one can certainly jump from the first year of King Hezekiah in 726 BC-725 BC to his last year of reign in 698 BC-697 BC. Having developed a biblical chronology from the disruption of King Solomon's *United Kingdom*, to the *last year of King Hezekiah's reign*, it is now a relatively simple matter to reconstruct the last years of the Southern Kingdom, regardless of the Babylonian invasion theories.

Hezikiah	29th Year	698	697	
Manasseh	1	697	696	
	55	643	642	
Amon	1	642	641	
	2	641	640	
Josiah	1	640	639	
	31	610	609	
Jehoahaz	1	609	608	3 Mo.
Jehoiakim	1	608	607	
	11	598	597	
Jehoiachin	1			3 Mo,10 days
Zedekiah	1	597	596	
	11	587	586	

It is instructive to show the details of the Southern Kingdom from the last year of Hezekih (Sept, 698 BC–Sept, 697 BC) to Zedekiah (Zedekiah was the last king of Judah). Zedekiah's last full year of reign was from Tishri 1, 587 BC to Tishri 1, 586 BC. The table on the next page provides details of the last 112 years of the Southern Kingdom of Judah. The basic structure was first suggested by McFall and later published by Finnegan in his *Handbook of Biblical Chronology*.

Recall that after the death of King Solomon, which likely occurred in the summer of 975 BC, the 12 tribes of Israel were split into two separate kingdoms: the Northern Kingdom of Israel, and the Southern Kingdom of Judah. The Northern Kingdom lasted about 255 years and vanished into history after being conquered and deported by Assyria. The Southern Kingdom of Judah lasted another 134 years. It was destroyed by the Babylonian Empire and all of the people were taken into captivity for 70 years. It is remarkable that the Southern Kingdom of Judah appeared to last exactly 389 years from the death of King Solomon in the summer of 975 BC to the final fall of Jerusalem on July 18, 586 BC. The exact date that Jerusalem fell has been well established and accepted by almost every biblical scholar based upon Babylonian historical documents.

It is now important to discuss a key biblical passage which has driven many biblical scholars to pursue a 390 year period of time for the Southern Kingdom of Judah.

Josiah was only 8 years old when he began to reign...(II Kings 22:1). Reigned 31 Years	

Josiah died in his 31st year of reign at Meggido in month of Tammuz, 609 BC
  Month of Tammuz (Tammuz 1=June 24 - Tammuz 29=July 23)
  Last year is Tishri 1, 610-Tishri 1, 609 BC.... (Sept 21, 610-Oct, 19, 609)
Jehoahaz reigned only 3 months (II Kings 22:30), but his last month of reign allowed him to assume the throne
  on Tishri 1, 609 Bc. This allowed him to claim the year 609 BC-608 BC as a full regnal year.
 Month 1 Tammuz (June 2 609 BC
Month 2 Ab (July 24-Aug 609 BC
Month 3 Elul (Aug 23-Sep 609 BC
Jehoiakim accession year was Tishri (Sept 21-Oct 19)-End of Elul (Sept 9), 608 BC
    Year 1   Sept 10, 608 BC to Sept 28, 607 BC
    Year 2   Sept 29, 607 BC to Sept 18, 606 BC
    ....
    Year 10 Sept 29, 599 BC to Sept 17, 598 BC
    Year 11 Sept 18, 598-Sept 6, 597
Jehoiakim died in late Fall 598 BC.....Likely Dec 16, 598 BC
Jehoiakin became King likely on Dec 17, 598 and reigned 3 months, 10 days
 Month 1 (Dec 17, 598 BC -Jan 16, 597 BC)
 Month 2 (Jan 17, 597 BC -Feb 15, 597 BC)
 Month 3 (Feb 16, 597 BC- 22-Mar 15, 597 BC)
..... Jehoiakin flees from Jerusalem and is captured 10 days later on Mar 25, 597
    The 10 days are: Dec 16, 597 BC-Mar 25, 597 BC
Since Jehoiakin was following an accession year system, and his 3 Mo, 10 day reign fell entirely within the
 last year of Jehoiakim, He never achieved a Tishri 1 Regnal start date. When Zedikiah started his reign in late
 spring of 597 BC he honored the ongoing last (11th) regnal year of Jehoiakim (Sept 18, 598 - Sept 6, 597 BC). His
 first officcial regnal year started Tishri 1, 597 BC.
Zedekiah reigned 11 years
    Year 1   Sept 7, 597 BC to Sept 26, 596 BC
    Year 2   Sept 27, 596 BC to Sept 14, 595 BC
    Year 3   Sept 15, 595 BC to Sept 3 , 594 BC
    Year 4   Sept 4, 594 BC to Sept 22, 593 BC
    Year 5   Sept 23, 593 BC to Sept 12, 592 BC
    Year 6   Sept 13, 592 BC to Sept 1, 591 BC
    Year 7   Sept 2, 591 BC to Sept 19, 590 BC
    Year 8   Sept 20, 590 BC to Sept 8, 589 BC
    Year 9   Sept 9, 589 BC to Sept 28, 588 BC
    Year 10 Sept 29, 588 BC to Sept 17, 587 BC
    Year 11 Sept 18, 587-Sept 6, 586
Zedekiah was taken prisoner in June/July of 586, and his last year of reign
    was given as Sept 18, 587 BC to Sept 17, 586 BC

The date that Jerusalem fell is well known as July 18, 586 BC

King Solomon died in 976 BC. His last year of reign was shown to be 977 BC - 976, BC. It was
suggested that Solomon died in the summer of 976 BC. It is now clear why this was suggested.
If Solomon died in mid July, it is likely that the Southern Kingdom of Judah lasted exactly 390
years.

Lie thou also upon thy left side, and lay the iniquity of the house of Israel upon it: according to the number of the days that thou shalt lie upon it thou shalt bear their iniquity. For I have laid upon thee the years of their iniquity, according to the number of the days, three hundred and ninety days: so shalt thou bear the iniquity of the house of Israel. And when thou hast accomplished them, lie again on thy right side, and thou shalt bear the iniquity of the house of Judah forty days: I have appointed thee each day for a year. Therefore thou shalt set thy face toward the siege of Jerusalem, and thine arm shall be uncovered, and thou shalt prophesy against it. Ezekiel 4: 4-7

To the best of my knowledge, there has never been a definitive interpretation of this mysterious event. Ezekiel is clearly acting out two prophetic times of severe iniquity and persecution concerning the corporate nation of Israel. He is told to lie on his left side for 390 days and upon his right side for 40 days. Each day represents one year. Several chronological researchers have proposed that the 390 year period of persecution and apostasy against Israel refers to a 390 year period of time in which the Southern nation of Judah existed from the death of King Solomon until the final fall of Jerusalem in 586 BC. In reconstructing this period of time in this chapter, complex synchronization with the regnal periods of both the Northern and Southern Kingdom kings resulted in a 389 year period of time. One is tempted to say that there is only a one year error and this is *close enough*, but this author steadfastly supports a 389 year period. It is also certain that Ezekial was prophesying of a 390 year period of time in which the nation of Israel would suffer apostasy and tribulation. Although certainly indicated, there is no real proof that this period of time (and the other 40 years) might run sequential. A possible explanation is that from the death of King Solomon to the final fal of Jerusalem on July 18, 586 BC was likely 389 Julian calendar years. Most would simply say that "this is close enough". Another possible explanation is that prophetic periods of time are always given in whole years...so if King Solomon died in the late spring of 975 BC, 390 years would be a rounded up period of time. It is this author's opinion that both explanations are feasible, but not necessarily correct.

Recall that the death of King Solomon resulted in the immediate disruption of the United Kingdom (Corporate Nation of Israel). Although Solomon built the Holy Temple of God (Solomon's Temple), his reign was not what one might expect. In his later years he fell into great apostasy. He ignored the Laws of God by taking to himself 700 wives and 300 concubines.... women of the Moabites, Ammonites, Edomites, Sidonians and Hittites (I Kings 11: 3, 1. He erected alters to foreign gods and worshipped Ashtoreth, goddess of the Sidonians (I Kings 11: 5-8) and he burned incense and offered sacrifices to foreign Gods. Solomon died in total apostasy and was an abomination to God. It is proposed that if the 390 years of Ezekiel represent a period of wickedness and apostasy which included the Divided Kingdom, that this period of time started with the last year of Solomon and ended with the destruction of Judah. I will not claim that this explanation can be proved, but it is a plausible and completely defensible explanation. There is certainly no biblical mandate to associate the entire 390 year period of iniquity described by Ezekial with the duration of the Divided Kingdom.

Finally, if the initial period of time played out by Ezekiel is the period of time just postulated, then when Ezekiel turned to his other side for 40 days... where is this 40 year period of time? It is my opinion that this 40 year period of time can only apply to the 40 years between the crucifixion of Christ in 30 AD to 70 AD when the Roman forces let by Titus completely destroyed Herod's Temple and conquered the City of Jerusalem. The Nation of Israel then ceased to exist until May 18, 1948 AD when it once again became a sovereign nation. Many prophecy teachers proposed that the Rapture would occur in 1988 based upon that event. They have, of course, all been proved wrong. Any attempt to predict when the rapture of the church might occur is a waste of time, but it may not be far off.

We have now developed and documented a continuous sequence of historical and biblical events from when Adam and Eve were expelled from the Garden of Eden until the Southern Kingdom of Judah and Jerusalem fell on July 18, 586 BC. The unbroken sequence of events from Adam's departure to the final fall of Jerusalem has been sequentially recorded without violation of a single biblical record. The following graphic illustrates key AY-year identification of several key events between when Adam left the Garden of Eden and the final fall of Jerusalem and the Northern Kingdom of Judah.

AY Year		Julian Year
1	Year Adam Left Eden	Sept, 3944-Sept, 3933
		2454 years
2454	Year of the Exodus	Sept, 1491-Sept, 1490
2454	Year of the Exodus	Sept, 1491-Sept, 1490
		480 years
2933	Solomon's 4th Year	Sept, 1012-Sept, 1011
2930	Solomons 1st Year	Sept, 1015-Sept, 1014
		4 years
2933	Solomon's 4th Year	Sept, 1012-Sept, 1011
2930	Solomons 1st Year	Sept, 1015-Sept, 1014
		40 years
2969	Solomon's 40th Year	Sept, 976-Sept, 975
2970	Divided Kingdom	Sept, 975-Sept, 974
		389 years
3358	Final Fall of Judah	Sept, 587-Sept, 586

The AY years have been cross referenced to Proleptic Julian calendar years. Every other biblical event up to the fall of Jerusalem in 586 BC can now been uniquely assigned both an AY number and a Julian year. It should be clearly understood that the offered chronology and the derived AY dates is a *relative chronology*. It is relative to when the AY count of years started and whether the first AY year was AY=0 or AY=1. However, it is also *an absolute chronology* because even if a 40 year period of trial and testing for Adam and Eve is added to the AY year count, one can verify that this would only add years to the AY count and would *not* affect any Julian year dates of major events in this offered chronology. Many chronographers have started an AY count with when they thought *Adam was created*. Such assumptions have no biblical basis whatsoever and are completely arbitrary. It should also again be noted that the use of any AY starting point, or whether that point is AY=0 or AY=1, is merely to establish a counting mechanism to uniquely assign an AY year identification to consecutive and unbroken record of biblical events. The critical step in identifying an associated sequence of Julian or Gregorian calendar years is to uniquely and absolutely establish a biblically identified AY year with a corresponding, fixed

Julian or Gregorian year. We have chosen to equate AY 1 with the expulsion of Adam and Eve from the Garden of Eden. Which results in AY 3358 contains July 18, 586 BC. This Julian date anchor point is almost universally accepted among biblical chronographers; what is not universally accepted is how to determine the exodus, period of the Judges and the period of the divided kingdom. We have shown how each can be reconstructed using biblical records.

Finally, In developing a chronology of the 389 year Divided Kingdom, the astute biblical scholar has undoubtedly noted that except for accepting the final fall of Jerusalem as July 18, 586 BC, there was no need to place any dependency whatsoever on either the Assyrian historical and archeological records or the ancient Babylonian records. It is also true that the existence, interpretation and use of any such records do not play a part in developing the sequence of events and their relationship to one another. The chronology presented here can be developed strictly from the biblical records. The entire purpose of the detailed analysis of Chapters 3 and 4 was to show that the Biblical records are trustworthy, accurate and divinely inspired.

Aside from the belief that the biblical records are God-inspired and that the King James Bible is a complete and reliable source of information, *why would any biblical literalist want to accept the validity of secular historical and archeological records over the inspired word of God?* This is not a casual or contrived statement of belief. Over the past 100 years, the biblical records have time and again been tossed aside and called inaccurate based upon information recovered from multiple Assyrian and ancient Egyptian records. The chronology presented in this study assigns a complete and unbroken sequence of linked, historical events from the expulsion of Adam and Eve from the Garden of Eden to the fall of the Southern Kingdom. *It was not even necessary to address the two invasion theory of Zachariah to derive the chronology offered up to the end of the Northern Kingdom.* For completeness, the problems associated with matching Assyrian and Babylonian Records to those given in the Holy Bible during the reign of Hezekiah have been addressed and a solution to how events transpired over this complicated period of time have been proposed and analyzed by this author; but this investigation is not given in this book.

We will now show how to extend the results given so far to the crucifixion of Christ. In order to do this, we will need to address a historical event which has been hotly debated for over 2000 years. What year did the 490-year prophecy of Daniel the prophet recorded in Daniel 9:27 take place? Before we tackle this difficult task, it will be advantageous and helpful to determine when Sabbatical and Jubilee years were divinely ordained for the corporate nation of Israel

Chapter 5
Sabbatical and Jubilee Years

The key to unlocking the remaining years between when Judah finally fell to the crucifixion of Jesus Christ is the proper identification of what Julian year the remarkable 70 week of year's prophecy given to Daniel the prophet in Daniel 9:20-27 actually started. In order to fully understand the prophecy of Daniel's 70 weeks, it will help to understand the concepts of a Sabbatical year, a Sabbatical cycle and the year of Jubilee. Using the chronology previously developed, and doing a little *biblical detective work*, we can identify when the Sabbatical and Jubilee years were *supposed to have occurred*.

Sabbatical Years

God ordained and established the sabbatical year, and instructed Moses and Israel to honor these years. The command to observe Sabbatical years is found in Lev 25.

> *"And the LORD spake unto Moses in Mount Sinai, saying, Speak unto the Children of Israel, and say unto them, When ye come into the land which I give you, then shall the land keep a sabbath unto the LORD. Six years thou shalt sow thy field, and six years thou shalt prune thy vineyard, and gather in the fruit thereof; but in the seventh year shall be a sabbath of rest unto the land, a sabbath for the LORD: thou shalt neither sow thy field, nor prune thy vineyard. That which groweth of its own accord of thy harvest thou shalt not reap, neither gather the grapes of thy vine undressed: for it is a year of rest unto the land. And the sabbath of the land shall be meat for you; for thee, and for thy servant, and for thy maid, and for thy hired servant, and for thy stranger that sojourneth with thee, And for thy cattle, and for the beast that are in thy land, shall all the increase thereof be meat."*
> Lev 25:1-7

In the *Torah*, it was written that no trees could be planted, pruned or harvested during a Sabbatical year. However, irrigation was permitted to keep trees alive. During the time that Herod's temple was standing, rabbinical law forbade Jews to work in the fields one month before a Sabbatical year. This was not a part of the *Law*, but an attempt by the rabbis to *fence in the law* to keep it from being violated. The Sabbatical year has three primary aspects. The *first* is religious; The Sabbath Year was to be a *Sabbath unto the Lord*. It is a holy observance ordained by God. The *second* aspect is agricultural; the seventh year is to be a *Sabbath for the land*, in which the land would rest and renew itself. A *third* aspect is added to the agricultural principles in Deuteronomy 15:1-11. *All debts are to be forgiven* during that year, and those to whom money is owed no longer have the right to demand it back. This aspect of the commandment is designed to enable the impoverished to make a fresh start.

Since the land could not be planted and harvested in a Sabbatical year, the question arises as to how the Children of Israel were to eat during that year. Not only that, since the land could not be planted until the planting season of the eighth year, there were about two years without produce. God provided for these two years in a miraculous way.

"And if you say "what shall we eat in the 7th year, since we have not sown or gathered in our produce?" Then I will command my blessing on you in the 6th year, and it will bring forth produce enough for three years. And you shall sow in the 8th year, and eat old produce until the 8th year, until its produce comes in you shall eat of the old harvest."
Leviticus 25: 20-21.

The Lord is faithful and true, and he will take care of those whom he calls and those who respond. This covenant promise was conditional upon allowing the land to rest. The Sabbatical year has many Messianic overtones (Phillips, *The Book of Revelation*). The Sabbatical years were to continue forever (as long as the Children of Israel were in the land).

Year of Jubilee

The Sabbatical year was to be observed every seventh year. The sabbatical year started on Tishri 1 (just as the Jewish civil year). A sequence of seven Sabbatical years was 49 complete years. The 50th year was to be both a Year of Jubilee and the start of the next Sabbatical cycle. Interestingly, the Year of Jubilee started on Tishri 10 on the Feast of Atonement. This unusual start date also has Messianic and prophetic implications (Phillips). The Jubilee will start at the end of Daniel's 70th week, and will begin the 1000-year millennial kingdom.

"And thou shalt number seven Sabbaths of years unto thee, seven times seven years; and the space of the seven Sabbaths of years shall be unto thee forty and nine years. Then shalt thou cause the trumpet of the Jubilee to sound on the tenth day of the seventh month, in the Day of Atonement shall ye make the trumpet sound throughout all your land. And ye shall hallow the fiftieth year, and proclaim liberty throughout all the land unto all the inhabitants thereof: it shall be a jubilee unto you; and ye shall return every man unto his possession, and ye shall return every man unto his family. A jubilee shall that fiftieth year be unto you: ye shall not sow, neither reap that which groweth of itself in it, nor gather the grapes in it of thy vine undressed. For it is the jubilee; it shall be holy unto you: ye shall eat the increase thereof out of the field. In the year of this jubilee ye shall return every man unto his possession. Wherefore ye shall do my statutes, and keep my judgments, and do them; and ye shall dwell in the land in safety."
Lev 25 8-55

In the year of Jubilee; just as in a sabbatical year, the land shall rest; it shall not be planted, pruned or harvested. The English word *jubilee* comes from the Hebrew word *yobel* meaning a trumpet or a horn. The year of Jubilee is a Sabbath of Sabbaths. It is a special year among special years. The year of Jubilee is unique to all other Sabbatical years in that it is initiated on Tishri 10. This is a *feast day*, a *high Sabbath*, and a *fast day*. Tishri 10 represents the most holy day of the year for Jews. It is the great *Day of Atonement* (Lev. 23:26-32). On the Day of Atonement, the high priest would first make atonement for his sins, and then for the sins of the people. He would then offer incense to the Lord on the altar of Incense just outside the Holy of Holies. He would then enter into the very presence of the Lord as He dwelt above the Tabernacle in a thick cloud. There were three other things which happened on that day in ancient Israel:

> ➤ All Hebrews slaves were set free.
> ➤ All land returned to its original owner or owner's family.
> ➤ All debts are to be forgiven.
Deuteronomy 15

For 215 years before the Exodus, the Israelites had been slaves in the land of Egypt, without freedom and without possessions. Everything in Egypt belonged to the Pharaoh. After the Exodus, the Children of Israel wandered in the desert for 40 years as a result of not trusting the Lord (Deut. 1:19-46).We have shown that after crossing the river Jordan, it took Joshua and his army between 5 years, 2 months; and 6 years, 2 months to conquer the land. Once the land was conquered, the land of Canaan was divided among the 11 tribes (the Levites had no land inheritance). Every adult male became a land owner. This land could not be permanently sold. If a man became poor he could sell part or all of his land, but *only temporarily.* It would *always* revert to him or his descendants at the year of *Jubilee.* If he became poor and was unable to pay his debts, he could sell himself into slavery, and work to pay off his debts. Again that slavery could only be temporary. When the great *Day of Atonement* and the *Year of Jubilee* came around, he became a free man once again and repossessed his inheritance. What a wonderful promise this was! How many hopeless slaves to debt and poverty in the poorest countries of the world today would wish they lived under such laws! The lord said that *the land is mine*; you are only a sojourner on *my land.* The land was a unique Hebrew inheritance that was never intended to depart from the Children of Israel; the land was to be handed down from generation to generation (Lev 25:23).

When did Sabbatical and Jubilee years start to be *observed*? Over the last 2500 years, there have been many debates and interpretations of this question. Most have been based upon a complete misunderstanding of when Sabbatical years were to be *initiated.* One of the most recent hypotheses has been based upon an ancient non-canonical manuscript called the *Book of Jubilees.* The Book of Jubilees is generally recognized as one of the oldest manuscripts in existence. The Book of Jubilees contains a comprehensive chronology and record of the generations that were born between when Adam and Eve were created, to the giving of the law on Mt. Sinai. The chronology given in the *Book of Jubilees* is based on multiples of seven years duration. A Jubilee is a period of 49 years or seven *weeks of years,* into which all of time has been divided. The Book of Jubilees defines a *Jubilee* to be the 49th year in a 49-year cycle. According to the book, Adam and Eve were in the Garden of Eden for exactly seven years. At the end of the seventh year they sinned, and were expelled. The correct concept of every seventh year being a *Sabbatical Year,* and the 50th year after 7 consecutive Sabbatical cycles being a *Year of Jubilee,* is never defined or used in the Book of Jubilees.

Several biblical scholars have insisted that the Sabbatical and Jubilee years started when Moses led the Exodus out of Egypt. An even larger group of chronological researchers have proposed that the year Joshua crossed the river Jordan after a 40-year Exodus was both a year of Jubilee and the first year in the first seven-year Sabbatical cycle. The basis for this assumption is:

> **"When you come into the land which I give you, then shall the Land keep a Sabbath onto the Lord."**   Lev 25:2-b

Either interpretation of Lev 25:2-b demonstrates a complete misunderstanding of why a Sabbatical year was given by God to Moses. The primary purpose of a Sabbatical year is to *rest the land from cultivation and harvest by the Jewish land owner.* When Joshua crossed the river Jordan after Moses had led the Israelites through the wilderness for 40 years, the *land* did not belong to Israel (although it did belong to God and had been promised to Israel as an inheritance). Joshua shortly embarked on a campaign to conquer the land and then give it to the 11 tribes of Israel (excluding the Levites). It is impossible to initiate any Sabbatical year cycle until the land has been conquered, divided, cultivated and planted for harvest. Remember that both the Sabbatical years and the subsequent year of Jubilee is a *corporate commandment to all of Israel,* and both are intended to *let the land rest* from six consecutive years of planting and harvesting. The 50th or Jubilee year is a Sabbath of Sabbath years; the Jubilee includes an extra year of rest for the land, and involves forgiving debts.

A large number of chronologists have determined from Jewish Rabbinical records, the Works of Josephus, and the Holy Bible when several Sabbatical years *might* have occurred, and built a sequence of Sabbatical years around those records. However, there are no *definitive records* anywhere as to when Jubilee years actually occurred. By all indications, Israel *never* observed a single year of Jubilee. However, we do know that if an initial set of seven seven-year Sabbatical cycles could be discovered, then the 50th year would be a Jubilee, and all other 49-year Sabbatical cycles and 50th Jubilee years would follow. Before we attack this problem, we should note that exactly when a Jubilee cycle occurs is a debated topic. The debate is not that the Jubilee is the 50th year following a 49-year (seven-seven's) Sabbatical cycle, but how the 50th year is to be counted. The first interpretation is that the 50th (Jubilee) year is the *first year* of the next Sabbatical cycle. The second interpretation is that the 50th year is a *separate year*, and that the next Sabbatical cycle starts following the 50th year. Rabbi Judah states: *The Jubilee year counts both ways,* meaning it is counted as both the 50th year and the first year of the next seven-year cycle. We agree with Rabbi Judah. This assumption will be proven correct when we compare our derived sequence of Sabbatical years to historical records, and to when the Jewish people seemed to observe Sabbatical years. In order to determine the chronological ordering of Sabbatical years, it is necessary to trace the Exodus from when Moses left Egypt in 1490 BC (AY 2454) to when the Jordan River was crossed 40 years later in 1450 BC (AY 2494) We have already studied this journey in Chapter 3, but for clarity and completeness we will again trace the exodus.

The Exodus Journey

The Chronology of the 40-year exodus sojourn is clearly recorded in the Books of Genesis, Exodus, Leviticus and Joshua. The nation of Israel left at midnight on Nisan 15, which was the day following Nisan 14. Recall that Nisan 15 began at 6:00 pm; the evening of Nisan 14. The journey from leaving Egypt until the river Jordan was crossed 40 years later consisted of three major time periods: The *first* was the departure from Egypt, followed by the giving of the law at Mt Sinai and construction of the tabernacle. The *second* was the failure at Kadesh-barnea to trust God, and an 8 month delay. The *fourth* was a period of 38 years wandering in the wilderness. The entire journey took 40 years. We have already shown that under the leadership of Joshua, the land was conquered in about 6 years. To prove this, we needed to do a little *detective work.* Looking at the table on the following page, we can trace the main events of the Exodus from Egypt. Note that it took about 47 days for Moses and the children of Israel to reach Mt. Sinai. God gave the 10 commandments and the laws for spiritual and social behavior on the 50th day. After building the tabernacle, they camped just south of the Promised Land, and Moses sent out members from each tribe to spy the land. After bad report spawned by disbelief, God sentenced Israel to a total of 40 years wandering in the wilderness. It would be more than 38 more years before Israel would enter the Promised Land. After Moses is taken away by God, Joshua assumed leadership and started conquest of the land.

Timeline	Event	Reference
1st Day....Nisan 15	Exodus starts just after midnight	Ex 12:40-42, Num 33:3
47 Day journey	Arrival at Mt Sinai	Ex 19:1
50th day after departure	God speaks the 10 commandments	Ex 20:1-20, Deut 5:22
2nd year, 1st Month, First Day	Tabernacle set up after 7 Months, 3 days Construction	Ex 40:2, 40:17
2nd year, 2nd month, 20th Day	Depart from Mt. Sinai 50 days after tabernacle is completed	Num 10:11
2nd year, 3rd Month, Day 8	Arrive at Kadesh-barnea after a 18 day journey including a 7 day delay to heal Miriam. Spies sent out to Promised Land	Deut 1:2, Num 12:15
2nd year, fourth Month, 18th Day	Spies return. Only Joshua & Caleb give a good report. God condemns them to wander 40 years (total since Exodus) in the wilderness.....One year for each day.	Num 13:25
	Moses stays at Kadesh-barnea for almost 9 Months	Deut 1:46 Deut 2:14
3rd year, 15st Day, 1st Month	Moses departs Kadesh-barnea for 38 years in the Wilderness	Deut 2:14
40th year, 5th Month, Day 1	Aaron dies and is buried on Mt. Hor	Num 33:38
40th year, 12th month, 1st Day	Moses dies and is taken to Mt. Nebo by God. He recites all of the law to Israel before he is taken away. He anoints Joshua as the new leader	Deut 34:1, Deut 34:7-8 Josh 1:1-5
41st year, Month 1, Day 1	Camp at River Jordan....Spies sent out a second time	Deut 34:8 Josh 2:1
41st year, Month 1, Day 10	River Jordan is crossed on Nisan 10 All men circumcised	Josh 4:19 Josh 5:2-5
41st year, Month 1, Day 14	Exodus completed....Manna ceases	Josh 5:12

It is amazing how many different time periods (years) have been proposed for Joshua and the army of God to conquer the various nations and Kings in Canaan. Of course, the land was never fully conquered and after the initial period of conquest, the Children of Israel became complacent and failed to fully fulfill their destiny. The author has seen estimates ranging from five years to more than 40 years required to conquer the land, divide the land and release each of the tribes home to claim their allotted inheritance. If studied carefully, the biblical record is quite clear on how long this actually took.

Moses led the nation of Israel out of Egyptian bondage; starting shortly after midnight (Exodus 12:29-30) on Nisan 15, a Thursday. This was the first day of the seven day *Feast of Unleavened Bread* (Ex 12:17). They crossed the Red Sea seven days later on the last day of the Feast of Unleavened Bread and emerged a new, free nation (a type of rebirth which was a shadow and type of our Lord's resurrection). On the 47th day after they left Egypt, they arrived at Mt. Sinai and on the 50th day (Exodus 19:1) God gave them the law (a shadow and type of when the New Covenant was initiated as the Holy Spirit fell on the day of *Pentecost*). The tabernacle was finished on the 20th day of the second month in the second year, and on that day Moses and the Children of Israel departed for the Promised Land. They arrived at Kadesh-barnea one year, two months and 15 days after leaving Egypt (Num 10:11). The journey took 40 days, including a seven-day delay for Miriam to be cleansed (Num 12:15). Moses immediately sent 12 men to spy the land (Lev 13:2-3), and after 40 more days they returned. Upon their return, 10 of the spies gave a bad report, and only Joshua and Caleb gave a good report (Num 13:25-33). In one of the most tragic events in biblical history, the 10 spies who gave the bad report were killed by a plague; the Lord sentenced the nation of Israel to wander a total of 40 years in the wilderness (Deut 2:7); and none of the generation that rebelled were allowed to see the promised land (Num 26:64-65): Only Joshua and Caleb would enter Canaan of all those who were at Kadesh- barnea (Num 14:22-24, 30, 37-38, Deut 1:1-38). This is a stark testimony to anyone who refuses to trust in the Lord and not respond to a sacred calling.

Moses stayed at Kadesh-barnea for about eight months and 5 days (Deut 2:14). He finally departed on or near the first day of the third year after leaving Egypt (Deut. 2:13). He then led the nation of Israel through the wilderness for 38 more years. In the 40th year, on the first day of the 12th month, Moses gathered all the people to him. He reviewed all of the events that had transpired since they had left Egypt, and he read all of the Law. Moses was 120 years old that very day (Deut 31:1-2). Having been instructed by God, he inaugurated Joshua as the new commander-in-chief (Deut 31:23), recorded the law in a *book* (Deut 31:24), and was then taken to Mt Nebo by God where he died (Deut 32: 48-50). The entire nation of Israel wept for 30 days (Deut 34:8) and on Nisan 1, 39 years, 11 months and 15 days after leaving Egypt they broke camp and prepared to cross the river Jordan. They crossed the river Jordan; Joshua circumcised every male; and then they pitched camp at Gilgal on Nisan 14; exactly 40 years after leaving Egypt (Josh 5:1-12). Manna ceased the next day (Nisan 15) and Joshua began the conquest of Canaan at Jericho (Josh 5:12-15, Josh 6). It was necessary to examine in detail the Exodus journey to establish how long it took to conquer the land. The duration of the conquest, which terminated in a division of the Promised Land, is determined as follows.

Joshua, Caleb and the other 10 men were sent to spy on the enemy one year two months and 15 days after leaving Egypt. They were gone for 40 days, and returned one year three months and 25 days after leaving Egypt. Most chronologist stumble on this point, but after God passed judgment on the nation of Israel, Moses remained at Kadesh-barnea for eight months and five days. At this point, Moses broke camp and began 38 additional years wandering in the wilderness. When Caleb was sent to spy the land, he was 40 years old. Caleb said:

> *I was 40 years old when Moses the servant of the Lord sent me from Kadesh Barnea to spy out the land.*   Josh 14:7.

The period of time required to conquer the land of Canaan can also be determined with scriptural help. We now move forward to the Division of Canaan by Joshua.

> *So Joshua conquered* **all the land**: *the mountain country and the lowland and the wilderness slopes, and all their Kings.; he left none remaining, but* **utterly destroyed all that breathed**, *as the Lord of Israel had commanded. Then Joshua returned, and all Israel with him, to the camp at Gilgal (Josh 10:43). So Joshua took the whole land,*

according to all that the Lord had said to Moses; and Joshua gave it as an inheritance to Israel, according to their divisions by tribes. Then the land rested from war.
Joshua 11:25

Note carefully that the tribes did not inherit the land until this point in time. Both the Sabbatical year and the year of Jubilee were designated to let the land rest. Both were *corporate* commandments to the nation of Israel and both were not to be observed until the tribes of Israel had conquered the land, inherited the land, and started to live on the land. In the Book of Numbers the Lord's instructions are given as to *when* the land was to be divided and inherited by the tribes of Israel.

> *Speak to the Children of Israel, and say to them: When you have crossed the Jordan into the land of Canaan… you shall dispossess the inhabitants of the land and dwell in it…and (then) you shall divide the land by lot, as an inheritance among your families.*
> Numbers 33:51-54.

God gave these instructions for possessing the land just before Joshua crossed the river Jordan. Many chronographers have assumed, based upon this passage, that this first year in the land was both a Jubilee year and a Sabbatical year. Nowhere is this implied in these instructions. The land was not to be inherited until (1) the land was conquered and (2) the land is divided by lots. When was the land divided? Chapter 13 in the book of Joshua provides a detailed account of how the land was to be divided. At that time: "***Joshua was old*** (between 90-100 years old), ***and was stricken in years*** (Josh 13:1). The narrative continues as the Lord admonishes Joshua for not fully completing the conquest (Josh 13:2-5). But the Lord said, ***I will drive (all them) out before the Children of Israel; only divide it by lot to Israel as I have commanded you*** (Joshua 13:6). Here is another great object lesson. Even though we are weak and sometimes falter, when God has a plan he will bring it to completion. When the Lord calls, he will see you through. So Joshua divided the land as command in Josh 13:11, and recorded in Joshua 13:1-33 and Joshua 14:1-6. But here something unusual happens. Caleb approaches Joshua and says:

> *"Then the children of Judah came unto Joshua in Gilgal: and Caleb the son of Jephunneh the Kenezite said unto him, Thou knowest the thing that the LORD said unto Moses the man of God concerning me and thee in Kadesh-barnea. Forty years old was I when Moses the servant of the LORD sent me from Kadesh-barnea to spy out the land; and I brought him word again as it was in mine heart. Nevertheless my brethren that went up with me made the heart of the people melt: but I wholly followed the LORD my God. And Moses sware on that day, saying, Surely the land whereon thy feet have trodden shall be thine inheritance, and thy children's for ever, because thou hast wholly followed the LORD my God. And now, behold, the LORD hath kept me alive, as he said, these forty and five years, even since the LORD spake this word unto Moses, while the children of Israel wandered in the wilderness: and now, lo, I am this day fourscore and five years old."* Joshua 14:6-10

Can you just imagine this confrontation between Caleb and Joshua, who was the most powerful and respected man in all of Israel. Caleb is saying to Joshua, *Moses promised me a piece of this land and I want it now!* Caleb now provides the following justification.

And now, behold, the Lord has kept me alive, as he said, these forty and five years, even since the LORD spake this word unto Moses, while the children of Israel wandered in the wilderness: and now, lo, I am this day fourscore and five years old. Josh 14:10-11

There you have it! On that very day, Caleb is 85 years old. It is now time to do a little math.

- ➢ Joshua was sent to spy on the land one year, three months and 25 days after leaving Egypt.
- ➢ Joshua is 40 years old when he was sent to spy the land
- ➢ The children of Israel remained at Kadesh–barnea for eight months and five days before leaving on a 38-year wilderness journey (Deut 2:14)
- ➢ It is 45 years until Caleb's confrontation with Joshua
- ➢ Caleb is exactly 85 years old when he confronts Joshua

If Joshua has *just turned* 40 years old when he returned from spying the land, and was promised an inheritance by Moses, there were 45 years between this event and his confrontation with Joshua. This leaves six years, three months and 25 days that were spent conquering the land. If, in fact, Caleb was 40 years old when he was sent to spy the land, but *one day later* he would be 41 years old, the conquest of the land would have taken five years, three months and 25 days. We do not know exactly how old Caleb was when he was sent to spy the land, but following scriptural clues we can state with certainty that the average time to conquer the land can be determined as five years, nine months and 25 days. The following graphic gives a snapshot of the years between the Exodus and when the land was divided.

5 yrs, 3 Mos, 25 days ≤ time to conquer the land ≤ 6 yrs, 3 Mos, 25 days

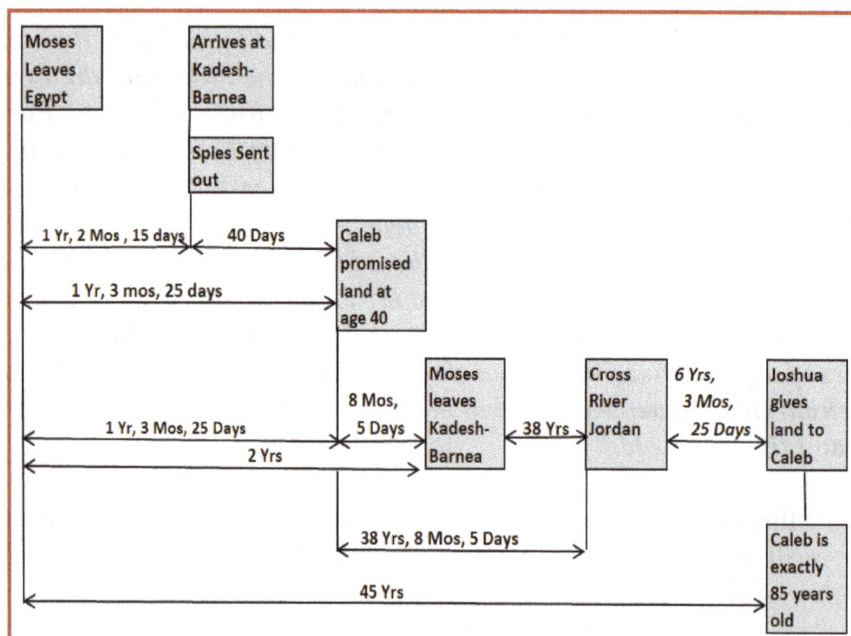

We can now state the following facts surrounding the Exodus and conquest of the land.

> Joshua assumed commander-in-chief of Israel upon the death of Moses in AY 2494 Adar 1, 1450 BC
> The conquest started shortly after Nisan 15 in AY 2494, 1450 BC
> Conquest of land took no more than 6 years 4 months. Using this duration of time, this would bring us to the summer of 1444 BC, AY 2500
> The land was divided sometime in late AY 2500; likely Early summer
> The tribes of Israel inherited land and returned home. The first Sabbatical cycle was initiated in AY 2501, Sept, 1444 BC-Sept, 1443 BC
> The first Sabbatical year was seven years later; AY 2507, Tishri 1, 1438 – Tishri 1, 1437.

We have previously shown that the Exodus occurred in the Julian year 1490 BC. Note that this corresponded to the Jewish civil calendar year of AY 2454, Tishri 1 (Sept/Oct) 1491 – Tishri 1(Sept/Oct). The Exodus took place on Nisan 15, 1490. The Exodus account can be traced from Egypt to Mt. Sinai, a period of 47 days, and it can be verified that the Exodus *had to have occurred on a **Thursday***. The exodus year of 1490 BC was determined by a consistent and biblical sound methodology. When was Nisan 15, 1490 BC? Amazingly, it falls on *Thursday, April 1* (Julian date)! This is an astounding result and is a very strong indication that the exodus did occur in 1490 BC. It is worth noting that there is no Nisan 15 Thursday date within 6 years of 1490. A second witness is that Christ had to be crucified on a Wednesday to fulfill the ***Sign of Jonah***. This is shown in *The Birth and Death of Christ* (Phillips, 2014). This resulted in the first day of the Feast of Unleavened Bread being Nisan 15, a Thursday. The *sign* was that He would lie in the grave for three days and three nights, just as Jonah was in the belly of a great fish for three days and three nights (Jonah 1:17). After exactly three days and three nights, Christ arose from the grave. We will subsequently verify that Christ was crucified on Wednesday, Nisan 14 on April 5 (Julian date) in 30 AD. In 1490 BC, the Passover Lamb was slaughtered on the afternoon of Wednesday, Nisan 14, just as Christ was also crucified on that *same day*. Christ expired at 3:00pm, the *same hour* that the High Priest had slaughtered the Passover lamb for over 1500 years! The day that the children of Israel left Egypt was later designated as the first day of the Feast of Unleavened Bread (Nisan 15). Christ is our Passover Lamb, and the Firstfruit of all who will rise from the grave: He was sinless (without leaven). The first day that Christ had departed from this earth was Nisan 15, which was the first day the Children of Israel departed from Egypt.

The Jordan River was crossed on Nisan 10 (Joshua 4:19) in 1450 BC (AY 2494). All the men were circumcised (Joshua 5:4) and camp was broken on Nisan 15 (Joshua 5:10-12) … exactly 40 years to the day that the Children of Israel left Egypt. The conquest of the land was started almost immediately. We have shown that conquering the land took a minimum of about 5 years, 3 months, 25 days and a maximum of 6 years, 3 months and 25 days. The shortest and longest time periods yield an average of about five years and nine months. We chose to use 6 years, but either the upper or lower bound would still give the same AY year in which the land was divided. The land would be divided in AY 2500, most likely in the late spring or early summer of 1444 BC. At that point in time, the tribes would all inherit the land as God promised, return home, and start to work the land. Of course, there was never an end to wars because of Israel's rebellion. But God's promise had been fulfilled under Joshua. It is now almost certain that the conquest of the land took *less* than God's number of completeness, seven years. It was not the number of completeness, because the Children of Israel never fully possessed all of the land that God gave to them. The first year of the first Sabbatical cycle occurred as soon as the tribes began to inherit and work the land. Sabbatical Years ran from Tishri 1 to Tishri 1, and coincided with the Jewish traditional civil year. Since the first Sabbatical year count started on AY 2501 (Tishri 1 in Julian Year 1444 BC), the first *week of years* ended on Elul 29, 1438 BC; so 1438 BC to 1437 BC was the *first Sabbatical year*. This is shown in the following graphic. The Julian year dates that correspond to the given AY years will be fully substantiated in Chapter 6; they are shown here for ease of future reference.

1	2451	1494	1493	2452	1493	1492	2453	1492	1491	2454	1491	1490	2455	1490	1489	2456	1489	1488	2457	1488	1487
2	2458	1487	1486	2459	1486	1485	2460	1485	1484	2461	1484	1483	2462	1483	1482	2463	1482	1481	2464	1481	1480
3	2465	1480	1479	2466	1479	1478	2467	1478	1477	2468	1477	1476	2469	1476	1475	2470	1475	1474	2471	1474	1473
4	2472	1473	1472	2473	1472	1471	2474	1471	1470	2475	1470	1469	2476	1469	1468	2477	1468	1467	2478	1467	1466
5	2479	1466	1465	2480	1465	1464	2481	1464	1463	2482	1463	1462	2483	1462	1461	2484	1461	1460	2485	1460	1459
6	2486	1459	1458	2487	1458	1457	2488	1457	1456	2489	1456	1455	2490	1455	1454	2491	1454	1453	2492	1453	1452
7	2493	1452	1451	2494	1451	1450	2495	1450	1449	2496	1449	1448	2497	1448	1447	2498	1447	1446	2499	1446	1445

52	1			2			3			4			5			6			7		
1	2500	1445	1444	2501	1444	1443	2502	1443	1442	2503	1442	1441	2504	1441	1440	2505	1440	1439	2506	1439	1438
2	2507	1438	1437	2508	1437	1436	2509	1436	1435	2510	1435	1434	2511	1434	1433	2512	1433	1432	2513	1432	1431
3	2514	1431	1430	2515	1430	1429	2516	1429	1428	2517	1428	1427	2518	1427	1426	2519	1426	1425	2520	1425	1424
4	2521	1424	1423	2522	1423	1422	2523	1422	1421	2524	1421	1420	2525	1420	1419	2526	1419	1418	2527	1418	1417
5	2528	1417	1416	2529	1416	1415	2530	1415	1414	2531	1414	1413	2532	1413	1412	2533	1412	1411	2534	1411	1410
6	2535	1410	1409	2536	1409	1408	2537	1408	1407	2538	1407	1406	2539	1406	1405	2540	1405	1404	2541	1404	1403
7	2542	1403	1402	2543	1402	1401	2544	1401	1400	2545	1400	1399	2546	1399	1398	2547	1398	1397	2548	1397	1396

Red Dates: *Exodus beginning and end*
Brown Dates: *Conquering the land; dividing the land; inheriting, settling and planting the land*
Blue Dates: *The first Sabbatical year cycle of 7 years. Last maroon date is first Sabbatical year*

Having determined when the Sabbatical years started and ended, it is now easy to determine when all other Sabbatical years occurred, or at least when they were supposed to occur. Since the first sabbatical cycle of seven years has been determined, it is also easy to determine when all the Jubilee years were to be observed. The following Table shows the Sabbatical years between 1438 BC-1437 BC (AY 2507) and 222 AD-223 AD. Note that the years of Jubilee are also shown in the *columns* labeled *Jubilee*, and that each Sabbath and Jubilee Year always spans two Julian calendar years; starting in September/October on Tishri 1. The year shown is the first year.

First Sabbatical Year..1438-1437							First Jubilee Year..1396-1395									
Sabbatical Years							Jubilee	Cycle	Sabbatical Years							Jubilee	Cycle
1	2	3	4	5	6	7			1	2	3	4	5	6	7		
1438	1431	1424	1417	1410	1403	1396	1395	1	1389	1382	1375	1368	1361	1354	1347	1346	2
1340	1333	1326	1319	1312	1305	1298	1297	3	1291	1284	1277	1270	1263	1256	1249	1248	4
1242	1235	1228	1221	1214	1207	1200	1199	5	1193	1186	1179	1172	1165	1158	1151	1150	6
1144	1137	1130	1123	1116	1109	1102	1101	7	1095	1088	1081	1074	1067	1060	1053	1052	8
1046	1039	1032	1025	1018	1011	1004	1003	9	997	990	983	976	969	962	955	954	10
948	941	934	927	920	913	906	905	11	899	892	885	878	871	864	857	856	12
850	843	836	829	822	815	808	807	13	801	794	787	780	773	766	759	758	14
752	745	738	731	724	717	710	709	15	703	696	689	682	675	668	661	660	16
654	647	640	633	626	619	612	611	17	605	598	591	584	577	570	563	562	18
556	549	542	535	528	521	514	513	19	507	500	493	486	479	472	465	464	20
458	451	444	437	430	423	416	415	21	409	402	395	388	381	374	367	366	22
360	353	346	339	332	325	318	317	23	311	304	297	290	283	276	269	268	24
262	255	248	241	234	227	220	219	25	213	206	199	192	185	178	171	170	26
164	157	150	143	136	129	122	121	27	115	108	101	94	87	80	73	72	28
66	59	52	45	38	31	24	23	29	17	10	3	5	12	19	26	27	30
33	40	47	54	61	68	75	76	31	82	89	96	103	110	117	124	125	32
131	138	145	152	159	166	173	174	33	180	187	194	201	208	215	222	223	34

As previously stated, there is no indication that *any* Jubilee Years were ever observed. It is also true that the failure to observe 70 Sabbatical and Jubilee years between 1438 BC and 586 BC resulted in God destroying Jerusalem and deporting the entire nation of Israel except for the old and weak to Babylon for 70 years. The critical question that begs to be asked is: *do historical, biblical and written records support these dates?* The answer is convincingly, *YES*. We offer only a few verifications using Tishri 1 (Sept-Oct)-Tishri1 (Sept-Oct) sabbatical years. A Jubilee year follows 7 full cycles of sabbatical years and starts on Tishri 10 (Lev 25: 8-10).

> ➤ Jack Finnegan, one of the most-respected chronographers of our time, and author of the *Handbook of Biblical Chronology,* has proposed that the beginning of the Bar Kokhba rebellion and the first year of Israel's liberation was 131-132 AD. He further identifies 131-132 AD as a Sabbatical year. The previous table of sabbatical years agrees with his conclusion.

> ➤ August Strobel and others have suggested that 458-457 BC was a Sabbatical year. Jewish tradition and rabbinical opinion also hold that this was a Sabbatical year (The Shemitah). Maimonides, a respected and reliable ancient historian wrote: *"With Ezra, the Shemitah (Sabbatical years) began to be counted, and after seven Sabbatical years they sanctified the 50th year; for even though the Jubilee year(s) were not observed, these years were nevertheless counted in order to satisfy the Shemitah"*. We concur with 458-457 BC being a Sabbatical year.

> ➤ The historian Josephus has identified several Sabbatical years in his history of the ancient world. 136 BC-135 BC (Antiq. Book 13:8:1); 45 BC-44 BC (Antiq. Book 14:10:5) and 38 BC-37 BC (Antiq. Book15:1:2) ...... We concur with all of these Sabbatical years.

> ➤ In the first full year of the Ministry of Jesus Christ, He attended a temple service in his home town of Nazareth He opened the Book of Isaiah the Prophet and read the following passage:

> *"The Spirit of the Lord is upon me, because he hath annointed me to preach the gosple of the poor; he hath sent me to heal the brokenhearted, to preach deliverance to the captives, recovering of sight to the blind, to set at liberty them that are bruised. To preach the acceptable year of the Lord."*   Luke 4:18-19

This passage was taken from Isa. 61:1-2(a). Our Lord Jesus Christ stopped reading in the middle of verse 61:2 because the first part of Verse 61:2 dealt with the message of *preaching the acceptable year of the Lord,* while the second part of 61:2 dealt with *the Day of Vengence of our Lord.* The Day of Vengence is the *second coming of Jesus Christ,* when he will fight the battle of Armageddon (Revelation Chapter 19). He chose not to announce that event at that time. The Jubilee year was to be observed as a Sabbatical year, but with the added condition to: *proclaim a release through the land to all its inhabitants* (Lev. 25:10). All land would be returned to its original owner, and all slaves would be set free. It is the proclaiming of release in the Jubilee that is tied to proclaiming release to the captives in the words of Isaiah and Jesus. Therefore, the Jubilee is equated with the *favorable year of the Lord.* Did Jesus read this passage on a Jubilee year at the tabernacle in Nazareth? We will show in the next chapter that Jesus Christ began his

3.5-year ministry at the river Jordan in September of 26 AD. From our list of Sabbatical years, 26-27 AD is a Sabbatical year and 27-28 AD is a year of Jubilee. The

proclamation of Isa 61:1-2 is to be read on the Day of Atonement, Tishri 10. Since in 26 AD, after his baptism, Jesus went to be tempted by Satan for 40 days; he could not have been in Nazareth in 26 AD, so *it must have been in 27 AD, and 27-28 AD was a year of Jubilee as we have previously shown.*

➤ In 70 AD the Roman general Titus attacked Jerusalem and on Av 9, August 4 (Julian date). Herod's temple as burned to the ground. Josephus was an eye witness. He and others record that 70 AD was a year immediately following a Sabbatical year. Since we use Jewish years from Tishri 1-Tishri 1, the year Tishri 1, 69-Tishri 1, 70 AD was the year that Herod's temple was destroyed. The previous year is Tishri 1, 68-Tishri 1, 69 AD, and we show this as a Sabbatical year!

Ab 9, Aug 5 AD 70 was fall of temple to Titus…This was a year immediately following a Sabatical year.

➤ Finnegan has researched several papyrus fragments recently found at a place called Murabba'at, and known collectively as the Mur 24 papyri. They are written in Hebrew, and reflect what is equivalent to a sequence of *bank notes* in today's economy. The Bar Kokhba revolt was a revolutionary revolt against the oppression of the Roman Empire. This was a critical battle in Hebrew history, for after the Roman Empire put down the rebellion, there was never another insurrection of the Hebrew nation until Israel became a country in the 20th century. Assembling data from these papyri Finnegan has constructed the following Table.

Date	Description
131-132 AD	**Year of the revolt… A Sabbatical Year**
132-133 AD	**" First year of the liberation of Israel"**
133-134 AD	**"Second year of the liberation of Israel"**
134-135 AD	
135-136 AD	
136-137 *AD*	
137-138 AD	
138-139 AD	**A Sabbatical Year**

We agree with Finnegan: Both 131 AD-132 AD and 138 AD-139 AD are Sabbatical years.

➤ It has been suggested that by divine appointment, Alexander the Great conquered Jerusalem and began to reign in 331 BC. This appears to be true since 332-331 BC was a Sabbatical year.

332 BC-331 BC was believed to be a Sabbatical Year Alexander the Great started to rule Jerusalem in 331 BC

All of the Evidence presented suggests that our list of Sabbatical years is correct. This would also make our sequence of Jubilee years correct.

Scholarly Support

In 1856, Benedict Zuckermann published a table of sabbatical years based upon both historical and biblical evidence. His table of Sabbatical years has been recognized as a standard since that time. One objector to the Zuckermann dates was Ben Zion Wacholder, who in 1973 published a study on the same subject. He concluded that the Zuckermann dates were all one year too early. In 2007, Bob Pickle published a scholarly investigation of both the Zuckermann and Wacholder dates. Using ten reference points, he showed convincingly that the Zuckermann dates were correct. Both Pickle and Zuckermann conclude that 458 BC-457 BC was a Sabbatical year (the Wacholder date would be 457 BC-456 BC). Finally, Jack Finnegan… who is one of the most respected chronographers of the modern era… concluded in his widely acclaimed *Handbook of Biblical Chronology* that the Zuckermann dates were verifiable and correct. It should be easily recognized that the sequence of Sabbatical years produced by Zuckermann are identical to those determined in this book, but we independently derived the Sabbatical years based only upon biblical chronological evidence. Our sequence of Jubilee years and when they occur appear to be unique to the offered chronology in this book.

The Consequence of Failure

The Lord had made incredible provisions for his people as part of the Sabbatical and Jubilee years. Sadly, it is not known how many of these years were actually observed by the corporate nation of Israel. The Bible only hints at several of these years being observed, and there is no undisputed biblical record of when they were observed. Leviticus 26:34-35 says the land will take her Sabbath even if the nation of Israel ignored God's word. Prophets and leaders regularly called Israel to account for neglecting the demands of the Sabbatical and Jubilee ordinances (Neh. 5:1-13, Jer. 34:8-18, Amos 2:6-7, 8:5-6, Eze.18: 7-9, Isaiah 58). Whether the Sabbatical and Jubilee years were ever adequately observed is a secondary question; the Jewish nation was called to accountability, regardless. This is a basic Christian principle today. God will not be mocked, nor will he sleep. We will all be held accountable for our deeds, good and bad, at the *Judgment Seat of Christ*. Thank God that we are living under the grace of our Lord Jesus Christ. We may suffer loss for bad works, but we will all be saved; all of those who accept Jesus Christ as their Savior. What is known for sure is that *God was keeping track* of his holy years, and that the house of Israel refused to observe a combination of 70 Sabbatical and Jubilee years between when they were started and the final fall of Judah on July 18 in 586 BC (Finnegan, Thiele).

"Yet ye have not hearkened unto me, saith the LORD; that ye might provoke me to anger with the works of your hands to your own hurt. Therefore, thus saith the LORD of hosts; Because ye have not heard my words, behold, I will send and take all the families of the north, saith the LORD, and Nebuchadnezzar the king of Babylon, my servant, and will bring them against this land, and against the inhabitants thereof, and against all these nations round about, and will utterly destroy them, and make them an astonishment, and an hissing, and perpetual desolations. Moreover I will take from them the voice of mirth, and the voice of gladness, the voice of the bridegroom, and the voice of the bride, the sound of the millstones, and the light of the candle. And this whole land shall be a desolation, and an astonishment; and these nations shall serve the king of Babylon seventy years.
And it shall come to pass, when seventy years are accomplished, that I will punish the king of Babylon, and that nation, saith the LORD, for their iniquity, and the land of the Chaldeans, and will make it perpetual desolations."   Jeremiah 25:9-12

"For thus saith the LORD, That after seventy years be accomplished at Babylon I will visit you, and perform my good word toward you, in causing you to return to this place".
Jeremiah 29:10.

This is an *amazing* prophecy made by Jeremiah. He received his prophetic call in the thirteenth year of King Josiah's reign around 628-627 BC (Jer. 1:2-3). This prophetic word proclaimed that the nation of Israel would be conquered by a Babylonian king named Nebuchadnezzar, and that the entire Jewish nation would serve the nation of Babylon for a period of 70 years. After the 70 years had been fulfilled, Babylon would be punished (fall to the nation of Assyria), and the Jews would be allowed to return to their land. All of this came true starting in 605 BC with the deportation of a large number of Jews; including Daniel, Shadrach, Meshach and Abednego by King Nebuchadnezzar of the Babylonian Empire. There were actually three deportations:

➢ 605 BC - This is when Daniel and other members of Judah's elite were taken into captivity (Daniel 1:1 & 2 Kings 24:1-2),

➢ 597 BC - Jehoiakim was taken into captivity (2 Chron. 36:5-6). Three months and ten days later Jehoiachin, along with other members of the royal family, were taken into captivity (2 Chron. 36:9-10 & 2 Kings 24:15-17),

➢ 586 BC - After a 3-year siege, Jerusalem was conquered and destroyed, and most of the remaining people were taken into captivity, along with articles from the temple. Only the poorest people remained (2 Kings 25:12). July 18, 586 BC is widely accepted as the final fall of Jerusalem and the Nation of Israel.

The following passage is taken from Finnegan who references Thiele.

*In King Zedekiah's ninth regnal year, in the 10th month, on the tenth day of the month, Nebuchadnezzar came against his faithless appointee, and with his whole army laid siege to Jerusalem (I King 25:1). The 9th year of Zedekiah was Tishri 1, 589 BC (Oct 10) to Elul 30, 588 BC (Sept, 28). The siege went on for slightly more than two and one-half years until at last famine was unbearably severe in the city. A breach was made in the city (wall). The king and men of war fled by night, but was overtaken in the plains of Jericho. Zedekiah was captured and taken to Nebuchadnezzar at Riblah, where his sons were slain before his eyes and he was blinded and taken off to Babylon to prison until the day of his death (II King 25:3-7, Jer 52:5-11). The date of the final fall of Jerusalem was in the 11th year of Zedekiah, on the 9th day of the 1st month (II King 25:2-3, Jer 52:5-6). The 11th year of Zedekiah was from Tishri 1, 587 BC (Oct 18) to Elul 30, 586 BC (Oct 30). The 4th month is Tammuz (June/July), and in 586 BC the 9th day is equivalent to July 18, and is determined to be a Saturday. This, then, is the highly probable date of the final fall of Jerusalem... **July 18, 586 BC.***

July 18, 586 BC is chosen to be our ***anchor date*** from which working backward (or forward) all Julian years can be determined from the AY years previously derived from the Biblical records.

Establishing Calendar Dates for the Full Chronology

Having established and verified a 389 year epoch of time for the reign of all Southern Kingdom Kings (Judah), an unbroken chronology from the AY year that Adam and Eve were cast out of the Garden of Eden (AY 1) to the destruction of the Southern Kingdom and the exile of Israel to the city of Babylon (AY 3358) has been completed. The subsequent Babylonian exile lasted 70 years, because there were 70 Sabbatical and Jubilee years that the land was not allowed to rest. The following table provides a summary of important events which occurred between AY 1 and AY 3358. The final fall of Jerusalem was on July 18, 586 BC and the year that Adam and Eve left the Garden of Eden was determined to be 3944 BC. Note again that 3944 BC is NOT when the world was created, nor is it when Adam was created and placed into the Garden of Eden.

Event	AY Year	Julian Years
Adam and Eve leave the Garden of Eden	1	Sept/Oct 3944-Sept/Oct 3943
The Great Flood (Noah is 600 years old)	1657	Sept/Oct 2288-Sept/Oct 2287
Abraham Leaves Haran @ Age 75	2024	Sept/Oct 1921-Sept/Oct 1920
Jacob Dies	2256	Sept/Oct 1689-Sept/Oct 1688
Joseph Dies	2310	Sept/Oct 1635
Moses Born	2374	Sept/Oct 1571-Sept/Oct 1570
Exodus from Egypt	2454	March/April 1490
Law is Given @ Mt. Sinai	2454	May/June 1490
Moses dies at Age 120	2494	Feb/March 1450
Exodus Ends & River Jordan is Crossed	2494	March/April 1451-March/April 1450
Promised Land is Conquered and Divided	2500	Late spring or summer of 1444 BC
First Sabbatical Year	2507	Sept/Oct 1458-Sept/Oct 1457
First Jubilee Year	2550	Sept/Oct 1395-Sept/Oct 1394
First Year of King Solomon's Reign	2930	Sept/Oct 1015-Sept/Oct 1014
4th Year of King Solomon's Reign	2933	Sept/Oct 1012-Sept/Oct 1011
Solomon's Temple Started in Month of Ziv	2933	April/May 1011
Last Year of King Solomon's Reign	2969	Sept/Oct 976-Sept/Oct 975
First Year of Divided Kingdom	2970	Sept/Oct 975-Sept/Oct 974
Last Year of Northern Kingdom of Israel	3224	Sept/Oct 721-Sept/Oct 720
Jerusalem Falls to the Babylonian Empire	3358	July 18, 586 BC

Conclusion

Following the final fall of Jerusalem in 586 BC, the nation of Israel ceased to exist except for remnants of the 12 tribes of Israel which were left behind. All of the able bodied men and their families were exiled to Babylon for a period of 70 years. Total or partial deportation of conquered foes was a common practice by both the Assyrian and Babylonian empires after a conquest to prevent insurrections. Although the bulk of 10 tribes of Israel vanished into history when the Northern Kingdom of Israel was conquered by the Assyrians in 721 BC, a few from every tribe survived. We will not go into any great detail concerning the 70 years of servitude under the Babylonian Empire. It is stated in the scriptures that the 70 year exile of the children of Israel were a direct result of not allowing the land to rest for some combination of 70 Sabbatical and Jubilee years (II Chronicles 36: 20-21). The starting and ending dates of the exile are not important to our study, or when the holy years were failed to be observed; but the fact that

Daniel was carried into Babylon and remained there throughout the full 70 years is important. While Daniel was in Babylon, he was given a series of prophetic visions which would outline history between when the command *to the remnant of Israel went forth to restore and rebuild Jerusalem* to the crucifixion of Christ (Dan 9:24-27). The story of Daniel and his prophetic revelations are given in the Book of Daniel. It is impossible to understand the book of Revelation without understanding Daniel, and any serious student of prophecy should spend a great deal of time studying the Book of Daniel. As we will see, the sequence of Sabbatical and Jubilee years determined in this chapter will prove to be important components of when the 490 year prophecy of Daniel's 70th week started, and will help to verify the correct dates for the earthly ministry of Christ and His crucifixion. We will now turn our attention to the most important prophecy in the Old Testament: the *70 weeks of Daniel*.

Thoughts and Things………

Chapter 6
Daniel's 70 Week Prophecy and the Crucifixion of Christ

Daniel's Prophecy of 70 Weeks

Daniel is one of the most remarkable persons in the entire Bible. He was never rebuked or criticized for departing from the word of the Lord. He was deported from Jerusalem by Nebuchadnezzar in the first group of exiles in 605 BC, along with Shadrach, Meshach and Abednego (Danial 1:6-7). God gave him the gift of interpreting visions and dreams, and he became the third most powerful man in Babylon. After the Persians conquered Babylon in 539 BC under Darius I, he continued to serve in the King's palace. In the first year of Darius, he *understood by books* that the Jewish Babylonian exile would shortly come to an end (Dan 9:1-2). The *books* were the writings of the prophet Jeremiah. Jeremiah began prophesying at age 20 during the 13th year of the reign of King Josiah. At the age of 33 (23 years later), he predicted that the Southern Kingdom of Judah would be conquered, and that Israel would serve the king of Babylon for 70 years (Isa 25:11). As Daniel studied the books of Jeremiah (Jer 29:10-11), he realized that 70 years had almost passed since he was deported. Daniel began a remarkable prayer (Dan 9:1-18) in which he petitioned the Lord to end the captivity as prophesied, and *turn* (His) *fury from the Holy City of Jerusalem* (Dan 9:16). His prayer was answered by the Archangel Gabriel (Dan 9:20). The response from Gabriel should be carefully noted: *Oh Daniel, I am now come forth to give thee skill and understanding*. Gabriel clarified his mission: *I am come to show you; for thou art greatly loved: therefore understand the matter and consider the vision.* (Dan 9:23). Oh what a wonderful greeting! Daniel is said to be *greatly loved* by the Lord. The vision was then presented.

> *"Seventy weeks are determined upon thy people and upon thy holy city, to finish the transgression, and to make an end of sins, and to make reconciliation for iniquity, and to bring in everlasting righteousness, and to seal up the vision and prophecy, and to anoint the most Holy. Know therefore and understand, that from the going forth of the commandment to restore and to build Jerusalem unto the Messiah the Prince shall be seven weeks, and threescore and two weeks: the street shall be built again, and the wall, even in troublous times.*
>
> *And after threescore and two weeks shall Messiah be cut off, but not for himself: and the people of the prince that shall come shall destroy the city and the sanctuary; and the end thereof shall be with a flood, and unto the end of the war desolations are determined.*
>
> *And he shall confirm the covenant with many for one week: and in the midst of the week he shall cause the sacrifice and the oblation to cease, and for the overspreading of abominations he shall make it desolate, even until the consummation, and that determined shall be poured upon the desolate."*   Dan 9:24-27

This prophecy is considered to be one of the most important in the entire Holy Bible. It spans a period of time from when it was issued to the second coming of Jesus Christ. It also predicts when the coming Messiah would be crucified. Note that this prophecy begins with the *going forth of the commandment to restore and to build (rebuild) Jerusalem.*

The Commandment to Restore and Rebuild Jerusalem

It is crucial that we determine exactly when this commandment went forth. There are two basic things to consider. The *first* is that we are able to look back in time and determine the most likely time and place that this commandment occurred. *Second*, the decree which will initiate the 70 week prophecy of Daniel must lead to the *beginning* of the ministry of Christ when he came to the River Jordan to be baptized by John at the end of 483 years. There are four decrees to consider.

The Decree of Cyrus

In 536 BC, the Persian King Darius conquered Babylon and installed Cyrus (a Mede) to act as king. This happened after the prophet Daniel had almost completed his 70 years of exile, which had previously been prophesied by Jeremiah (Jeremiah 29:10). In Ezra 1:1 we read: *Now in the first year of Cyrus king of Persia, that the word of the Lord by the mouth of Jeremiah might be fulfilled, the Lord stirred up the spirit of Cyrus, king of Persia, that he made a royal proclamation.* This proclamation authorized the return of Israel to Jerusalem to *build (rebuild) the house (temple) of the Lord.* From 536 BC, a span of 483 years *unto the Messiah the Prince (Jesus Christ)*, would take us to 53 BC. This is way too early, so we must look elsewhere.

The Decree of Darius

The rebuilding of the temple authorized by Cyrus did not go well. The *people of the land* (Ezra 4:4) resisted the project, and it is recorded in Ezra 4:24 that the work *ceased until the second year of the reign of Darius, king of Persia.* Darius succeeded Cyrus in 518 BC. The work resumed in 520 BC under Haggai and Zechariah. The governor of the province surrounding Jerusalem came to the temple site and inquired: *Who hath commanded you to build this house?* (Ezra 5:3). They replied that King Cyrus had authorized the project. The governor then sent a letter to the king asking him to produce such a decree, if indeed one existed. A search was made and the original decree was found. Darius then reinforced this decree with one of his own. *Let the governor of the Jews and the elders of the Jews build this house of God in His place.* So Darius simply reissued the decree of Cyrus authorizing that the Temple of God be rebuilt. Based upon Ezra 4:24 and biblical/archeological research, this event likely occurred in 520 BC. Again moving forward 483 years, we find an ending date of 37 BC. This was about when King Herod began to reign in Jerusalem, and is again much too early. We must search further.

The First Decree of Artaxerxes

In Ezra 7:1-10, we read that Ezra the scribe, who was a descendent of Aaron, approached King Artaxerxes I and petitioned the king to allow him and a band of Israelites to return to Jerusalem. Biblical scholars are in almost universal agreement that this occurred in either 457 BC or 458 BC. We will later show that this occurred in the spring of 458 BC in the seventh year of Artaxerxes reign. Ezra wanted to *set magistrates and judges* in place, *teach the laws of God,* and *let judgment be executed speedily*, upon all who would not obey the laws of God (Ezra 7). The petition was granted, and Ezra left *on the first day of the first month of Artaxerxes Seventh year*, and arrived in Jerusalem *on the first day of the Fifth month.* We will later show that the departure from the city of Babylon was on Nisan 1 in 458 BC (Ezra 7:9). After a short delay to find some

Levites to serve as priests, he arrived in Jerusalem after a journey of just less than five months; one month before Tishri 1, 458 BC (Ezra 7:8). Ezra assembled all of the people and read the proclamation and the law. The *decree went forth* at this time to all the people, and was put into effect. Synchronizing with Sabbatical years, the 70 weeks of Daniel would have started on *Tishri 1, 458 BC.* Subtracting 483 years from this date, we arrive at 26 AD. Please note that to arrive at 26 AD; we must subtract a total of 484 years because when one crosses from BC to AD, there is no year zero. 26 AD is considered by many to be the year in which Jesus Christ came to the river Jordan and started his ministry of 3.5 years. This would demand that Christ was crucified on Nisan 14 in 30 AD. This is a strong candidate, but we will consider the final possible decree.

The Second Decree of Artaxerxes

In the 20th year of King Artaxerxes (Neh. 1:1) word came to Nehemiah that things were not going so well in Jerusalem: *The remnant that are left of the captivity there in the province are in great affliction and reproach. The wall of Jerusalem also is broken down, and the gates thereof are burned with fire* (Neh. 1:3). Nehemiah wept, mourned, fasted and petitioned God to turn the heart of Artaxerxes to let him go to Jerusalem and rebuild, for he was the King's personal cupbearer (Neh. 1:11; 2:1). God moved Artaxerxes' heart, and he gave Nehemiah permission to return. He also sent a letter to *Asaph* informing him to supply timber to rebuild the gates, the walls and the temple (Neh. 2:6-8). This commission was issued to Nehemiah in the month of Nisan (Neh. 2:1). In 1882 Sir Robert Anderson published a book called *The Coming Prince.* In this book he determined that the month of Nisan in 445 BC must have been in the 20th year of Artaxerxes reign. Hence, Anderson declared that the decree was issued in the month of Nisan, 445 BC. After a five month trip to Jerusalem and installing a judiciary, Daniels 70th week would start on Tishri 1, 445 BC. If we subtract 484 years from this date we would arrive at September of 39 AD. The death of Christ would be on Nisan 14 in 43 AD. This is much too late for the death of Christ. At this point, Anderson made a rectifying assumption. Using the flood account of Gen 6-8, he determined based upon Gen 7:11, 7:24 and 8:4 that a *prophetic month* was only 30 days long, and a *prophetic year* was 360 days long. He supported this theory by referring to the Book of Revelation, which equates 1260 days to 42 months (Rev 11:2-3). Using a year as 360 days, he multiplied 360 days times 483 years. He then converted this number of prophetic days into a *Gregorian* calendar year, even though the Gregorian calendar had not even been implemented in Daniel's time. After adjusting for leap years, Newton arrived at Nisan 10, Psalm Sunday in 32 BC. The subsequent date for the crucifixion of Christ worked out to be on Thursday, Nisan 14, in 32 AD. The 7 years remaining in Daniel's 490-year prophecy were then given to the tribulation period of John's Revelation. However, the Roman Catholic Church has decreed for many centuries that Christ was crucified on a Friday in 33 AD. To accommodate this date, Hoehner assumed that the month of Nisan in 444 BC must have been in the 20th year of Artaxerxes reign. Hoehner then assumed that the 70 weeks of Daniel commenced on Nisan 1, 444 BC. Using an approach similar to Isaac Newton, Hoehner arrived at Psalm Sunday, Nisan 10 in 33 AD as his *terminus quo* of the first 483 years. It then followed that Friday, Nisan 14, 33 AD was the crucifixion date of Jesus Christ. Since the Roman Catholic Church dogmatically holds to a Friday crucifixion day, Hoehner's work has been widely accepted.

We can only applaud Sir Robert Anderson and Harold Hoehner for using such a clever approach to arrive at either 32 AD (Newton) or 33 AD (Hoehner) as a crucifixion year. Both dates have been widely acclaimed as correct by two large groups of followers. However, the basic assumptions and methods used by both Anderson and Hoehner have been critically assailed and claimed in error by Pickle, Ice and Jones to name a few. *First*, the flood account in Genesis *does* state that over a period of 150 days, five months elapsed, but this does not guarantee that *each month* was 30 days in duration. In fact, if anyone wants to carefully study the narrative in Gen 7 & 8 they will find that from when Noah entered the ark until he left the ark was 365 days, and it could have been exactly one solar year of 365.2422 days which would imply a normal year. *Second*, the book of Revelation would not be written for about another 620 years, so Daniel would have no access to that text. *Third*, Daniel was nearing the end of the 70-year period of Babylonian exile when he received the prophecy. He was not experiencing 360-day prophetic years during his exile, but full solar years. He was also well aware that the 70 years of exile were almost over when he petitioned God in prayer and fasting. There would be no confusion whatsoever in associating full solar years with the 70 week prophecy given to Daniel (Dan 9:24). *Fourth*, if Daniel *understood* (Dan 9:23) that the 490-year prophecy was *not* based upon the Babylonian calendar year, which was very close to a modern solar year, there was certainly no indication of that in his response to Gabriel nor in the Biblical record. There is no proof or any revelation whatsoever that a 360-day year prophetic ever existed in the Holy Scriptures. In fact, to keep the Passover every year in the correct month at the correct time of year, a 360 year *could not* be in use. Of course, the 360 day year proponents never suggest that anything but a full solar year was in use following the exodus. They simply state with a great deal of confidence that the *360 year prophetic year* was a *mystery* hidden until Sir Isaac Newton discovered it! Finally, everyone today does have access to the book of Revelation, and there is no doubt that the last 3.5 years of the tribulation period is 1260 days, and this is equated to 42 months (Rev 11:2-3). Ah ha! They say, Daniel was told this by Gabriel and he knew it all along. After all, Gabriel told Daniel that he would *understand*. This is *high conjecture* at best. We will show in the next section that these 1260 days involving 42 months can and should refer to a 365.2425 solar year, and not a 360 day lunar year. In this author's opinion, the assumption of a 360-day *prophetic year* is simply unwarranted.

The conclusion of this investigation is that the only decree which makes logical sense, and fits all the requirements of a normal 490-solar year prophecy, is the one issued by Artaxerxes in either 457 BC or 458 BC. We will now show that 458 BC is the correct year.

The Seventh year of Artaxerxes

We believe that after examining the available options, the commandment to restore and to rebuild Jerusalem (Dan 9:25), which initiated the 70-week prophecy of Daniel is most likely the decree from Artaxerxes I to the scribe, Ezra. This decree *went forth* to the people of Israel when Ezra arrived in Jerusalem. Ezra left Babylon *on the first day of the first month* (Ezra 7:9). After gathering the people together and assembling a group of Levites to conduct temple services, he *departed from the River of A-Haya on the 12th day of the first month* (Ezra 8:31). He arrived in Jerusalem on the *first day of the 5th month.* Hence, the journey took almost four months. Ezra left in the first month and arrived in the fifth month of Artaxerxes seventh year. The key question is: *when was Artaxerxes seventh year?* And *when was the first month?* From the context of Ezra 7, the *first month* is undoubtedly the first month of the 7th year of Artaxerxes reign. To determine the seventh regnal year of Artaxerxes, we need to discuss two fundamental issues. Artaxerxes was a Persian king: (1) In what month of the year did Persian kings begin to count their regnal years? (2) How did Persian kings transition from the death of one king to the next?

The Beginning of Regnal Years

Each ancient kingdom had their own calendar system which was used to mark the beginning of a king's reign. Each ancient kingdom employed a slightly different calendar, but most had learned that the length of a solar year was determined by the sun; which we now know is exactly 365.2422 days. A year was composed of 12 months (13 in a Leap Year), and a week of seven, 24-hour days. The number of days in each month varied from kingdom to kingdom, as did the actual number of months in each year. The length of a month in ancient times was usually set at either 29 or 30 days. This is because the actual length of a lunar month is determined by the rotation of the moon and is 29.53059 days, which was from one *new moon* to the next *new moon*. Calendars are designed to mark time by the passage of months, with the number and initiation of each month designed so that a series of 12 or 13 months would coincide with the solar year. However, there is no combination of 30 and 29 day months that can equate to a solar year on a yearly basis. There were two common solutions to the problem: the first was to add days at the end of each year; the second is to periodically add an extra (13th) month to the normal 12-month year. For example, the Egyptians used a simple 12-month calendar consisting of 12 months of 30 days per year. This would total to 360 days per year. They then added 5 days at the end of the 12th month, so that their year was 365 days. This was close to the actual solar year, but fell short about 0.2422 days per year. Hence, the calendar *drifted backward* about one day every four years. After about 1460 years, the Egyptian year would move back in sync with a true solar year. For example, if today was Christmas using this calendar, in about 730 years Christmas would be in July! The calendar used by the Jews was also a *lunar-Solar* calendar. It consisted of 12 alternating 30 and 29 day months. Simple math shows that a Hebrew year was only 354 days, which is about 11.25 days short of a solar year. About every three years, the calendar would drift back approximately 33.75 days. To keep the lunar-based 12-month year in sync with the solar year, it was discovered that by adding seven extra months over a 19-year period of time, 19 lunar calendar years of 12 (13) months would almost exactly equal the solar calendar over the same period of time. This 19-year period of time with seven inter-calculated months is called a *Metonic cycle*.

With some minor adjustments to prevent back-to-back Sabbaths and other anomalies, the same calendar is in use today. The Babylonians seem to be the first to discover the *Metonic cycle* and put it into formal use. However, it must again be stressed that since the seven feasts of Israel were ordained by God, and were to be observed every year following agricultural cycles, the Hebrews after the exodus also had to keep their 12-month lunar calendar in sync with the solar year. Whether this was done by a formal method such as the one just described, or done by observation of crop maturity, is unknown. However, after the Babylonian exile, the Hebrews almost surely adopted and used a Metonic cycle. Each civilization had its own names for each month of the year, but after the 70-year Babylonian exile, the Hebrews adopted the Babylonian calendar names with only slight variations. The calendar we use today is called the *Gregorian calendar*. It was derived from the *Julian calendar*. The Gregorian calendar is very accurate, as is the modern Jewish calendar. The modern Jewish calendar was first implemented by the Patriarch Hillel II in 358 AD. The following table is a summary of the Julian, Gregorian, Babylonian and Hebrew calendars.

Month	Julian Name	Gregorian Name	Hebrew Name	(Civil) Months	Babylonian Name	Months
1	Januarius	Jan	Tishri	Sept/Oct	Nisanu	Mar/Apr
2	Februarius	Feb	Heshvan	Oct/Nov	Aiaru	Apr/May
3	Martius	Mar	Chislev	Non/Dec	Simanu	May/Jun
4	Aprilus	April	Tebeth	Dec/Jan	Duzu	Jun/July
5	Maius	May	Shevat	Jan/Feb	Abu	July/Aug
6	Junius	June	Adar	Feb/Mar	Ululu	Aug/Sept
7	Julius	July	Nisan	Mar/Apr	Tashritu	Sept/Oct
8	Augustus	Aug	Iyyar	Apr/May	Arahsamnu	Oct/Nov
9	Septembris	Sept	Sivan	May/Jun	Kislimu	Non/Dec
10	Octobris	Oct	Tammuz	Jun/July	Tebetu	Dec/Jan
11	Novembris	Nov	Ab/Av	July/Aug	Shabatu	Jan/Feb
12	Decembris	Dec	Elul	Aug/Sept	Addaru	Feb/Mar

Ancient Civil Calendar Years

*The Hebrew Civil year was used from antiquity to the Exodus. Month 1 was always Tishri. After the Exodus,   God ordained that the Religious year would begin in Nisan. All festivals and "Month 1" in the scriptures always referred to the month of Nisan. Before the Exodus in scripture, all "Month 1" references referred to Tishri.

**Egyptian years always began on Thoth 1. The Julian date of Thoth 1 has to be calculated using modern computers. It "drifts" back across Julian months at a rate of about 1 day every 4 years.

After Medo-Persia overthrew the Babylonian empire in 539 BC, the Persian Empire also adopted the Babylonian calendar for their own use. The Babylonians, Hebrews, Egyptians and Persians all used a common method for determining when a king came to reign, and this was to use the first day of the first month in the civil year. The Babylonians and the Persians used Nisan 1 and the Egyptians used Thoth 1. The Hebrew Southern Kingdom of Judah used Tishri 1 until the Babylonian destruction and exile. This was proved and published by Edwin Thiele, and is now widely accepted.

Determining the Seventh Year of Artaxerxes Reign

The Book of Ezra records that the decree which launched the 490-year prophecy of Daniel was given by King Artaxerxes I. Ezra left for Jerusalem in the 7th year of his reign.

> *"…in the reign of Artaxerxes, King of Persia, the King granted him all his requests… This Ezra went up from Babylon…. for upon the first day of the first month began he to go up from Babylon… In the 7th year of Artaxerxes the King."*   Ezra 7:1-10

From Ezra 7, we only know that Ezra left Babylon in the seventh year of Artaxerxes I reign, but the Biblical record is silent in recording any *calendar year* or the *name* of the *first month* for this event. Based upon a wide range of Biblical scholarly investigations, almost everyone agrees that *Persian kings used an accession year system and that Persian kings began their regnal years on Nisan 1*. It is also generally agreed that contemporary with Artaxerxes reign; *Hebrew Kings also used an accession-year system, but used a Tishri 1 regnal start date*. Ezra was a Hebrew writing for his Jewish people, but he was in Persian exile. So which system did Ezra use in the Biblical records? Ezra and Nehemiah were Hebrew contemporaries, and at least according to some sources the Biblical records of both Ezra and Nehemiah were originally one document and that both must have referenced Persian events using Hebrew dating schemes. Whether that is true or not, the book of Nehemiah as it now stands clearly indicates that Nehemiah cross referenced Persian events to a Hebrew Tishri 1-Tishri 1 regnal year system, and *NOT* the Nisan-Nisan Persian system (compare Neh. 1:1 to Neh. 2:1). If Nehemiah and Ezra were originally one document, the problem would be solved. However, no reliable data exists to prove or disprove this theory. Pragmatically, Ezra and Nehemiah were both serving in the King's court, and both were likely good friends; but this only suggests that both would use the same system to reference the reign of each king. Depending upon which system is being used by Ezra; the seventh year of Artaxerxes could be off by one year at Nisan 1. Hence, imminent scholars are divided upon exactly when Ezra left Babylon in the seventh year of Artaxerxes reign. Some defend a 458 BC date and some dogmatically defend a 457 BC date. So which is to be believed?

The most acceptable solution is to carefully examine historical and archeological records to determine when Ezra left in the seventh year of Artaxerxes. We are quite certain that a Persian King named Xerxes preceded Artaxerxes. It is also known that the Persian King Xerxes was assassinated in 465 BC. Scribes recorded Xerxes assassination date on a clay tablet known as the *Babylonian Astronomical Text*. Scholars have translated the text and determined that the murder of Xerxes occurred sometime between August 4-August 18, 465 BC. Two other dates are recorded in the ancient literature, which indicate either late July or early August of 465 BC. By all historical accounts known to exist, Xerxes was murdered before Tishri 1, 465 BC. Xerxes was assassinated by a courtier of his court called Artabanus who wanted to usurp the king. He then had the brother of Artaxerxes assassinated, and also tried to assassinate Artaxerxes; but his plan was discovered and Artabanus was executed. No record has ever been found that credits Artabanus as a reigning king of Persia, but a second-century historian called Mantheo wrote that a power struggle did indeed take place between Artabanus and Artaxerxes. However, Mantheo wrote his comments more than 500 years after the fact. Turning to archeological records, in the 20th century evidence surfaced from a community of Jews living in Egypt on the upper Nile River. They were called the *Elephantine Community*, and records of financial and social transactions were found which provides important data for this investigation. Out of a number of documents found and restored, two are of great importance: They are known as *AP 6* and *AP 8*.

The Jewish document, called *AP 6* from the Elephantine community of Jews fails to resolve the issue. Scholars all agree that *AP 6* was written on Jan 2/3, 464 BC. Unfortunately, the document is severely damaged and a key phrase is partially missing. Paleographic science has been used to reconstruct the missing word(s), and it was found that it could be reconstructed in one of two ways. The first would indicate that Jan 2/3 is *in the first year* of Artaxerxes reign; the second is that it would read *in the acession year* of Artaxerxes. We now need to determine exactly when Artaxerxes assumed the throne and started his official reign. Clearly, if AP 6 was written in early January of 465 BC, and that date is in Artaxerxes *acession year*, the first year of Artaxerxes reign would either start on Nisan 1 (March/April) of 464 BC using Persian reckoning, or on Tishri 1(Sept/Oct) of 464 BC using Hebrew rekoning. If that date is in the *first year* of Artaxerxes, then Artaxeres would have *had* to assumed the throne on Tishri 1 (Sept/Oct) of 465 BC, and the document had to have used the Hebrew regnal years The following diagram graphically displays the relevant timeline.

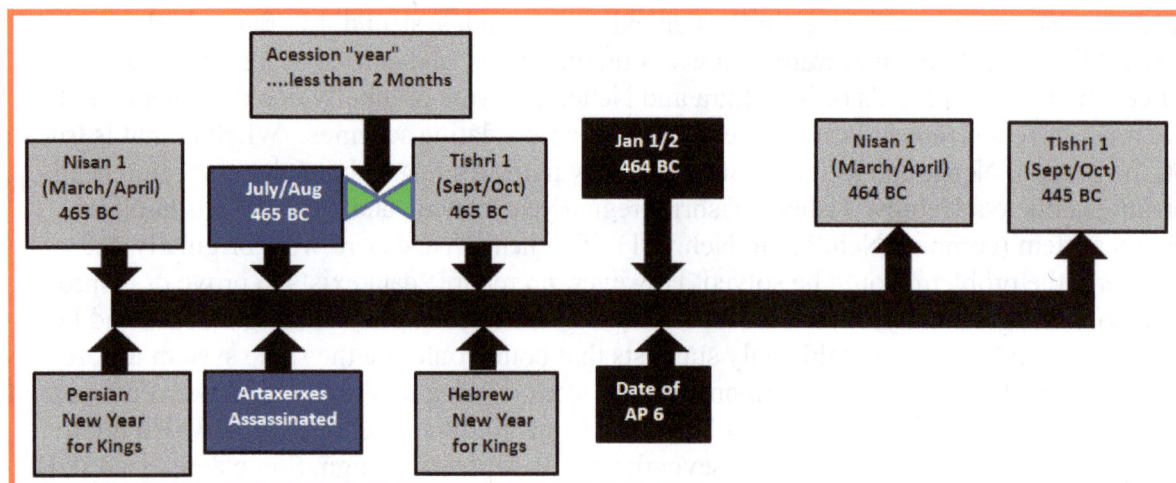

Recall that both the Persians and Hebrews used an acession year system: The Persians started their Kings reign on Nisan 1, and the Hebrews on Tishri 1. Also recall that AP 6 was written Jan 1 or Jan 2, 464 BC.

The conondrum can be stated as follows. If the throne became vacant with the assassination of Xerxes in July/August of 465 BC, regardless of the power struggle that ensued the following possibilities present themselves.

> If AP 6 recorded that Artaxerxes was in his **acession year** as of Jan 1 or Jan 2 of 464 BC, then using the **Hebrew** *acession year system*, something unusual would have had to occur between the death of Xerxes in July/Aug of 465 BC and Jan 2, 464 BC, such that Artaxerxes was not able to start his first year of reign until Tishri 1, 464 BC. If AP 6 is written using the Hebrew acession year viewpoint, this would create an unlikely situation of Artaxerxes not claiming a short acession year period between July/Aug of 465 BC and Sept/Oct of 465 BC, and then start his first credited year of reign on Tishri 1, 465 BC as was the normal custom. In addition, who would get credit for the full year of reign between Tishri 1, 465 BC and Tishri 1, 464 BC? Since all kings wanted to claim as many years in office as possible it is extremely likely that Artaxerxes would want to claim this year. Xerxes would be credited with his last full year ending on Tishri 1, 465 BC, leaving no gap in the regnal records. Why did Artabanus never even appear in the official records? The answer is probably buried in a cloak of political intrigue. Artabanus had Xeres killed and tried to blame it on Artaxerxes: he then killed the brother of Artaxerxes, and plotted to kill him also. So it is likely that when Artaxerxes ascended to the throne, he would remove any historical reference of Artabanus….after all, Atabanus was both a murderer and a usurper. Artaxerxes could then claim that short period of political upheavel as his *accession year* under the acession year system. No record exists of any Persian King or Hebrew king using a non-acession system. The conclusion is that if AP 6 was written using an acession year system, and all traces of Artabanus were stricken from the King's records, it is logical (and likely) that Artaxerxes started his first year of reign on Tishri 1, 465 BC.

116

> If AP 6 recorded that Artaxerxes was in his *first year of reign*, then he would have *had* to start that first year on Tishri 1, 465 BC.

Both scenarios seem to indicate that the first year of Artaxeres began on Tishri 1, 465 BC. However, neither of these scanarios can be absolutely proved using only AP 6, although several researchers have tried to do so. In particular, Horn and Wood emphatically and mysteriously state that only the acession year reconstruction of AP 6 makes any sense They are equally emphatic that Artaxeres first year of reign did not start until Tishri 1, 464 BC. So who is right? We will look for further information. A second document recovered from the Elaphantine community was *AP 8* . The AP 8 papyrus is well preserved and intact. In that document the following dateline is recorded.

Kislev 21= Mesore 1 in Year 6 of Artaxerxes reign

Kislev corresponds to November/December on both the Babylonian and the Julian or modern Gregorian calendar. Mesore 1 is the 12th month in the ancient Egyptian calendar that was in use in Egypt at that time. Note that the Jewish regnal New Year of Tishri 1 had occurred almost two months earlier. The Egyptian New Year at that time was a month called *Thoth,* which was at least 30 days after Mesore 1. Both the Hebrews and the Egyptians counted the reign of Artaxerxes from their own New Year day. Hence, both Kislev 21 and Mesore 1 were *within year 6 of Artaxerxes reign;* but again the question arises: Which year? From AP 8, the 6th year of Artaxerxes reign is said to contain Kislev 21. The following Table illustrates the three possible occurrence of Artaxerxes 6th year using AP 6.

Year	Hebrew System: Artaxerxes in Acession Year for Less than 2 Mos....AP 6	Persian System: Artaxerxes in Acession Year Till Nisan 1, 464 BC....AP 6	Hebrew System: Artaxerxes in Acession Year Till Tishri 1, 464 BC....AP 6
1	Tishri 1, 465 BC - 464 BC	Nisan 1, 464 BC - 463 BC	Tishri 1, 464 BC - 463 BC
2	Tishri 1, 464 BC - 463 BC	Nisan 1, 463 BC - 462 BC	Tishri 1, 463 BC - 462 BC
3	Tishri 1, 463 BC - 462 BC	Nisan 1, 462 BC - 461 BC	Tishri 1, 462 BC - 461 BC
4	Tishri 1, 462 BC - 461 BC	Nisan 1, 461 BC - 460 BC	Tishri 1, 461 BC - 460 BC
5	Tishri 1, 461 BC - 460 BC	Nisan 1, 460 BC - 459 BC	Tishri 1, 460 BC - 459 BC
6	Tishri 1, 460 BC - 459 BC	Nisan 1, 459 BC - 458 BC	Tishri 1, 459 BC - 458 BC
7	Tishri 1, 459 BC - 458 BC	Nisan 1, 458 BC - 457 BC	Tishri 1, 458 BC - 457 BC
8	Tishri 1, 458 BC - 457 BC	Nisan 1, 457 BC - 456 BC	Tishri 1, 457 BC - 456 BC

Tishri 1... September/October   Nisan 1 ...... March/April

Since Kislev occurs in the month of November/December, and by AP 8 it must be in Artaxerxes 6th year of reign, then the only possible, feasible alternative is that AP 8 must be referencing the Hebrew system, and that Artaxerxes *acession year* was only the short period of time between the death of Xerxes in July/Aug of 565 BC to Tishri 1 in Sept/Oct of 565 BC. While this is convincing evidence, we can show that this conclusion can be reached in another way.

	Regnal Years of Artaxerxes
1	Tishri 1, 465 BC - 464 BC
2	Tishri 1, 464 BC - 463 BC
3	Tishri 1, 463 BC - 462 BC
4	Tishri 1, 462 BC - 461 BC
5	Tishri 1, 461 BC - 460 BC
6	Tishri 1, 460 BC - 459 BC
7	Tishri 1, 459 BC - 458 BC
8	Tishri 1, 458 BC - 457 BC
9	Tishri 1, 457 BC - 456 BC
10	Tishri 1, 456 BC - 455 BC

The 7th year of Artaxerxes Reign was Tishri 1, 459 BC to Tishri 1, 458 BC

Ezra left Babylon on Nisan 1, 458 BC
Ezra Arrived in Jerusalem 5 months later
Daniel's 70 Week Prophecy started on Tishri 1, 458 BC.
Tishri 1, 458 BC -Tishri 1, 457 BC was a Sabbatical Year

Using modern computer software, the calendar date for the Egyptian Mesore 1 can be calculated for the year 460 BC. In that year, Mesore 1 occurred on Nov 11. This date must coincide with Kislev 21 by AP 8. Note that the Jews living in Egypt would most certainly know what the date was for Mesore 1, and it is highly likely that being a Jewish community they would also know the correct Hebrew calendar date. On the Hebrew calendar, every new month started with a new moon. Hence, working backwards a new moon must have occurred on Kislev 1, which would be October 21. Using new modern computers and NASA software, the new moon dates far back in time can be accurately determined, since the cycle of days from new moon to new moon is a constant. One can verify that in 460 BC, the New Moon of Kislev 1 occurred in close proximity to 3:22 AM on October 21 ! Hence, using two witnesses we have shown that Kislev 21 on November 11 occurred in the 6th year of Artaxerxes reign. We then conclude that the 6th year of his reign had to be from Tishri 1, 460 BC to Tishri 1, 459 BC…using non inclusive recogning on Tishri 1 in 459 BC. The 7th year of his reign is determined to be Tishri 1, 459 BC – Tishri 1, 458 BC. Using this information relative to AP 6, it is concluded that the broken/missing segment of the AP 6 document should read *In the first year of Artaxerxes reign*, and not *in the acession year of Artaxerxes reign*. We also conclude that Ezra was using the Hebrew regnal, accession year system as did Nehemiah. The above table shows the first 10 years of Artaxerxes reign.

To summarize: We have established with reasonable evidence….. including ancient documents double dated from a Jewish community in Egypt (AP 6 and AP 8) ….. that Ezra wrote his records from a Hebrew perspective, and that the first year of Artaxeres reign was Tishri 1, 465 BC – Tishri 1, 464 BC. Starting from that date, the 7th year of Artaxeres reign is Tishri 1, 459 BC to Tishri 1, 458 BC. Artaxerxes acession year was a short time between when Xerxes was murdered in July/Aug of 465 BC to Sept/Oct of 465 BC (Tishri 1).

Ezra the scribe left Babylon in the seventh year of Artaxerxes reign (Ezra 7:7) on first day of the first month (Ezra 7:9),which was Nisan 1, 458 BC. This date was likely April 8, 458 BC as confirmed by Finnegan. He arrived in Jerusalem on the first day of the fifth month…..both in the seventh year of Artaxerzes reign. (Ezra 7:8). We should now note that according to our AY chronology and the determined sabbatical years, 458 BC–457 BC *was a sabbatical year*. This is a confirming sign, since several Jewish rabbis have recorded that the first year following Ezra's departure was the year 458 BC–457 BC, and it was a sabbatical year: Our previous determination of Sabbatical years is in agreement.

The Decree of Artaxerxes
We have spent a great deal of detective work to prove that the first year of Artaxerxes reign referenced by Ezra the scribe followed Hebrew convention, and that it was between Tishri 1, 459

BC and Tishri 1, 458 BC. The following statements have been substantiated using Biblical records supported by archeological and historical documents.

- The decree which started the 70 Weeks of Daniel's prophecy (490 years) was that of Artaxerxes I in his 7th year of reign (Ezra 7)
- The Decree was issued sometimes just before Nisan 1 of 458 BC in the 6th year of Artaxerxes' reign. The most likely date was April 8, 458 BC.
- Ezra left Babylon with a decree that authorized hum to rebuild the temple (Ezra 1:1-4). It should be noted that in the 20th year of Artaxerxes, he (Nehemiah) was given permission to rebuild the walls. This second decree of Artaxerxes was not a completely new decree: it only reinforced the one given to Ezra, which in turn was originally given by Cyrus. The decree given to Ezra certainly implied that Ezra thought that the Temple had to be protected by a new wall, and that the city inside had to have dwellings for the men and their families.
- Ezra left after Nisan 1 in 458 BC (March/April), and arrived before Tishri 1, 458 BC (Sept/Oct).
- After Ezra arrived, he gathered the people and declared a fast. He then established the judicial system, organized the exiles, reinstated Levitical temple service and corrected intermarriage problems. The entire decree had *gone forth* by Tishri 1, and Daniels first week of years began on Tishri 1, 458 BC....Which began a *Sabbatical year*.
- The first year of Daniel's 70 week prophecy was therefore Tishri 1, 458 BC – Tishri 1, 457 BC.

To this may be added (Pickle):

1. Daniel 9:25 specified two things for the decree that must be used for the beginning of the prophecy: 1) "restoring" and 2) "building" Jerusalem.
2. It was prophesied of Cyrus that he would command Jerusalem to be built: "*That saith of Cyrus, He is my shepherd, and shall perform all my pleasure: even saying to Jerusalem, Thou shalt be built; and to the temple, Thy foundation shall be laid*" (Is. 44:28; cf. 45:13).
3. It was also prophesied by Isaiah that God would "*restore*" Jerusalem's judiciary: "*And I will restore thy judges as at the first, and thy counselors as at the beginning: afterward thou shalt be called, The city of righteousness, the faithful city*" (Is. 1:26).
4. While Cyrus' decree of Ezra 1:2-4 and Darius' decree of Ezra 6:1-12 called for building, it is only in Artaxerxes' decree from his 7th year, as recorded in Ezra 7:12-26, that we find a call for restoring the judges.
5. The decrees of Cyrus, Darius and Artaxerxes in his 7th year of reign are referred to in Ezra 6:14 as if they are but one decree. It is as if Cyrus began the decree and Artaxerxes finished it; which may explain why Daniel 9:25 spoke of "*one commandment to restore and build.* Once the original commandment was initiated, the 70 week prophecy of Daniel could begin. Remember that all Sabbatical years start on Tishri 1, and not on Nisan 1. All Jubilee years are officially declared to start on Tishri 10, on the Feast of Yom Kippur (Lev 25:9).

The Table on the right shows Sabbatical and Jubilee years. Every entry in this table starts a Sabbatical Year, except the years shown in Column 8 which start *Years of Jubilee*. The years shown are Tishri 1 start years. For example, Row 1, Col 1 Tishri 1, is 1438 BC–Tishri 1, 1437 BC, which is the *first Sabbatical year*. Tishri 1, 458 BC–Tishri 1, 457 BC is shown as *a Sabbatical year* as previously indicated. The first year of the next sabbatical cycle is Tishri 1, 457 BC–Tishri 1, 456 BC, which is also the *first year of Daniel's 70 weeks of years*. Recall that The Daniel prophecy predicted that there would be 69-7's = 483 years *unto Messiah the Prince*. In other words, Jesus Christ would begin His earthly ministry *immediately after* 483 years have elapsed.

Starting in Tishri 1, 458 BC, 483 Solar/Julian years would elapse on Tishri 1, 26 AD. Note that 458 BC to 26 BC appears to be 484 years. This is because there is no year zero, and when passing from BC to AD, one extra year must be added. Jesus Christ came to Jordan River to be baptized when he was *about 30 years of age*. It may come as a surprise to many, but Christ was *NOT* born on December 25. This date was contrived by the Roman Catholic Church. It is easy to show that Christ was born in the month of Tishri, likely on the Feast of Trumpets (Tishri 1) or on the Feast of Tabernacles (Tishri 15). He came to the Jordan River to be baptized by John the Baptizer in the month of Tishri, likely on the Feast of Atonement, Tishri 10 or shortly thereafter on the Feast of Tabernacles. In either case, Christ was *about 30 years of age* (Luke 3:23). The days between Tishri 1 and Tishri 10 are known as the *Days of Repentance*, during which every Israelite must repent of any sins committed over the previous year, in order to have their name inscribed in the *Book of Life* for the coming year.

First Jubilee..1395-1394								
Sabbatical Years							Jubilee Yr	Cycle
1	2	3	4	5	6	7		
1438	1431	1424	1417	1410	1403	1396	1395	1
1389	1382	1375	1368	1361	1354	1347	1346	2
1340	1333	1326	1319	1312	1305	1298	1297	3
1291	1284	1277	1270	1263	1256	1249	1248	4
1242	1235	1228	1221	1214	1207	1200	1199	5
1193	1186	1179	1172	1165	1158	1151	1150	6
1144	1137	1130	1123	1116	1109	1102	1101	7
1095	1088	1081	1074	1067	1060	1053	1052	8
1046	1039	1032	1025	1018	1011	1004	1003	9
997	990	983	976	969	962	955	954	10
948	941	934	927	920	913	906	905	11
899	892	885	878	871	864	857	856	12
850	843	836	829	822	815	808	807	13
801	794	787	780	773	766	759	758	14
752	745	738	731	724	717	710	709	15
703	696	689	682	675	668	661	660	16
654	647	640	633	626	619	612	611	17
605	598	591	584	577	570	563	562	18
556	549	542	535	528	521	514	513	19
507	500	493	486	479	472	465	464	20
458	451	444	437	430	423	416	415	21
409	402	395	388	381	374	367	366	22
360	353	346	339	332	325	318	317	23
311	304	297	290	283	276	269	268	24
262	255	248	241	234	227	220	219	25
213	206	199	192	185	178	171	170	26
164	157	150	143	136	129	122	121	27
115	108	101	94	87	80	73	72	28
66	59	52	45	38	31	24	23	29
17	10	3	5	12	19	26	27	30
33	40	47	54	61	68	75	76	31
82	89	96	103	110	117	124	125	32
131	138	145	152	159	166	173	174	33

It is then no coincidence that John was *preaching repentance* at that time (Mat 3:1-2). The prophecy of Daniel also predicted that Jesus Christ would be *cut off* or crucified *in the midst of the 70th week*. The duration of Christ's ministry was 3.5 years, and ended on Nisan 14, 30 AD on the cross of Calvary. Looking at the table once again, we see a remarkable thing. Christ began His ministry in a *sabbatical year* (Tishri 1, 26 AD–Tishri 1, 27 AD). Even more remarkable is that the next year is a *Year of Jubilee*. It is even more interesting when the Gospel of Luke is studied.

In Luke 4:19, Christ is attending a service in his home town of Nazareth on the next Feast of Yom Kippur. We know that this visit took place on that particular feast day because the book of

Isaiah was always read on that day. He stood to read in the synagogue and the book of Isaiah the prophet was given to Him. He then turned to Is 61 and began reading.

> *"The Spirit of the Lord is upon Me, because He hath appointed me to preach the gospel to the poor: He hath sent me to heal the brokenhearted, to preach deliverance to the captives, and recovering of sight to the blind, to set at liberty them that are bruised, to preach the acceptable year of the Lord."* Is. 61:1-2(a)

Christ stopped reading in the middle of Isaiah verse 2. The next words proclaimed that a *Day of Vengeance* was coming, which will not occur until His Second Advent. The message that Jesus proclaimed is *Jubilee*. The *Jubilee* that Jesus proclaimed was at the very heart of His earthly ministry. Jesus then added: ***This day is this Scripture fulfilled in your ears*** (Luke 4:21). Jesus not only announced that it was time for a Jubilee. He announced that He *WAS* the Jubilee. He had come to do all of those things written by Isaiah the prophet and more. From that point on, he publically set about healing the blind, causing the deaf to hear, commanding the lame to walk, setting people free from their spiritual bondage, and proclaiming the message of salvation to Jews and Gentiles alike. The *fullness of time* had surely *arrived*. This message was a *Jubilee message* and it was read in a *Jubilee year*, important to the efficacy of our offered chronology.

The Crucifixion of our Lord Jesus Christ

According to the prophecy of Daniel (Dan 9:26), *after threescore and two weeks* (after 483 total years) had been completed, Christ would be *cut off* (crucified). Exactly when this would occur can now be determined. According to Dan 9:27; Christ was prophesied to be killed *in the midst* of the 70th and (last) week. This is perfectly consistent with the known 3.5 year ministry of Christ. The midst of this last week was on *Nisan 14, 30 AD* on a *Wednesday*, which is the *Feast of Passover*. The offered chronology points to this date, but is there other evidence that this is the correct year? The answer is, *YES*.

- The apostle Paul was converted on the road to Damascus by Jesus Christ, who appeared in his risen body shortly after he was crucified; which we have just shown was in 30 AD. Fourteen (14) years after his conversion, Paul records in Gal. 2:1 that he, Barnabus, and Titus journeyed to Jerusalem. While Paul, Barnabus, and Titus were in Jerusalem, King Herod Agrippa died. This date is known to be during or shortly after the Passover Feast of 44 BC (March/April). The apostle Luke records that John the Baptist came to the Jordan River baptizing and preaching repentance in the 15th year of Tiberius Caesar (Luke 3:1-3). Tiberius was the successor to Augustus Caesar, who became the Emperor of Rome on Jan 13, 27 BC after the assassination of Julius Caesar. The last five years of his life (AD 10-14) were untroubled by war or disaster. Augustus was aging fast, and was more and more disinclined to appear personally in the senate or in public. Yet in AD 12 he consented, reluctantly we are told, to yet one more renewal of his imperial reign for ten years. Roman emperors were appointed in January, and officially conferred in March. He consented with a demand that his stepson, *Tiberius*, now over fifty years of age, should be equated with himself, both in power and authority, in the administration of the empire. He retreated to an island villa and hardly ever appeared again in public between 12 AD and his death in 14 AD. Augustus died on Aug 19, 14 AD and Tiberius became sole ruler. If Luke measured the 15 years from the co-reign of Tiberius starting in the spring of 12 BC, the 15th year would be the spring of 26 AD to the spring of 27 AD. Christ was baptized by John in September of 26 AD. There is no reason to think that Luke would not have counted the reign of Tiberius from 12 BC. Jerusalem was effectively under the iron boot of Tiberius between 12 AD -14 AD, when the death of Augustus occurred.

March/April		March/April	Year
12 BC	to	13 BC	1
13 BC	to	14 BC	2
14 BC	to	15 BC	3
15 BC	to	16 BC	4
16 BC	to	17 BC	5
17 BC	to	18 BC	6
18 BC	to	19 BC	7
19 BC	to	20 BC	8
20 BC	to	21 BC	9
21 BC	to	22 BC	10
22 BC	to	23 BC	11
23 BC	to	24 BC	12
24 BC	to	25 BC	13
25 BC	to	26 BC	14
26 BC	to	27 BC	15

The 15th year of Tiberius Reign was Spring of 26 AD to Spring of 27 AD. Christ came to the river Jordan to be baptixed in the Fall of 26 AD

- Just before the first Passover of Christ's ministry (John 2:13), following his baptism at the Jordan River, Christ foretold of his death and resurrection in three days.

Destroy this temple (his body) and in three days I will raise it up John 2:1

But the Jews thought that Christ was referring to Herod's temple and replied:

Forty and six years was this temple in building, and wilt thou raise it up in three days? John 2:20

In the Works of Josephus (Book XV: 11:1), he records that construction on the temple was begun in the 18th year of King Herod's reign, which was 20 BC-19 BC. Leaping forward 46 years, we come to 27-28 AD. The first Passover in Jesus ministry was in Mar/April of 27 BC.

- Jesus was *about 30 years of age* when He was baptized by John. If the baptism of Christ took place in the month of Tishri in 26 AD, it was near his birthday and it can be shown based upon the testimony of Luke 1:1-33 that Christ was born on either the Feast of Yom Kippur or 5 days later on the Fast of Tabernacles, in September or October of 5 AD (remember to add one year when crossing from BC to AD). Until recently, everyone believed that Herod died in the spring of 4 BC. This birth date of Christ fits nicely within this theory. However, recent research by Filmer places the death of Herod in either 1 BC or 1 AD, but that date is not without controversy. A 1 BC or a 1 AD date for the death of Herod is necessary to support a Friday crucifixion in 33 AD. If Herod died in 4 BC, then Christ could not have been born after that date. This research indicates that Christ was born in 5 BC and was crucified in 30 AD.

- Shortly before the last Passover of Christ's ministry, Jesus was delivering the Olivet Discourse to his disciples. At that time, He prophesied that Herod's Temple would be destroyed and when the destruction would take place.

"Verily I say unto you, this generation shall not pass till all these things be fulfilled." Mat 24:34

This prophecy was given in the spring of 30 AD the night before He suffered on the cross of Calvary. Almost all biblical scholars agree that based upon the Exodus account, the entire generation of Hebrews who left Egypt would perish (die) within a 40 year period of time. This clearly indicated that a biblical generation was 40 years in duration. Adding 40 years to the spring of 30 AD, we arrive in the spring of 70 AD. This was precisely the point in time when Herod's temple was destroyed. Only a 30 AD crucifixion renders this destruction in exactly one generation.

Terminating Daniels 70th Week

We have proposed and presented reasonable arguments to support a Nisan 14 (Wednesday; April 5 (Julian date); 30 AD) crucifixion for Jesus Christ. The year 30 AD falls in the middle of Daniel's 70th week, that is after 486.5 years had elapsed since the 490-year prophecy started. Clearly, this leaves 3.5 years to finish the prophecy. Many modern prophecy teachers allow the 70-7's to expire on Tishri 1 (Sept/Oct) of 33 AD. The event designated to end the prophecy is proposed to be the stoning of Stephen in Acts 6. Proponents of this theory (rightly so) identify this event as the final act of rejection of Jesus Christ as the promised Messiah by the corporate nation of Israel. From this point on, the message of salvation in Jesus Christ under the new covenant passed to both Gentiles and Jews. We totally reject the logic which ends Daniel's 70th week in 33 AD at the death of Stephen based upon three platforms. *First*, a careful study of the Book of Daniel will identify several things which must be completed before Daniel's 70 weeks of years expires which can only be accomplished at the second advent of Jesus Christ (such as the rise of the antichrist in the end times). This reason alone is enough to reject the *Steven hypothesis*. A *second* and more compelling reason is in the stoning of Steven. In Acts 1-2 we are told how the Holy Spirit fell on the Feast of Pentecost, 50 days after the resurrection. Chapter 3 records a post-Pentecost miracle, the healing of a lame man, followed by Peter's sermon. Chapters 4:1-6:7 are concerned with the beginning of persecutions and the preparation for spreading the gospel. Acts 6:8 records how Steven *full of faith and power* did *great wonders and miracles*. The Jewish leaders turned against him, fearing that he would *destroy this place, and change the customs*. At this point Stephen delivers perhaps the most powerful sermon ever preached (Acts 7:1-53). When he finished his discourse, the Jews *cast him out of the city and stoned him*. So, Steven became the first apostle named in the New Testament to be martyred after the day of Pentecost. The *third* concerns the conversion of Paul (Saul) is recorded in Acts 9. However, considering the sequence and duration of the events recorded in the Book of Acts, his conversion on the road to Damascus was likely within a year after Christ was crucified. If this is true, then it is impossible that the stoning of Steven took place 3.5 years after the crucifixion. We therefore conclude that there has been a *gap* of almost 2000 years since the midpoint of Daniel's 70th week. The termination of Daniel's 70th week will not occur until the second coming of Jesus Christ at the end of the great tribulation period. The fact that the tribulation period described in the book of Revelation is only 3.5 years in duration and not 7 years as is commonly taught is not a large leap of faith. In either case, there is a gap in time which represents the church age. For a more detailed discussion of this conclusion see Phillips (*Revelation: Mysteries Revealed : Second Edition*).

The Chronology Extended

This chapter has addressed two important issues: (1) When the 390 year prophecy to Daniel started and (2) the year in which our Lord Jesus Christ suffered and died on the Cross of Calvary. With these two dates secured, we are now able to extend the AY years from the final fall of Jerusalem in AY 3358 to the ministry and death of Jesus Christ. This extension is straightforward and is given in the table on the following page.

AY Year		Julian Dates
1	Year Adam left Eden	Sept/Oct, 3944-Sept/Oct, 3943
		2454 Years
2454	Year of the Exodus	Sept/Oct, 1491-Sept/Oct, 1490
2454	Exodus	Sept/Oct, 1491-Sept/Oct, 1490
		480 Years
2933	Solomon's 4th Year	Sept/Oct, 1012-Sept/Oct, 1011
2930	Solomon's 4th Year	Sept/Oct, 1012-Sept/Oct, 1011
		4 Years
2933	Solomon's 1st Year	Sept/Oct, 1015-Sept/Oct, 1014
2930	Solomon's 1st Year	Sept/Oct, 1015-Sept/Oct, 1014
		40 Years
2969	Solomon's 40th Year	Sept/Oct, 976-Sept/Oct, 975
2970	Divided Kingdom (Judah)	Sept/Oct, 975-Sept/Oct, 974
	Jerusalem fell, July 18, 586 BC	389 Years
3358	Last Year of Judah	Sept/Oct, 587-Sept/Oct, 586
3358	Last Year of Judah	Sept/Oct, 587-Sept/Oct, 586
		129 Years
3487	Start of Daniel's Prophecy	Sept/Oct, 458 Tishri 1
3487	Start of Daniel's Prophecy	Sept/Oct, 458-Sept/Oct, 457
		483 Years
3970	End of Daniel's 69th Week	Sept/Oct, 25 AD-Sept/Oct, 26 AD
3971	Beginning: Ministry of Christ	Sept/Oct, 26 AD-Sept/Oct, 27 AD
		3.5 Jewish Years
3974	*Crucifixion of Christ*	Nisan 14, 30 AD
		Wednesday, April 5

The Ministry and Crucifixion of Christ

This author has suggested that the 3.5 years earthly ministry of Christ started at the River Jordan when Christ came to be baptized by John. This was at or near the Feast of Yom Kippur, when John was baptizing the Jews *unto repentance*. The first full year of Christ's 3.5 year ministry was Tishri 1, 26 AD – Tishri 1, 27 AD; and his crucifixion occurred in 30 AD on Wednesday, April 5. The associated AY year of AY 3974 was determined by following the sequence of key Biblical events shown in the previous table. It is this author's belief that these dates are true and accurate. However, it should be noted that many other respected and capable Biblical researchers will not agree with this offered chronology. In this author's mind, the value in this research has been to show that all critically assailed Biblical dates can be justified and shown to be true. It has been shown that *all* the Biblical records from the King James Bible have all been shown to fit into a rational and sequential sequence of AY years from the expulsion of Adam and Eve from the Garden of Eden to the crucifixion of Christ.

Notwithstanding the results of this study, the earthly ministry and the subsequent crucifixion of our Lord Jesus Christ in 30 AD will not be universally accepted. For over 1500 years the beginning and end of Christ's earthly ministry have been hotly debated. Nevertheless, probably over 95% of all opinions locate the death of Christ between 30 AD and 34 AD. Between this narrow range of years, the majority of researchers have supported 30 AD - 33 AD; and the two most popular choices are 30 AD or 33 AD. Of those who have seriously studied the first advent of Christ, two outstanding Biblical scholars stand head and shoulders above the rest: (1) Sir Isaac Newton and (2) Dr. Harold Hoehner. Although the dates presented from this study do not agree with either of these two individuals, it is straightforward to modify the AY dates in this study to embrace both conclusions. For completeness, this will now be accomplished. A summary of how Sir Robert Anderson arrived at a 32 AD crucifixion date, and how Harold Hoehner arrived at a 33 AD crucifixion date is taken with much gratitude from *The Words and Works of Jesus Christ*, by J. Dwight Pentecost.

Sir Isaac Newton
The following is quoted from *The Coming Prince;* Robert Anderson, 1909.

*"From the going forth of the commandment to restore and rebuild Jerusalem unto Messiah the Prince shall be seven weeks and threescore weeks. An era of sixty-nine weeks, or 483 **prophetic years** reckoned from the 14th of March, 445 BC, should close with some event to satisfy the words unto the Messiah the Prince. No student of the gospel narrative can fail to see that the Lord's last visit to Jerusalem was not only in fact, but in the purpose of it, the crisis of His ministry .... now the twofold testimony of His words and His works had been fully rendered, and His entry into the Holy City was to proclaim His Messiahship and to receive His doom. And the date of it can be ascertained. In accordance with the Jewish custom, the Lord went up to Jerusalem upon the 8th of Nisan, six days before the Passover. But as the 14th, on which the Paschal supper was eaten , fell that year upon a Thursday, the 8th was the preceding Friday. He must have spent the Sabbath, therefore at Bethany; and on the evening of the 9th, after the Sabbath had ended, the supper took place in Martha's house. Upon the following day, the 10th of Nisan,He entered Jerusalem as recorded in the Gospels. The Julian date of that 10th of Nisan was Sunday the 6th of April, AD 32. What was the length of the period intervening between the issuing of the decree to rebuild Jerusalem and the public advent of Messiah the Prince. ---- between the 14th of March, 445 BC and the 6th of April, AD 32 the interval contained exactly and to the very day 173,880 days, or 7 times 69 **prophetic years of 360 days.**---the first 69 weeks of Gabriel's prophecy"*.

The period of 173, 880 days is determined as follows.

> Assume that a prophetic year was implied by the angel Gabriel when he gave the prophecy of the 70 weeks of years to Daniel. Sixty-nine weeks of prophetic years are:

> (69 years)*(360 days/yr) = 173,880 days (Prophetic Days)

He then stated that the actual (Julian year) period was 476 yrs and 24 days. :

> (173,880 days) / (365.25 days/yr) = 476.0575 years or 476 years and 24 days.

To this total he then added 116 days for leap years, and 24 days between March 14 and April 6. Having made these adjustments, He then triumphantly declared that Christ was crucified on Thursday, April 16 in the year 32 AD.

The calculations of Anderson include problems. The first major problem is that a *year* was only 360 days (a *prophetic year*), and that despite the difference between this and a 365.25 Julian calendar year, Daniel clearly understood all of the complex calculation previously discussed when he received the prophecy. We know this because Gabriel specifically stated that he was *come to give Daniel understanding of the vision*. Second, he then superimposed a 365.25 Julian year upon the 365.24219879 day Gregorian year; and then adjusted by adding in leap days. But the most damaging criticism was clearly recorded by Pentecost.

> *"The 32 AD date for the crucifixion is untenable. It would mean that Christ was crucified on either a Sunday or Monday. In fact, Anderson realized this dilemma and he has to do mathematical gyrations to arrive at a Friday crucifixion. This makes one immediately suspect. Actually, there is no good evidence for a 32 AD crucifixion date"*
> The Words and Works of Jesus Christ, J. Dwight Pentecost, P. 375

Harold Hoehner

Hoehner was convinced that the crucifixion occurred in 33 AD (So do all Roman Catholic theologians). Realizing that the work and conclusions of Anderson were untenable but perhaps on the right track; Harold Hoehner made the following remedial calculations. Instead of using 445 BC for the 20th year of Artaxerxes, he chose to use Nisan 1, March 4 in 444 BC as the day that the prophecy was initiated. Following Anderson, Hoehner corrected Anderson's solar year to 365.24219879 days and also declared that Gabriel was speaking of a 360 day prophetic year. Again multiplying 69 weeks of years by 360 days, he also arrived at 173,880 days. He then declared the difference between 444 BC and 33 Ad to be 476 years, and multiplying 476 years by the length of a Gregorian year he arrived at 173,885.28662404 days, or 173,855 days, 6 hours, 52 minutes and 44 seconds. This left only 25 days to be accounted for between 444 BC and 33 AD. By adding these 25 days to March 5 of 444 BC and moving forward 173,880 days he arrived at Nisan 10, 33 AD. This date would coincide with the entry of Christ into Jerusalem on Psalm Sunday. The crucifixion was then triumphantly declared to be on Friday, Nisan 14.

Exegesis and Comments

Much of the theory of modern dispensationalism and a 7 year tribulation period rests upon the assumption that we can make the first 69 weeks of Daniel's 70 weeks fit into some sort of timeline from Artaxerxes' 20th year to Christ's death. Often when one discusses the details of the first 69 weeks with a dispensationalist, the dates and theories of Sir Robert Anderson arise, as outlined in his book, *The Coming Prince*. A critical examination of Anderson's work can be found by Bob Pickle at http://www.pickle-publishing.com/papers/sir-robert-anderson.htm

It is important to recognize that as just discussed, there is a large group of prophesy teachers and theologians who start Daniel's 70th week in either 445 BC (Sir Robert Anderson and others) or in 444 BC (Harold Hoehner and others). As previously discussed, they resort to using a *prophetic year* based largely upon facts that are in the book of Revelation. If 42 months is to be equated to 1260 days, it must follow that a *prophetic month* is 30 days long and a *prophetic year* is 12 months of 30 days or 360 days long. Everyone who follows this line of thought, multiplies the number of years in Daniel's 70th week by 360 days, and then converts these prophetic years into either Julian years (360.25 days long) or to Gregorian years (360.2524 days long).

A Friday crucifixion date has been widely accepted ever since the work of Harold Hoehner was published, particularly by Roman Catholics, since the Roman Catholic Church doggedly holds to a Friday crucifixion date. Although both Anderson and Hoehner should be highly commended for innovation and believable results, we must reject both crucifixion dates as being interesting but not acceptable. *First*, Daniel did not have all of these complex numbers running through his mind when he received the prophecy. We have argued that he was no doubt relating the prophecy to full calendar years with sabbatical year milestones. *Second*, to make the 445 BC or the 444 BC departure dates for Daniel's prophecy work, Daniel would have had to anticipate (or know) the exact number of days in either a Gregorian or Calendar solar year. Daniel was told that he would *understand* when he received this prophecy, and there is no hint in the biblical record that he would understand this complex system of calculation. Finally, both Anderson and Hoehner claim that the book of Revelation substantiates their approach…. But the book of revelation would not be written until about 500 years later! *Third*, and most compelling, is that the concept of a 360-day prophetic year cannot be accepted. The only precedence that a prophetic month was to be only 30 days was from the biblical account of the flood. Using Gen 7:24 and Gen 7:11 with Gen 8:4; one can equate 5 months with 150 days… Bingo! However, the fact that it rained for 150 days over a 5 month period does not specifically prove that each month was 30 days in duration. For example, two months of 31 days, two of 29 days and one of 30 days will yield the same result. *Finally*, to accept a Friday crucifixion of Christ is to completely ignore the straightforward and simple statements of Christ on several occasions that He would be in the grave three days and three nights, and Christ banked the belief of his entire ministry on this statement.

> *"Then certain of the Scribes and of the Pharisees answered, saying, Master, we would see a sign from thee. But he answered and said unto them, An evil and adulterous generation seeketh after a sign; and there shall no sign be given to it, but the sign of the prophet Jonah: For as Jonah was three days and three nights in the whale's belly; so shall the son of man be three days and three nights in the heart of the earth."*   Mat 12:37-49

It is impossible to have Christ in the grave a full three days and three nights using a Friday crucifixion and a Sunday morning resurrection without a very clever part-day accounting scheme; and even this stretches the imagination. To get three days, one must resort to equating the short time that Christ was in the tomb late Friday afternoon to a full 24-hour day (one 12 hour night and one 12 hour day). The next day (Saturday) is a whole day and whole night. Things get worse. The second night is 6:00 pm-6:00 am on Friday (Saturday night actually), and the third night is obtained by assuming that Christ rose just before dawn on Sunday. So where is the third day? Simple they say. Sunday night (following Saturday-day) was connected to Sunday-day, and so the third day is counted concurrent with Sunday night. The entire scenario is preposterous! Christ clearly said He would be in the grave for *three days and three nights*, and He banked the validity of who He was on this statement. He was not trying to be clever or cause confusion; He meant what He said. The 30-day month, 360-day year prophetic year theory, is not based upon solid biblical evidence as we have previously discussed. However, even if we concede that this theory may have some basis in the book of Genesis (flood account), can it really be supported by the periods of time just studied in which the great tribulation period lasts exactly 1260 days and 42 months? On the surface, there seems to be no question about it: However, let us examine the facts that we have put forth in our chronological study.

Recall that we propose a natural and plausible start of Daniel's 70th week on Tishri 1, 458 BC; which was the first year of a Sabbatical year (458 BC - 457 BC). It would not stretch our imagination to assume that Daniel evidently immediately *understood* that normal years were in view, and that they were tied to 70 Sabbatical year cycles. Seventy Sabbatical year cycles are exactly 490 years in duration; which is 49 full sabbatical cycles of 7 years. After all, violation of 70 sabbatical years by the Nation of Israel is why he was there in the first place. He (and anyone else) would simply count off 483 years to when Messiah the Prince would appear. The only confusion or *mystery* is in what Julian year would the 490 year cycle begin?

 Daniels 70 weeks of years is rooted in the Jewish feast days; known to everyone of that time. Daniel could easily assume that the decree which initiated the 490 year count would coincide with Tishri 1, the Feast of Trumpets, and it is conceivable that he knew that 458 BC – 457 BC was a sabbatical year. It is interesting that ancient Jewish rabbinical writings reflected the belief that at that time, an entirely new sequence of Sabbatical and Jubilee years were restarted. What Daniel could not have known is the calendar year on which the 490 year count would begin. Looking back, we have determined that the prophecy started on the Feast of Trumpets (Tishri 1, 458 BC) and would terminate 490 years later on another Feast of Trumpets. We can now state that: (1) Christ came to the River Jordan to be baptized by John shortly after 483 years had elapsed in August/September of 26 AD ….. Just as predicted. (2) After an earthly ministry of 3.5 years, *in the middle of Daniel's 70th week* Jesus Christ was crucified on Wednesday, April 5 on Nisan 14 in 30 AD; and He died on the cross at 3:00pm…at exactly the same hour that the high priest was standing in Herod's Temple and killing the Passover lamb. As the priest cut the lamb's throat, blood was shed for the atonement (covering) of sin. At exactly that same time, a Roman soldier thrust a sword into the side of Jesus Christ…and water and blood came forth. At this very moment, the Jewish sacrificial system was ended forever. Christ had shed his precious blood for once and for all to carry our sins away. On the afternoon of Nisan 14 the Passover lamb was to be slain at 3:00 pm, and then prepared for the Passover Feast that evening. (3) Recall that Nisan 14 ended at 6:00 pm that day, and the next day, Nisan 15, was the first day of the Feast of Unleavened Bread. The 70th week of Daniel was interrupted at that time *in the midst of Daniels 70th week*; approximately 3.5 years into the last 7 years of the 490 year prophecy.

A complete chronology has been constructed from the year that Adam and Eve were expunged from the Garden of Eden to the crucifixion of Christ. The following tables were constructed from the Authorized King James biblical records with confirmation from the ancient Book of Jasher.

Name	Lived (Yrs)	Had Son	At Age		AY YEAR Year Born	Biblical Reference
Adam	930	Seth	130	Creation Yr	1	Gen 5:3
Seth	912	Enosh	105		131	Gen 5:6
Enosh	905	Cainan	90	Methusalah	236	Gen 5:9
Cainan/Kenan	910	Mahalalel	70	Dies	326	Gen 5:12
Mahalalel	895	Jared	65	1657	396	Gen 5:15
Jared	962	Enoch	162	Creation	461	Gen 5:18
Enoch	365	Methuselah	65	Year of Flood	623	Gen 5:21
Methuselah	969	Lamech	187	1657	688	Gen 5:25
Lamech	777	Noah	182	Shem Birth	875	Gen 5:28
Noah-600 @ Flood	950	Shem	502	1559	1057	Gen 5:32
Shem-Gen 11:10-Lived 600 yrs	600	Arphaaxed	100	Arphaaxed Birth	1559	Gen 11:10
Arphaaxed-Born 2Yrs after flood	438	Salah	35	1659	1659	Gen 11:12
Selah	433	Eber	30	Abram Covenant	1694	Gen 11:14
Eber	464	Peleg	34	1729	1724	Gen 11:16
Peleg	239	Reu	30	Abram 75 when	1758	Gen 11:18
Reu	239	Serug	32	enters Canaan	1788	Gen 11:20
Serug	230	Nabor	30	2024	1820	Gen 11:22
Nahor	148	Terah	29	Terah died in	1850	Gen 11:24
Terah	205	Abraham	70	2084	1879	Gen 11:26
Abraham...75 entered Canaan	175	Isaac	100	Abram 100 when	1949	Gen 21:5
Isaac	180	Jacob & Esau	60	Issac born	2049	Gen 25:26
Jacob	147	Joseph	91	2049	2109	See Below
Joseph	110				2200	Gen 50:22

Joseph sold into slavery at age 17	2217
13 Yrs later at age 30 he is called	
before Pharoh (Gen 41:46)..............	2230
7 Years of Plenty follow	2237
Followed by 7 by years of famine	2244
Jacob moves to Egypt at age 130 in	
second year of famine..........	2239
Jacob lives for 17 Yrs in Egypt, then dies	
at age 147 [enters at 130, (130 +17)]=147	2256
Joseph lives to age 110, and then dies in Yr	2310
Now, Abram left at age 75	2024
It is exactly 430 years to the day that Exodus starts..	2454
Since Exodus was in year 2454	
Moses was born in year........... 2374	
The number of years between	
Josephs death & Moses birth is	64 / 2374
Aaron was 3 Years younger, Born in 2371	
Note that Terah, Abram's father died in Yr ..	2377

One of the key assumptions is that Terah had Abram at age 70. There has been a long-standing debate concerning the birth date of Abraham. There are two choices which seem almost equally viable. Up until Abraham, the book of Genesis records the ages of the fathers at the births of selected, individual sons, so that one can simply add up the years to construct a clear and uncontroversial chronological sequence. At Abraham, that unbroken chain seems ambiguous.

The verse which we expect to be definitive is subject to interpretation: *And Terah lived seventy years, and begat Abram, Nahor, and Haran* (Gen. 11:26). Was Terah age 70 when he begat Abram (whose named was later changed to Abraham)? Were the three brothers triplets? Was Abram really born first or later? For all of the preceding patriarchs, a unique reference to the birth of a son was listed, usually followed by a statement that the father also begat other sons and daughters. Gen 11:26 breaks this pattern because other sons are named. The natural interpretation seems to be that Terah was age 70 at Abraham's birth, and that he later had two other sons named Nahor and Haran. However, this need not necessarily be true.

An alternate interpretation arises because shortly after the statement that Abraham's father died in Haran at age 205 (Gen 11:32), it says that Abraham departed from Haran at age 75 (Gen 12:4). If one assumes that Abraham left immediately after Haran died, then Terah was 130 (205-75=130) at Abraham's birth. So was Terah age 70 or 130 at Abraham's birth?

The Book of Jasher explicitly states that Terah was age 70 at Abraham's birth (Jasher 7:51) and that Noah didn't die until Abraham was 58 years old (Jasher 13:9), which agrees with the first interpretation of the Genesis account. Jasher and other biblical accounts seem to indicate that Terah was an idol worshipper and followed after strange gods. Why was Abraham so righteous when his father worshipped idols? Jasher explains that Abraham was raised and taught by Noah for 39 years, from age 11 to 49 (Jasher 8:36, 9:6, 11:13). If the testimony of Asher is true, it provides a key to the spiritual maturity of Abraham and why he left his idol worshipping father in Haran.

Counting years from the flood in AY 1657, Noah died in AY 2007. The two choices for Abraham are either that he was born in AY 1949 when Terah was 70 or in AY 2009 when Terah was 130. If Abraham was born when Terah was 130, then Noah could not have known Abraham because Abraham would have been born two years after Noah died. If Abram (Abraham) had lived with Noah when he was a child, Abram would have dwelt there between the ages of 10 and 49 years and Noah would have been between 902 to 941 years old. Noah died just nine years later at age 950. The chronology found in Bibles published during the last three centuries generally follows that of Bishop Ussher, who decided that Terah was age 130 at Abraham's birth.

Another ancient manuscript that was held in high esteem by the church fathers was the Book of Abraham, which contains the following narratives. We are indebted to the fine biblical scholar John Pratt, who has written the following observations (Pratt).

> ***"While Abraham was still living in Ur of the Chaldees (in modern Iraq), he was saved by an angel from being sacrificed to a pagan god. At that time he was told that the Lord would lead him away from his father's house into a strange land (Abr. 1:16). Sometime later there was a famine in Ur and it was then that the Lord commanded Abraham to***

begin his journey. Abraham states: "Therefore I left the land of Ur, of the Chaldees, to go into the land of Canaan" (Abr. 2:4). That statement indicates that from Abraham's point of view, the journey was from Ur to Canaan (modern Israel & Palestine). He mentions that his father followed after him, but that when they arrived in Haran (modern Syria), the famine abated; and my father tarried in Haran and dwelt there .The book continues to say: "and my father turned again unto his idolatry, therefore he continued in Haran" **Abraham 2:4-5**

If this account is indeed accurate, it provides a logical explanation to both of two popular beliefs. The first is that Terah and Abraham left together for Canaan; and the second is that Abraham left Terah in Ur (Babylonia) and went to Canaan with Lot. The Book of Abraham actually supports both views.

"The record states that he left Haran at age 62 (Abr. 2:14). The main point is that both the Book of Jasher and the Book of Abraham record that Terah was not dead when Abraham was called out of Ur, and that he actually died some time later. That removes all of the support for the interpretation that Terah was age 130 at Abraham's birth" **(Pratt).**

Hence, our interpretation of the biblical records, supported by both the Book of Asher and the Book of Abraham, is that Abraham was born in AY 1949 when his father Terah was age 70. Abraham left his father behind because he (Terah) chose to worship his idols in Haran rather than follow God's command. Abraham then entered Canaan at age 75 in AY 2024. The biblical key to determining the AY in which the exodus from Egypt occurred is found in Genesis 12.

> *"Now the sojourning of the children of Israel, who dwelt in Egypt, was four hundred and thirty years. And it came to pass at the end of the four hundred and thirty years, even the selfsame day it came to pass, that all the hosts of the LORD went out from the land of Egypt".* Exodus 12:40-41

The apostle Paul confirmed this testimony in Gal 3:15-17. The Genesis account clearly states that this period of time concerned the *children of Israel*. This is a Hebrew idiom that always means the *nation of Israel*, starting with Abraham, Lot and all those who followed them into the Land of Canaan. The 430 years encompasses the total sojourn of Abraham and all of his descendants from when Abraham left Mesopotamia until the exodus from Egypt. In fact, the biblical records record that this period of time started and ended on exactly the same day! Using this *Rosetta stone*, if Abraham left in AY 2024, the Exodus occurred on Thursday, Nisan 15 in AY 2454.

The Conquest of the Land, Sabbatical Years and Jubilee Years

At Mount Sinai God gave the Law to Moses and the children of Israel. Part of God's commandments were to ordain sabbatical and jubilee years during which the land was to rest and regenerate. A sabbatical year was to be observed every 7th year and a jubilee year was to be observed every 50th year. This was a national and corporate to all of the tribes of Israel. The sabbatical year was to be observed after 6 years of working the land, and the jubilee year after 7 full sabbatical year cycles. Leviticus 25: 3-5 makes this clear. This means that the first sabbatical year could not begin until the land had been conquered, the land divided among the 11 tribes (Levites received no land), and the fields cultivated, planted and reaped for 6 years.

> *"Six years thou shalt sow thy field, and six years thou shalt prune thy vineyard, and gather in the fruit thereof; But in the seventh year shall be a sabbath of rest unto the land, a sabbath for the LORD: thou shalt neither sow thy field, nor prune thy vineyard. That which groweth of its own accord of thy harvest thou shalt not reap, neither gather the grapes of thy vine undressed: for it is a year of rest unto the land."*
> **Leviticus 25: 3-5**

It was determined from the Holy scriptures that after the River Jordan was crossed in 1490 BC; it took about 6 years to conquer the land. The land was divided at Shiloh by Joshua in early summer of AY 2500, and each tribe finally inherited the Promised Land. The first *sabbatical cycle* began in Sept/Oct of 1444 BC in AY 2501. The first *sabbatical year* took place in AY 2507, Sept/Oct 1438 BC – Sept/Oct 1437 BC. From this point in time, it is a simple task to determine when every Sabbatical and Jubilee year was *supposed* to be held. The following table provides a summary of when sabbatical and Jubilee years should have been observed from 1438-1437 BC to 223 AD.

Sabbatical Years							Jubilee	Cycle								Jubilee	Cycle
1	2	3	4	5	6	7			1	2	3	4	5	6	7		
1438	1431	1424	1417	1410	1403	1396	1395	1	1389	1382	1375	1368	1361	1354	1347	1346	2
1340	1333	1326	1319	1312	1305	1298	1297	3	1291	1284	1277	1270	1263	1256	1249	1248	4
1242	1235	1228	1221	1214	1207	1200	1199	5	1193	1186	1179	1172	1165	1158	1151	1150	6
1144	1137	1130	1123	1116	1109	1102	1101	7	1095	1088	1081	1074	1067	1060	1053	1052	8
1046	1039	1032	1025	1018	1011	1004	1003	9	997	990	983	976	969	962	955	954	10
948	941	934	927	920	913	906	905	11	899	892	885	878	871	864	857	856	12
850	843	836	829	822	815	808	807	13	801	794	787	780	773	766	759	758	14
752	745	738	731	724	717	710	709	15	703	696	689	682	675	668	661	660	16
654	647	640	633	626	619	612	611	17	605	598	591	584	577	570	563	562	18
556	549	542	535	528	521	514	513	19	507	500	493	486	479	472	465	464	20
458	451	444	437	430	423	416	415	21	409	402	395	388	381	374	367	366	22
360	353	346	339	332	325	318	317	23	311	304	297	290	283	276	269	268	24
262	255	248	241	234	227	220	219	25	213	206	199	192	185	178	171	170	26
164	157	150	143	136	129	122	121	27	115	108	101	94	87	80	73	72	28
66	59	52	45	38	31	24	23	29	17	10	3	5	12	19	26	27	30
33	40	47	54	61	68	75	76	31	82	89	96	103	110	117	124	125	32
131	138	145	152	159	166	173	174	33	180	187	194	201	208	215	222	223	34

The Babylonian exile of 70 years was a direct consequence of the failure of corporate Israel to observe 70 sabbatical and jubilee years from 1490 BC to 586 BC. It might be noted that there was no indication that a year of jubilee was ever observed.

The Exodus to the Last Year of King Solomon's Reign
If we simply follow the Holy Bible, the following passage of scripture will take us directly from the Exodus to the fourth year of King Solomon's reign.

> *"And it came to pass in the four hundred and eightieth year after the children of Israel had come out of the land of Egypt, in the fourth year of Solomon's reign over Israel, in the month of Ziv, which is the second month, that he began to build the house of the Lord."*   I Kings 6:1

There is no ambiguity or uncertainty in this statement. The inspired word of God specifically states that Solomon's temple was started in the 4th year of King Solomon's reign, and that this took place in the 480th year after the exodus from Egypt. Since the exodus started on Nisan 15 in AY 2454, each of the 480 years are from Nisan 15-Nisan 15. AY years are from Sept 1-Sept 1. The regnal years of King Solomon correspond to AY years. The record goes on to say that the temple of God was started in the 4th year of King Solomon's reign; in the second Hebrew month of Ziv, which always falls in April/May, in the 480th year after the exodus This brings us to the spring of AY 2933; Sept, 1012 BC-Sept, 1011 BC. It immediately follows that the first year of King Solomon's reign was AY 2930; Sept, 1015-1014 BC and his last year of reign was AY 2969; Sept, 976-975 BC.

The Last Year of King Solomon's Reign to the Destruction of Jerusalem

King Solomon died in AY 2969; likely in the late spring or early summer of 975 BC. Following his death the United Kingdom ruptured into the Northern and Southern kingdoms. If the unbroken record of all Southern Kingdom (Judah) kings is carefully traced through the Holy Scriptures, it can be determined that a total of 389 regnal years elapsed between the first and last king of the Southern Kingdom. The *Southern Kingdom* started in Sept/Oct of AY 2970 and fell to the Babylonian Empire in AY 3358. It was earlier shown that in all likelihood, the Southern Kingdom lasted about 389 years from the death of King Solomon. *The Northern Kingdom* had fallen in the summer of 721 BC to the Assyrian Empire, about 135 years earlier. Based upon pioneering research by Edwin Thiele and later accepted by McFall and Finnegan, the regnal years of each king in the Southern Kingdom started their reign on Tishri 1 and ended on Elul 29 (Tishri 1-Tishri 1 for convenience). The regnal years of all Kings in the Davidic Dynasty, starting with King David and ending 489 years later, exactly coincided with AY years.

At this point in time, it was clearly established that the Julian calendar date on which Jerusalem finally fell was July 18, 586 BC. The synchronization of AY 3358 to the Jewish civil year of Tishri 1 (Sept/Oct) of 587 BC-Tishri 1 (Sept/Oct) of 586 BC was the *Rosetta stone* that was needed to synchronize all AY years to Julian calendar years. This synchronization was then used to equate AY years between AY 1 and AY 3358 to a Julian calendar year. Partial results are given in the following table.

AY Year		Julian Dates
1	Year Adam left Eden	Sept/Oct, 3944-Sept/Oct, 3943
		2454 Years
2454	Year of the Exodus	Sept/Oct, 1491 - Sept/Oct, 1490
2454	Exodus	Sept/Oct, 1491 - Sept/Oct, 1490
		480 Years
2933	Solomon's 4th Year	Sept/Oct, 1012-Sept/Oct, 1011
2930	Solomon's 4th Year	Sept/Oct, 1012 - Sept/Oct, 1011
		4 Years
2933	Solomon's 1st Year	Sept/Oct, 1015 - Sept/Oct, 1014
2930	Solomon's 1st Year	Sept/Oct, 1015 - Sept/Oct, 1014
		40 Years
2969	Solomon's 40th Year	Sept/Oct, 976 - Sept/Oct, 975
2970	Divided Kingdom (Judah)	Sept/Oct, 975 - Sept/Oct, 974
	Jerusalem fell, July 18, 586 BC	389 Years
3358	Last Year of Judah	Sept/Oct, 587 - Sept/Oct, 586

Validating the Fourth Year of King Solomon

An important Biblical clue used in this book is the testimony of I Kings 6:1 that Solomon's temple was started in the fourth year of King Solomon's reign in the 480th year after the Exodus from Egypt. Recall that the Exodus occurred on Nisan 15 in AY 2454 which is defined as Sept/Oct, 1491 BC - Sept/Oct, 1490 BC. It immediately follows that the Exodus ended in AY 2494 on Nisan 15, in March/April of 1450 BC. Recall that in AY 2454, God instructed the children of Israel to *rotate their yearly calendar* of Tishri 1-Tishri 1 to Nisan 1-Nisan 1. It is important to recognize that nothing changed except that Nisan 1 now became the first month on their yearly calendar and Tishri 1 became the seventh month. After the exodus from Egypt, the Hebrew calendar contained two interlocking years; the Hebrew *Civil* calendar (Tishri 1 – Tishri 1) and the Hebrew *Religious* calendar (Nisan 1- Nisan 1) Looking back through time, we now know that the month of Tishri always started in September or October on both the Julian and Gregorian calendars; and Nisan 1 started in March or April. In either case, the month of Ziv (second month) always referred to the religious calendar and fell in April/May on the Julian calendar. A legitimate question to ask is did the holy scribe in I Kings 6:1 reference Tishri-Tishri years or Nisan-Nisan years?

Case I: Tishri 1 to Tishri 1 Civil Calendar Years

If the 480 years given in I Kings 6:1 were based upon Tishri 1-Tishri 1 years we would observe:

Sept/Oct, 1491 BC – Sept/Oct, 1490 BC

480 Years

Sept/Oct, 1012 BC – Sept/Oct, 1011 BC   *King Solomon's fourth year of reign*

The exodus started on Nisan 15 (March/April), 1490 BC and Solomon's Temple was started in the Month of Ziv (April/May) in King Solomon's fourth year of reign. Solomon's regnal years started on Tishri 1 (Sept/Oct). This would demand that the temple was started in March/April of 1011 BC. March/April of 1011 BC was within the 4th year of King Solomon's reign which was Sept/Oct, 1012 BC to Sept/Oct, 1011 BC. It is easy to determine that Solomon's first year of reign was Sept/Oct, 1015 BC-Sept/Oct, 1014 BC and his last (40th) year of reign was AY 2969, Sept/Oct, 976 BC-Sept/Oct, 975 BC.

Case II: Nisan 1 to Nisan 1 Religious Calendar Years

The first religious year ordained by God was Nisan 1 (March/April), 1490 BC-Nisan 1, (March/April), 1489 BC. If the 480 years of I Kings 6:1 started on Nisan 1, 1490 BC, the 480th year would be Nisan 1 (March/April), 1011 BC–Nisan 1, March/April, 1010 BC. Hence, the temple would have been started in the second month (April/May) of the 480th year; 479 years and no more than six weeks after the exodus from Egypt.

March/April, 1490 BC – March/April, 1489 BC

480 Years

March/April, 1011 BC – March/April, 1010 BC   *The 480th year after the Exodus*

As already determined, regnal years for every Hebrew king from the reign of King David through the reign of King Zedekiah always started on Tishri 1 (September/October). The fourth year of King Solomon's reign is therefore Tishri 1, 1012 BC–Tishri 1, 1011 BC. The Hebrew religious year starts and ends on Nisan 1 (designated month one since the exodus from Egypt). The month of Ziv is the second month of the religious calendar, which corresponds to April/May. Hence, the temple of King Solomon must have been started in April/May of 1011 BC. This coincides *exactly* with the same month and year previously determined by using the Hebrew *civil* calendar. This is fortunate since one need not be chosen over the other, but we believe that II Kings 6:1 is referencing actual years after the exodus starting with Nisan 15 (March/April) of 1490 BC....which was a Thursday.

The conclusion is decisive: Solomon's fourth year of reign was Sept, 1012 BC–Sept, 1011 BC; his first year of reign was Sept/Oct, 1015 BC-Sept/Oct, 1014 BC, and his last (40th) year of reign was Sept/Oct, 976 BC-Sept/Oct, 975 BC. Solomon's temple was started in April/May of 1011 BC, and the schism occurred following the death of King Solomon in AY 2970.

Further Confirmation using Julian and AY Dates

Finally, it should be noted once again that the Southern Kingdom of Judah ceased to exist when the city of Jerusalem fell to the Babylonian Empire on July 8, 586 BC. This was in AY 3358, Sept/Oct, 587 BC - Sept/Oct, 586 BC. We have previously conjectured that the actual calendar time which elapsed was *likely* a little more than 389 years from the death of King Solomon in the spring or summer of 975 BC of in AY 2969 to the fall of Judah on July 18, 586 BC. The number of regnal years that elapsed was 389 years. Hence:

AY 2969   Sept/Oct, 975 BC – Sept/Oct, 974 BC
                                        389 *Years*
AY 3358   Sept/Oct, 597 BC – Sept/Oct, 586 BC   *The Year Judah Fell*

It follows that AY 2969, which was Sept/Oct, 976 BC-Sept/Oct, 975 BC was the 40th and last year of King Solomon's reign. The first year of King Solomon's reign is therefore determined as Sept/Oct, 1015 BC-Sept/Oct, 1014 BC, and his fourth year of reign Sept/Oct, 1012 BC-Sept/Oct, 1011 BC. This demands that the temple of King Solomon was started in the month of Ziv (April/May) in 1011 BC. By the testimony of three witnesses, Solomon's Temple was started in April/May in 1011 BC, in King Solomon's fourth year, which was AY 2930; Sept/Oct, 1012 BC–Sept/Oct, 1011 BC. This locks in the first year of the divided kingdom as AY 2970.

The 300 Years between the Exodus and the Last Year of Jair

A remarkable narrative is recorded in Judges 11:12-26. A mighty warrior named *Jephthah* arose when *Ammon* was waging war against Israel. Jephthah was sought out to defend Israel and wage war against the *Ammonites*. The people made him head of all the tribes, and he sent word to the King of Ammon asking why the Ammonites were attacking Israel. The King of Ammon responded that just before the children of Israel crossed the Jordan River, they "***took away my land from the Arnon to the Jabbok as far as the Jordan River***" (Judges 11:13) and he wanted the land back. In a remarkable response to the King of Ammon, Jephthah responded decisively and authoritatively: "***Israel did not take away the land of Moab, nor the land of the Ammon.***

Israel turned aside and captured land which belonged to the Ammorites and not the Ammonites." To add insult to injury, Jephthah then asked a concise question.

> *"While Israel dwelt in Heshbon and its villages, in Aroer and its villages; and in all the cities along the banks of the Arnon, for 300 years, why did you not try to recover them within that time?"* Judges 11:26

In other words, Jephthah asked; *if your claim is true, why have you not said anything in 300 years? Jephthah was not uncertain*, nor did he say **about** 300 years; he said 300 years with authority. This is the main point to consider in advancing the chronology. The Holy scribe continued by recording that after explaining this to the King of Ammon, he would not go away; so Jephthah assembled all of his troops and defeated them soundly (Judges 11: 28-33). At that point in time, Jephthah became Judge over Israel. The following graphic shows how the chronology is advanced between when the Ammorites were subdued, just before the 40-year exodus ended, and the beginning of Jephthah's judgeship, which commenced following the Judgeship of Jair and the end of the 18-year Ammorite oppression and war against Israel.

The speech by Jephthah declared that a 300-year period of time had elapsed between just before the exodus ended in AY 2494 to the year that the reign of Jair ended. These years are all March/April years and actually span two Sept/Oct-Sept/Oct AY and Jewish Civil calendar years. Note that a 6 month period is shown between when AY 2454 started in Sept/Oct to when the exodus commenced on Nisan 15 in March /April of AY 2454. The graphic adds 40 years for the exodus, which when added to the 300 year of Jephthah accounts for 340 years; starting with when the exodus began and when the 22 years that Jair served as a judge over all of Israel ended in March/April of AY 2794. When Jair died, Jepethah was called out of the land of Tob to fight against the Ammonites. Jepethah agreed provided he would be appointed Judge and captain of the army (Judges 10: 1-10). The people agreed and Jepethah soundly defeated the Ammonites (Judges 11: 32-33).The 22 years of Jair's judgeship were immediately followed by the 6 years that Jepethah served as a judge over all Israel.

Jepethah to the end of King Solomon's 3rd year of Reign

This period of time must include the judgeship of Jephthah, Ibzan, Elon, Abdon and Sampson; followed by 1 year in which there was *no king* (judge) *in Israel* (Judges 17:6, 18:1, 19:1). The 3 years of Samuel as the last sovereign judge, the co-reign of Samuel with Saul for 27 years, and the 13 year reign of Saul after Samuel died moves the chronology forward to the first year of King David's reign. After Saul died, the Davidic dynasty was initiated and a Tishri 1 (Sept/Oct) to Tishri 1 regnal year system was initiated by King David. This system continued for another 470 years until the destruction of Judah by the Babylonian empire in 586 BC. Finally, the first 3 full years of King Solomon's reign are added to span a total of 139 years.

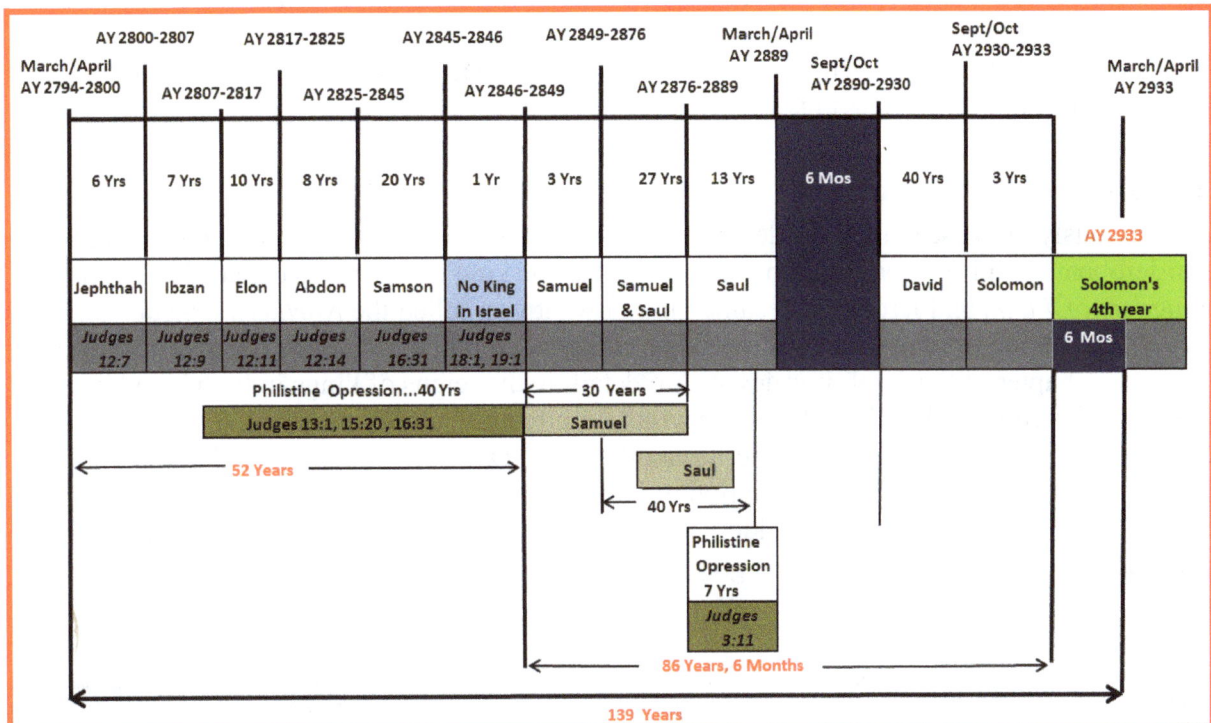

The 139 years added to the previous 340 years totals to (340+139) =479 years between when the exodus began in AY 2454 and the end of Solomon's 3rd year of reign, which was on Elul 29; the last day of AY 2929. The 4th year of King Solomon's reign coincided with AY 2933 (Sept/Oct), and contained the beginning of the 480th year after the exodus, which started in March/April of AY 2933. The temple started construction in the month of Ziv (April/May), which was in the 7th month of AY 2933.

In the fourth year of his reign, approximately 479 years and no less than 4 weeks or no more than 6 weeks after the exodus began; King Solomon began to build the temple of God. This was in the 480th year after the exodus from Egypt (I Kings 6:1). The temple took seven years to build (I Kings 6:38) and it was completed in the month of Bul (Oct/Nov). This temple stood until it was destroyed by the Babylonian Empire in 586 BC. Solomon died in AY 2969 (976 BC–975 BC). The documented chronology now brings us to the death of King Solomon, likely in the late spring or early summer of 975 BC.

Prior to the death of King Solomon, there arose a ***mighty man of valor*** (I Kings 11:28) called *Jeroboam*. King Solomon was so impressed with Jeroboam that he placed him in charge of all the labor forces in his kingdom (I Kings 11:28). At this time, the prophet Abijah met him on a road and prophesied that 10 of the 12 tribes would be given to him to rule (I Kings 11:31). He also prophesied that David would be given the Tribe of Judah (and the Levites) to rule over (I Kings 11:32). Hearing this, Solomon ***sought to kill*** Jeroboam (I Kings 11:40). But Jeroboam fled to Egypt where he remained until Solomon died. Upon Solomon's death, Rehoboam his son assumed the throne, expecting to rule over all 12 tribes (I Kings 11:43). But hearing of Solomon's death, Jeroboam returned from Egypt and by divine appointment became king of the Northern 10 tribes of Israel. So the United Kingdom was split into two pieces; the Southern Kingdom known as Judah ruled by Rehoboam; and the Northern Kingdom called Israel ruled by Rehoboam. Jeroboam ruled over the Southern Kingdom from Jerusalem, called the City of David: Rehoboam ruled over the Northern Kingdom from the City of Shechem in the mountains of Ephraim (I Kings 12:25). The Northern Kingdom of Israel was in rebellion against the House of David even unto today (I Kings 12:19)

The Divided Kingdom

As previously discussed, upon the death of King Solomon a power struggle ensued between his son Jeroboam and Rehoboam. Jeroboam emerged as the king of what was called *the Southern Kingdom of Judah* and Jeroboam became king of what was called the *Northern Kingdom of Israel.* The period of time which followed has confounded biblical scholars for over 1500 years. An entire chapter of this book was devoted to detailing the reigns of kings in both kingdoms. The Northern Kingdom of Israel fell to the Assyrian Empire after approximately 255 years. The Southern Kingdom of Judah continued for another 134 years until Jerusalem fell to the Babylonian Empire in 586 BC. The nation of Israel ceased to exist at that time, and all except the very old and a few that hid in the wilderness were carried to Babylon where they remained in servitude for 70 years. The following graphic summarizes this period of time.

AY Year	Event	Dates
AY 2969	The United Kingdom ruptures	Summer of 975 BC
AY 2970	Southern Kingdom of Judau begins (Rehoboam)	Sept/Oct, 975 BC-Sept/Oct, 974 BC
AY 2969 - AY 2970	Northern Kingdom of Judah begins (Jeroboam)	Mar/April, 975 BC-Mar/April, 974 BC
AY 3223	Northern Kingdom falls to Assyrian Empire	Summer of 721 BC
AY 3358	Southern Kingdom falls to Babylonian Empire	April 18, 586 BC (Julian date)

Note that the Southern Kingdom lasted from the schism in AY 2969 to the final destruction of Jerusalem in AY 3358.The following table gives a list of all of the Southern Kingdom monarchs and their regnal years.

Southern Kingdom Kings			
Name of King	**Duration of Reign**		
Rehoboam	17	Years	I Kings 14:21
Abijah	3	Years	I Kings 15:1-2
Asa	41	Years	I Kings 15:9-10
Jehosephat	25	Years	I Kings 22:41-42
Jehoram	8	Years	II Kings 8:16-17
Ahaziah	1	Years	II Kings 8:25-26
Athaliah	6	Years	II Kings 11:1-21
Joash	40	Years	II Kings 11:17-20, II Kings 18:1
Amaziah	29	Years	II Kings 14:1-2
Uzziah	52	Years	II Kings 15:1-2
Jotham	16	Years	II Kings 15:32-33
Ahaz	16	Years	II Kings 16:1-2
Hezikiah	29	Years	II Kings 18:1-2
Manasseh	55	Years	II Kings 21:1
Amon	2	Years	II Kings 21:19
Josiah	31	Years	II Kings 22:1
Jehoahaz	1	3 Months	II Kings 23:31
Jehoakim	11	Years	II Kings 23:34
Jehoiachin		3 Months, 10 Days	II Kings 24:8
Zedekiah	11	Years	II Kings 25:17-18
Total Years: 394 Years, 3 Months, 10 Days			

Note that the total number of regnal years is 394 Years, 6 Months and 10 days. In Chapter 3 we showed that *Jehoram* co-reigned with his father *Jehosephat* for four years. This reduces the number of independent regnal years to 390 years and 6 months. Finnegan has shown that while *Jehoahaz* only reigned 3 months, his time on the throne crossed Tishri 1 and so he was credited with one full year of reign. *Jehoiakin* actually ruled 10 days longer, but his 3 month 10 day reign fell completely within the last (credited) year of *Jehoiakim*. Hence, there were no official years of reign given to Jehoiakin. This strange sequence of events reduces the 393 years, 6 months and 10 days of the Southern Kingdom Davidic line to 390 Civil Calendar (Tishri1-Tishri1) years. Finally, when Jehu killed both the King of Judah and the King of Israel, Ahaziah immediately named herself king for a period of time that coincided with the last year of Jehoram. She was quickly assassinated. Since her one year of (claimed) reign coincided with the last year of Jehoram; this reduces the total number of sequential years to 389.

From the Babylonian Exile to the Death of Christ

We accept July 18, 586 BC as the final fall of Jerusalem and the Southern Kingdom of Judah. This date fell within AY 3358 which was Sept/Oct, 587 BC-Sept/Oct, 586 BC. Prior to that date, there were several deportations from Israel. Of primary importance was a deportation in 605 BC in which Daniel (Belteshazzar), Hananiah (Shadrach), Mishael (Meshach) and Azariah (Abednego) were deported. Daniel and his three young friends would spend the next 70 years in exile while living in the city of Babylon. These 70 years were decreed by God for failure to let the land rest during 70 Sabbatical years and years of Jubilee. We will not dwell upon the deeds of Daniel and his rise to a position of great importance, but toward the end of the 70 years of captivity, Daniel *understood by studying* the book of Jeremiah that the 70 years of captivity were almost over (Dan 9:1-2). In one of the most remarkable prayers recorded in the entire Bible, Daniel petitioned God to forgive the people and end the captivity as promised. He also sought to understand what would become of Israel and his people. Even while praying, the Archangel Gabriel appeared to answer Daniel's prayer and to *"give understanding"* (Dan 9:21-22). Gabriel then gave perhaps the most important prophecy in the entire Holy Bible, the 70-week prophecy of Daniel 9:24-27. The prophecy was far in scope and spoke of the promised Messiah and how He would be crucified. This prophecy would span 70 weeks of years (490 years).

Two important milestones must be identified from this prophecy. *First,* in what Julian year did the prophecy start? *Second,* when would it terminate? Both questions are complicated, and have been answered in many ways by many theologians. Both of these questions and their answers were addressed in Chapters 5 and 6. However, it is important to understand that not a single event in the Holy Bible was ever given with a Julian date. Hence, it is impossible to extend the AY date and the Julian year date past the final fall of Jerusalem in 586 BC without resorting to historical and archaeological records. It is the opinion of this author that using ancient records is perfectly acceptable provided that they do not conflict with the Holy Biblical Text. Of course, to offer credibility to any Julian calendar dates that can be directly associated with a biblical event, the extra-biblical source must be carefully scrutinized and studied for accuracy. In conclusion of this matter, even the most careful exegesis will always involve some degree of personal interpretation. Having stated the guiding principles to arrive at logical and biblically consistent chronological dates, the Julian calendar date on which the 490-year prophecy was initiated will now be addressed.

The Julian calendar year during which Gabriel gave the 70 week of year's prophecy to Daniel cannot be determined. We only know that it was given to Daniel toward the end of his 70-year captivity in Babylon. The date on which the prophecy was given to Daniel is interesting but not critical. The crucial piece of information is when it *began to run its course.* Once this is determined, the AY years and the calendar years can be extended to this point in time and beyond. There have been numerous attempts to determine when the prophecy was initiated, but the majority of biblical scholars believe that there were only two logical points of initiation. The *first* is in the seventh year of Artaxerxes, and the *second* is in the 20th year of Cyrus. These regnal years can be determined within one to two years from ancient records, but there is no universally accepted Julian calendar year for either event. There are two prevailing lines of thought, and both hold strong support. The *first* is that the *seventh year of Artaxerxes* started in either 458 BC or 457 BC. These two views will lead to a crucifixion as early as 30 AD or as late as 34 AD, depending on whether or not Daniel's 70th week is interrupted or runs its full course; and in what year the 490 year period begins. We support the view that the 490 years are full solar years of 365.2422 days. As previously stated, Daniel's 490-year prophecy is initiated in either 458 BC or in 457 BC. The 458 BC date will begin a 483 year period which would end in 26 AD when Christ began his three and one-half-year earthly ministry at the river Jordan. Some continue the prophecy to include a 486.5 year period which would terminate in 30 AD at the crucifixion of Christ; others conclude the full 490 years at the death of Steven assume as 3, 5 years later. Others interrupt the prophecy after only 483 years when Christ was baptized at the river Jordan to leave a full seven years for the Revelation period revealed to the apostle John. The 457 BC initiation date would start a 483 year period which would end at the river Jordan in 27 AD, or a 486.5-year period which would end at the crucifixion of Christ in 31 AD.

A *second* major group of biblical scholars believe that the 490-year prophecy given to Daniel did not represent full *calendar years* (365.2422 Julian calendar days) but was meant to be interpreted as *prophetic years* of only 360 days. The concept of a prophetic year which contained only 360 days was first exploited by Sir Robert Anderson in 1909 AD. He calculated the number of days in 483 prophetic years and then converted prophetic years to solar years. Using a very clever set of assumptions, he then determined that if the decree which initiated Daniel's 70 weeks of years was given on Nisan 1, in 445 BC, in the 20th year of Artaxerxes to Nehemiah, the 483 years would end in 32 AD which was Palm Sunday of the crucifixion week. He then determined that Nisan 14, the date of the crucifixion, fell on Thursday in 32 AD. The work of Anderson has been critically examined and challenged by a number of scholars. The most damaging criticism is that in 32 BC the crucifixion day of Nisan 14 did not fall on a Thursday. Hoehner has studied the calculations extensively, and after adjusting some errors he declared that Anderson's calculations will lead to either a Sunday or Monday crucifixion day, a clear impossibility. However, realizing that Anderson had discovered a possible key to determining when the first 483 years of Daniel's prophecy might expire, Hoehner assumed that Anderson was in error as to when the decree actually occurred, and he then showed that the decree would have been issued in 444 BC, March 4 or March 5. Hoehner then converted 483 prophetic years of 360-day duration into true solar years of 365.24219879 days. Using a set of corresponding clever assumptions, Hoehner determined that the crucifixion of Christ was on Nisan 14, 33 AD, which was on Friday. The work of Hoehner and a Friday crucifixion date has been widely accepted as correct.

The real crux of these matters is whether or not the Angel Gabriel communicated the prophecy to Daniel with Daniel *understanding* that the prophecy was in prophetic years of 360-day duration, or that Daniel understood Gabriel to mean that the prophecy engaged full 365.24219879 days. We will not pursue this important issue any more than already previously discussed. At this point we only want to recognize that *most* biblical scholars have arrived at 30 AD, 31 AD, 32 AD, or 33 AD for the death of Christ. Depending upon the assumptions of each individual, one will either be left with seven years, three and one-half years, or no years for the remainder of Daniel's 70th week. If either seven years or three and one-half years are left, this creates a *gap in time* between when Christ was crucified and the resumption of Daniel's 70-week prophecy. The remaining period of time represents the tribulation period found in the book of Revelation. This study concludes that there is a gap in Daniel's 70 week prophecy and that 3.5 years are left in the 490 year period. This is exactly the same period of time given in the book of Revelation for what we call the Great Tribulation (see Phillips: *The Book of Revelation: Mysteries Revealed*).

Our intent here is not to critically assess each approach in either initiating or terminating Daniel's 70th week. The only important issue is to determine from this study the impact on what year Christ was crucified. Following the chronology previously offered, we have determined that AY 3358 contains the Julian date July 18, 586 BC. It is a simple matter to extrapolate this *anchor point* to any other set of Julian or Gregorian years between AY1 and AY 3977.

In this study, we have previously presented convincing but not absolutely-certain evidence that Christ was crucified in 30 AD. This year has historically been suggested by many scholars. As we have just shown, the exact year and day simply provide a *terminus quo* to the offered chronology. Until either definitive and accepted biblical or Roman records of the crucifixion surface, there will be differing opinions. The following graphic summarizes the AY year count and corresponding Julian year date(s) for major events which occurred between the exodus from Egypt in 1490 BC to the four most popular crucifixion years of our Lord Jesus Christ.

AY Year	Event	Dates
AY 2454	The Exodus From Egypt	March/April, 1490 BC
AY 2494	Moses Dies	March/April, 1450
AY 2494	The River Jordan is Crossed	March/April, 1450
AY 2494	Joshua becomes Commander in Chief	March/April, 1450 - March/April, 1425
AY 2494 - AY 2500	Land is Conquered in 6 years	March/April, 1450 - March/April, 1444
AY 2494 - AY 2519	Joshua Rules the 12 Tribes	March/April, 1450 - March/April, 1425
AY 2519 - AY 2539	Period of the Elders	March/April, 1425 - March/April, 1405
AY 2539 - AY 2849	Period of the Judges	March/April, 1405 - March/April 1095
AY 2849 - AY 2969	Period of Saul, David and Solomon	March/April, 1095 - Sept/Oct, 975
AY 2969	Death of King Solomon	Summer of 975
AY 2969	The Shism of the United Kingdom	975
AY 3224	Northern Kingdom Destroyed by Assyria	Summer of 721
AY 3358	Southern Kingdom Destroyed by the Babylonians	July 18, 586
AY 3487	The 70 week (490 year) Prophecy is Initiated	Sept/Oct, 458 BC
AY 3974	Crucifixion of Christ in 30 AD	Nisan 14, Wednesday
AY 3975	Crucifixion of Christ in 31 AD	Nisan 14, Monday
AY 3976	Crucifixion of Christ in 32 AD	Nisan 14, Monday
AY 3977	Crucifixion of Christ in 33 AD	Nisan 14, Friday

Note that no Julian crucifixion date between 31 AD and 33 AD falls on a Wednesday.
It should again be noted that this author believes that Christ was crucified on Wednesday, April 5 (Julian date) in 30 AD, after 486.5 years of the 490-year prophecy of Daniel had elapsed. At that time, Daniel's 70th and final week of seven years was suspended, leaving three and one-half years for the duration of the future *tribulation* period. This hypothesis is supported by a wealth of biblical data, and is fully explained in *The Book Revelation: Mysteries Explained* by Philips.

Summary and Conclusions

The motivation for writing this book was to bring to a conclusion over five years of intensive investigation into the construction of a biblical chronology which would span the period of time between when Adam and Eve were expunged from the Garden of Eden to the crucifixion of Jesus Christ. It was my deep conviction that God would have left enough chronological data in the Holy Scriptures to accomplish this task. This belief resulted in the contents of this book. Initial efforts were focused upon the wide array of both partial and consecutive chronologies previously published over a long period of time. It was quickly discovered that there were many, many different opinions and interpretations of the biblical record and key chronological events. After a lengthy period of studying many published chronologies, it was decided that if a verifiable and biblically-supported chronology could be constructed from Eden to Calvary, there was only one way to accomplish that goal; the Bible itself would have to be the final authority and the Holy Spirit the source of understanding.

It became obvious that some sort of *counting mechanism* had to be initiated which would begin at either (1) the year that the world was created, (2) the year Adam was created, or (3) the year in which Adam and Eve were expunged from the Garden of Eden. Since it is impossible to know either exactly when the world was created or when Adam was created, the logical choice was to start a count of years from when Adam and Eve left the Garden of Eden, This year and all other subsequent years were called *Adam's Years*, or simply **AY** years. Corresponding to this

142

designation of years was whether to start at year zero or year one. Although certain to bring dissention and criticism, it was decided to start the yearly count at AY=1. This year was considered to be the *birth year of Adam* into this world. This was based upon the clear and unambiguous word of God which warned Adam:

> **"But of the tree of the knowledge of good and evil, thou shalt not eat of it: for in the day that thou eatest thereof thou shalt surely die."** **Gen 2:17**

When Adam and Eve were driven out of the Garden of Eden, they became like all other men and women to follow, they were *born* into a corruptible body and their flesh began to decay. True to God's word, they began to die on the very day, month and year that Adam (and Eve) were cast out of the Garden of Eden. Adam's *birth year into the world* was in accord with the birth years of all mankind to follow; the first *year that Adam spent in his new world* was called AY 1 and he was not one year old until 12 months later.

The next major decision was to choose which biblical authority would be used to develop chronological data. It was decided that the Authorized King James Bible (KJV) would be the biblical standard. Using the King James Bible, it was possible to construct a verifiable and accurate unbroken sequence of events between AY 1 and the exodus. It was established that the exodus from Egypt occurred in AY 2454. There were only three points of contention: (1) AY 1 was the first year that Adam and Eve spent outside of the Garden of Eden and not AY 0, (2) Abraham was born when his father Terah was age 70. Other biblical chronologies have assumed that Terah was age 130 years old when he had Abram, and (3) the time between when Abram left Haran at age 75 until the exodus was 430 years. Each of these major assumptions was justified, but each can and certainly will be challenged. Any variation from these three assumptions would simply cause the AY count to differ from that shown in this chronology. For example, if Terah was actually 130 years old when he had Abram (a fairly common assumption by other chronographers), the exodus would occur in AY 2514. If one also started the AY count at AY=0 rather than AY=1, it should be clear that the exodus would have occurred in AY 2513. It was interesting to find that if one chooses to believe that if Terah had Abram at age 110, *and* if the AY count started at AY=0, *and* if they left the Garden of Eden on Nisan 1, the Julian year that Adam and Eve left the Garden of Eden would turn out to be 4004 BC. This is the same date arrived at by Ussher in 1658 AD for the *creation of the world*. This is certainly an interesting coincidence, since his chronological listings in the *Period of the Judges* and in the *Divided Kingdom* differ considerably from this study.

The next major epoch of time was between the exodus from Egypt and the fourth year of King Solomon's reign. The duration of this time period is given in the following verse.

> **"And it came to pass in the four hundred and eightieth year after the children of Israel had come out of the land of Egypt, in the fourth year of Solomon's reign over Israel, in the month of Ziv, which is the second month, that he began to build the house of the Lord."** I Kings 6:1

The exodus occurred on Nisan 15, shortly after midnight in March/April of AY 2454; 1490 BC. I Kings 6:1 enables us to leap forward 480 years into the fourth year of King Solomon's reign. Since King Solomon reigned 40 years, we can also project forward to that point in time. The

480-year period of time given in I Kings 6:1 has been severely criticized and said to be an error by many, many scholars. This study has shown that the Biblical record can be verified. The period between when Moses lead the children of Israel out of Egypt contains the following sub periods of time: (1) the 40 year exodus, (2) the 25 years that Joshua served as commander-in-chief, (3) the 20 year period of the elders, (4) the 300 year period of Jephthah, (5) the years of the judges, (5) the 40-year reign of Saul, (6) the 40-year reign of David, (7) and the 40-year reign of Solomon. These periods of time have confounded many chronologists; they must be initiated at the exodus and terminate in the 480th year after the exodus in the 4th year of King Solomon's reign. A major study was undertaken to show that I Kings 6:1 is absolutely correct. This was shown to be true.

Following the death of King Solomon in the summer of AY 2969, the period of the Divided Kingdom commenced. The nation of Israel which had been unified under King Solomon was split into the *Southern Kingdom of Judah* and the *Northern Kingdom of Israel*. The Northern Kingdom was completely destroyed by Assyria, and years later the Southern Kingdom was destroyed by the Babylonian Empire. Historians have agreed that based upon ancient Babylonian records, the city of Jerusalem fell in the 11th year of King Zedekiah on July 18, 586 BC. The only remaining piece of the puzzle to be found was how many AY years elapsed between when King Solomon died, Israel split into two kingdoms, and Jerusalem fell. This period of time was 389.5 AY years. Verifying that the sequential regnal years of the Kings of Judah was 389 years proved to be a formidable task which required a biblical cross-synchronization of all Southern Kingdom kings and all Northern Kingdom kings. It was conjectured by looking at all the biblical clues that King Solomon probably died in the late spring or early summer of 975 BC. Since the final fall of Jerusalem was on July 18, 586 BC, it is likely that the period of time between when King Solomon died and the final fall of Jerusalem occurred was about 389.5 years by God's divine plan. The following graphic summarizes the progression of AY years between AY 1 and when Jerusalem fell.

AY Year		Julian Dates
1	Year Adam left Eden	Sept/Oct, 3944-Sept/Oct, 3943
2454	Year of the Exodus	Sept/Oct, 1491-Sept/Oct, 1490
2454	Year of the Exodus	Sept/Oct, 1491-Sept/Oct, 1490
2933	Solomon's 4th Year	Sept/Oct, 1012-Sept/Oct, 1011
2933	Solomon's 4th Year	Sept/Oct, 1012-Sept/Oct, 1011
2930	Solomon's 1st Year	Sept/Oct, 1015-Sept/Oct, 1014
2930	Solomon's 1st Year	Sept/Oct, 1015-Sept/Oct, 1014
2969	Solomon's 40th Year	Sept/Oct, 976-Sept/Oct, 975
2970	Divided Kingdom	Sept/Oct, 975-Sept/Oct, 974
	Jerusalem Fell on July 18, 586 BC	
3358	Last Year of Judah	Sept/Oct, 587-Sept/Oct, 586

The next chronological puzzle to be solved was to determine the most-likely year that the 490-year prophecy given to the prophet Daniel by the Angel Gabriel would be initiated. This required investigation into known Egyptian, Assyrian, Jewish and Babylonian historical records. The most-likely date determined from this investigation was shown to be Tishri 1 of 458 BC in the 7th year of the reign of Artaxerxes, and the basis of the 390-year prophecy was normal solar years. Both the AY year and the Julian year date that corresponded to when Christ was crucified on the cross of Calvary was then determined. It has been pointed out that almost all biblical scholars place the death of our Lord Jesus Christ on Nisan 14 in one of the years between 30 AD and 33 AD. The AY years associated with these four crucifixion years were previously summarized. The results of this study strongly support a Nisan 14, 30 AD crucifixion on Wednesday, April 5. A summary of major events between AY 1 and AY 3974 is as follows.

AY Year		Julian Dates
1	Year Adam left Eden	Sept/Oct, 3944-Sept/Oct, 3943
		2454 Years
2454	Year of the Exodus	Sept/Oct, 1491-Sept/Oct, 1490
2454	Exodus	Sept/Oct, 1491-Sept/Oct, 1490
		480 Years
2933	Solomon's 4th Year	Sept/Oct, 1012-Sept/Oct, 1011
2930	Solomon's 4th Year	Sept/Oct, 1012-Sept/Oct, 1011
		4 Years
2933	Solomon's 1st Year	Sept/Oct, 1015-Sept/Oct, 1014
2930	Solomon's 1st Year	Sept/Oct, 1015-Sept/Oct, 1014
		40 Years
2969	Solomon's 40th Year	Sept/Oct, 976-Sept/Oct, 975
2970	Divided Kingdom (Judah)	Sept/Oct, 975-Sept/Oct, 974
	Jerusalem fell, July 18, 586 BC	389 Years
3358	Last Year of Judah	Sept/Oct, 587-Sept/Oct, 586
3358	Last Year of Judah	Sept/Oct, 587-Sept/Oct, 586
		129 Years
3487	Start of Daniel's Prophecy	Sept/Oct, 458 Tishri 1
3487	Start of Daniel's Prophecy	Sept/Oct, 458-Sept/Oct, 457
		483 Years
3970	End of Daniel's 69th Week	Sept/Oct, 25 AD-Sept/Oct, 26 AD
3971	Beginning: Ministry of Christ	Sept/Oct, 26 AD-Sept/Oct, 27 AD
		3.5 Jewish Years
3974	Crucifixion of Christ	Nisan 14, 30 AD
		Wednesday, April 5

This concludes an unbroken chronology between when Adam and Eve were cast out of the Garden of Eden and the crucifixion of our Lord Jesus Christ. It is hoped that this study will help to convince any Christian that the word of God is true and it is reliable and historically accurate. However, if this study might somehow win only one soul to eternal salvation by believing that Jesus Christ is the only Son of God…He died on the cross for your sins….and He will return someday to claim those who believe upon His holy name; then all of the many hours and days spent on this study will have been worth it.

He which testifieth these things saith, Surely I come quickly. Amen.

*Thoughts and
Things………*

Appendix A

Evidentialism–The Bible and Assyrian Chronology

by Larry Pierce

April 1, 2001

Featured In

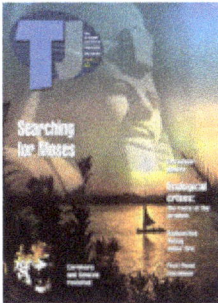

Summary

In the past 100 years, various reconstructions of Assyrian chronology have been used to undermine the accepted chronology of the period of the divided kingdom. Edwin Thiele's work on Hebrew chronology–as reinterpreted in the light of Assyrian chronology–has become widely accepted by evangelicals and secular historians. However, Assyrian chronology is not as simple as Thiele would have us believe, and there is no reason to bend the Bible to fit the current reconstructions of Assyrian chronology.

It is refreshing to see the creation movement maturing from the strictly evidential approach of the 1960s and 1970s to the Biblically based, axiomatic approach of recent years. This represents a shift in emphasis from science to philosophy, from looking at theories to looking at how to build theories and interpret facts. The emphasis is on the authority of the Bible. Our understanding of the sciences pertaining to origins has been greatly enhanced as a result of using this *Bible first* approach.

One area which has been almost totally untouched is the area of Biblical chronologies, especially for the period when Israel was divided into the kingdoms of Israel and Judah. Chronological problems are similar to the problems faced by the creation movement in dealing with the early chapters of Genesis. However, the arguments and logic are not simple, and most people surrender when confronted by a wordy argument. Reduced to the simplest terms, we have the same problem we face in Genesis, stated in a more complex way–**'What is your authority?'** In this article we will concentrate mainly on the latest accepted Assyrian chronology as popularized by Thiele. (There is little to be gained by examining previous reconstructions that have now been abandoned. These older, abandoned reconstructions should make us very wary of accepting newer models that likewise conflict with the Bible.) It will be shown how Thiele has manipulated the Biblical data to make it fit with the current understanding of Assyrian chronology. The following statement sets the tone for Thiele's work:

'Between the absolute chronology of the Hebrews and that of their neighbours there can be no conflict. If the Biblical chronology seems to be at variance with Assyrian chronology, it may be because of errors in the Hebrew records, but it may also be because the data preserved in these records are not correctly understood.'[1]

Thiele's book, *The Mysterious Numbers of the Hebrew Kings* has been published three times, 1951,[1] 1965[2] and 1983.[3] There are major revisions between each printing. Material from all three printings and, wherever possible, the latest printing will be referred to herein. Reference will also be made to the work by Leslie McFall,[4] which has some minor refinements to Thiele's chronology.

General problems with ancient history

Before we start, let us look at two well documented examples from ancient history that illustrate some of the problems we face in trying to reconstruct an accurate history. Both of these deal with the life of Alexander the Great and have abundant documentation from the ancient writers.

On the west side of the Hyphasis River in India, Alexander had his troops construct an oversized camp containing extra large furnishings. He did this to give an exaggerated impression of his army's stature and deeds to those who saw them in later times. If an Indian archaeologist discovered these a few hundred years later and did not have access to the historical accounts of Plutarch, Diodorus, Arrian and Curtius, he may be misled and come to wrong conclusions about the invading army of Alexander.

In attacking the citadel of the Mallians in India, Alexander was severely wounded. According to some accounts, even those who were present when this happened disagree among themselves in important details. The Latin historian Curtius wryly observed that so great was the carelessness of those old historians, it was hard to know what to believe!

These two items illustrate the problems faced when dealing with secular history. First, the accounts may have been deliberately misrepresented to glorify the doer of the deeds. Secondly, even eyewitness accounts may conflict. (Anyone who has sat on a jury will vouch for that.) Assyrian chronology suffers from all this, and more, as we shall see. Those who accept the authority of the Hebrew Scriptures know that only the records of the Bible are accurate when compared with secular accounts for the same historical period.

The problem

The problem with Biblical chronology is that it does not fit with our current understanding of Assyrian chronology. Depending on whom you read, the Biblical chronology is too long by about 40 to 50 years. The latest reconstruction by Thiele is but one of many attempts in the past 100 years to adjust the Biblical account to match the current conjectured chronology of the Assyrians. Thiele very creatively manipulated the Biblical data to eliminate about 40 years of history. He did this by constructing viceroy relationships to collapse the length of a king's reign by overlapping it with the king's predecessor. He is the first to have made such a detailed reconstruction of the divided kingdom using this approach, although variations on his scheme can be traced back at least 75 years before him. By this, he gave his shortened chronology much credibility. Having it published by a well-known university press, instead of by his church denomination, considerably helped his cause.

There are three dates where Assyrian and Biblical histories are supposed to intersect. They are the main reason for abridging the traditional Biblical chronology which is longer. These dates are 841 BC, 853 BC and 701 BC.[5] There is no mention in the Bible of the events that supposedly happened in the years of the first two dates. Their intersection with Biblical history rests entirely on secular interpretations of Assyrian records, not on Biblical data.

841 BC

This date is documented on the Black Obelisk of Shalmaneser III. Thiele states:

'The date of 841 is established by Jehu's payment of tribute to Shalmaneser III of Assyria in that year and, together with 853, becomes one of the basic dates in Hebrew history. Although the Bible makes no mention of Jehu's payment of tribute to Assyria, Shalmaneser III mentions that in the eighteenth year of his reign he went against "Hazael of Aram", shut him up in "Damascus, his royal city", and "received tribute of the men of Tyre, Sidon and of Jehu, the son of Omri".'

The 'Black Obelisk' inscribed with the account of the campaigns of Shalmaneser III, king of Assyria. The obelisk was discovered in 1846 in Kalhu (modern Nimrud).

From the Bible, it is easy to deduce that Jehu started to reign about 12 years after the death of Ahab. This would fix the date for the death of Ahab at 853 BC and the first year of Jehu at 841 BC.

At first glance, this seems to be impeccable evidence for discarding the longer Biblical chronology where Ahab died in 897 BC and Jehu started to reign about 885 BC If this were so, obviously Jehu would be dead and gone long before Shalmaneser III started to reign.

However, remember that very few archaeologists are Christians and most would reject the historicity and authority of the Word of God. Therefore, expect anything they find to be *interpreted* in a way that is unhelpful to Bible-believing Christians. Once these *interpretations* are published, they seem to get a life all of their own, and many *Christian* authors echo them without bothering to check what was actually found. This was the very reason the Christian Church caved in on billions of years then evolution, and why many churches ignore the historical portions of the Old Testament as being unreliable. It is a slippery road to liberalism that is well greased with the opinions of scholars.

Fossils and radiometric dating seemed to provide the *absolute* truth as to the age of the world until someone took the time to see what assumptions were involved. Likewise, in this case it is extremely important to determine what was actually found and ignore the *just-so stories* that became associated with the find. Many sources were researched before one was discovered that was honest enough to admit what was really found and what it meant.

The basis of what Thiele stated comes from the inscriptions found on the Black Obelisk of Shalmaneser III. We found the following in a Bible dictionary:

'The text depicts Shalmaneser's triumphs over several kingdoms of Syria and the West. Of special interest to Bible students is one panel in the second row in which a bearded Semite bows before the king while his servants present gifts. The text refers to the humble suppliant as Jehu, son of Omri (a name by which all Israelite kings were identified, whether of the Omride dynasty or not) and describes the gifts he brought. The event, apparently from the year 841 BC, gives us the earliest surviving picture of an Israelite and shows how such a person might have appeared to an Assyrian sculptor. There is no evidence, however, that the obelisk was actually depicting the Israelite monarch Jehu.'[6]

So, except for the fact we are not certain of the actual date of the obelisk and who is in the picture, we are in fine shape! Just as the Israelite kings were described as *sons of Omri*, when many were not, likewise many may have been identified with the name *Jehu*. This mode of expression seems to be common in Hebrewism. In Matthew 1, Christ himself is called the 'son of Abraham' and the 'son of David' when in fact He was separated from these men by many generations. Also, the name for a particular person may not resemble the name given to him in another country. Ancient history abounds with examples of this.

Much more damaging is the evidence uncovered by Faulstich. He documents that much of the information on the Black Obelisk that is attributed to Shalmaneser was taken from earlier monuments.[7] Are we so egocentric as to think historical revisionism is a recent phenomenon? This plagiarism was so common in Assyrian history that the father of Shalmaneser III pronounced a special curse on kings who tried to steal his fame by ascribing to themselves deeds he had done. Faulstich goes on to document inconsistencies among the Black Obelisk, the Tigris Inscriptions, the Statue Inscriptions and the Bull-Colossi.

This type of historical revisionism results in the collapsing of historical events into a shorter time frame. From the inspired Biblical accounts, we know this has happened. Rarely do we find historians mentioning the problems with Assyrian chronology when they use Assyrian data to amend the Biblical chronology. Thiele and McFall are very silent on this. As in the case of Alexander's wound, mentioned earlier, we will likely never know the correct story.

853 BC

This was the date of the famous battle of Qarqar that was fought between Shalmaneser III and an anti-Assyrian coalition. The Bible dictionary lists *A-ha-ab-bu Sir'-i-la-a-a* as supplying 2,000 chariots and 10,000 men for this battle. *A-ha-AB-Bu* is taken to mean *Ahab*. *Sir'I-la-a-a* is taken to mean *Israel*.[8] This is given as proof positive that the Ahab of 1 Kings was present at this battle.

This word may be translated *Ahab* but that does not prove that it was the King Ahab of the Bible. Several possibilities exist. In ancient history, it is the rule, not the exception, that different writers gave the same person different names. Consider this example:

'After Laborosoarchodus, who was disposed of by his subjects for his acts of villainy, Nebuchadnezzar's grandchild by his daughter succeeded him. The new king was his son by Evilmerodach and called by Berosus, *Nabonidus*, but by Herodotus, *Labynitus*, by Abydenus, *Nabannidochus* and by Daniel, *Belshazzar* or *Baltazar*.'[9]

Nebuchadnezzar's grandson had at least four or five different names depending on who wrote the history! Just because you see a historian use a name that is the same as a name mentioned elsewhere by a different historian, you cannot assume both historians are referring to the same individual.

You must study the context to be sure. This is the major failing of Assyrian history. Because the material is so scanty and fragmentary, we often do not have enough information to be absolutely sure of whom we are reading about and whether we are interpreting it correctly. However, that has never stopped a scholar from spinning a good story about what he thinks it says. If he has enough prestige, his story will soon become gospel.

Another possibility is that the person in command of the force was a general of a king of Israel and not the king himself. Saul, David, Solomon and Pekah had generals over their armies, and the names are recorded in the Scriptures.

The story may be improbable given the events that happened during Ahab's reign. He suffered a three-year drought that destroyed most of the livestock in the kingdom. A few years before this alleged event at Qarqar took place, Ahab was invaded by Benhadad. In that battle, Ahab was scarcely able to muster 7,000 soldiers much less any chariots or horsemen. In 1 Kings 20:1—21 there is a detailed description of this battle. However, the story is that he sent 10,000 troops and 2,000 chariots to this battle at Qarqar. This was no small force, especially considering the large number of chariots.

Another explanation was touched on previously–historical revisionism. The events described here likely happened, but at an earlier date, since the inscriptions were most likely doctored by a later king to enhance his glory. As mentioned previously, Assyrian kings made a practice of stealing inscriptions of glorious events from earlier Assyrian kings and adding them to their own monuments to enhance their glory.

No doubt some king from Israel sent an army to the battle of Qarqar. However, it was not likely King Ahab. We shall see later when we look at the Biblical problems, how much the texts of the Bible were twisted to force Ahab into this later time period when the battle of Qarqar took place.

701 BC

We are not certain why this date is essential to Thiele's chronology. If Thiele had not made this synchronization with Hezekiah, he would have had much less criticism of his scheme. Thiele conjectures that this was the date that Sennacherib attacked Hezekiah in the 14th year of his (Hezekiah's) reign (2 Kings 18:13). By forcing this synchronization, Thiele ignores several synchronizations of the Biblical text. We shall discuss this under the heading of the 'Third Biblical example'.

Biblical considerations

The main problem with all attempts to harmonize the Bible with Assyrian chronology is the violence it does to the Scriptures. To remove about 40 years from a chronology as well defined as the one we have in the Bible, requires some very creative exegesis or, worse, discarding numbers that do not fit our preconceived ideas. This is a classic case of starting with evidence outside the Bible and making the Bible conform to it. In the preface to the third edition, Thiele stated:

'The only basis for a sound chronology of the period to be discussed is a completely unbiased use of Biblical statements in the light of all other knowledge we can bring to bear on the problem, notably the history and chronology of the ancient Near East.'[10]

This statement indicates Thiele's approach to the Word of God and secular history. Thiele used the supposed dates from Assyrian chronology, which allegedly intersect with the Biblical chronology, to force-fit the Biblical data into the mould of secular chronology. We will only deal with the most serious problems in his work.

First Biblical example

To collapse the Biblical history, you must create overlapping reigns of kings so that the total length of the period is significantly shortened. The fun really begins with Uzziah. Up until then, the dates on Thiele and McFall's chronology are within a couple of years of the one derived from the longer Biblical chronology.

As we said, there is very little disagreement with the longer reconstruction for the first 150 years, even to the 12-year viceroyship of Jeroboam II with Jehoash. This is not only true for Thiele, but for all reconstructions done in the past 100 years that we have seen published. However, at this point, all the Assyrian-based chronologies diverge from the traditional chronology. Thiele stated that in the 27th year of Jeroboam, Uzziah became sole king and that, before this, he had a viceroy relationship with his father for 24 years. The only rationale for selecting a 24-year period is that Thiele can make it fit with current archaeological expectations. Again, Josephus and all the writers before 1850 never inferred that there was a viceroyship of any length, much less 24 years for Uzziah. The Bible says:

'And they brought him [Amaziah, Uzziah's father] on horses, and he was buried at Jerusalem with his fathers in the city of David. And all the people of Judah took Azariah [Uzziah] who was sixteen years old, and made him king in place of his father Amaziah' (2 Kings 14:20,21).

'In the twenty-seventh year of Jeroboam king of Israel, Azariah [Uzziah] the son of Amaziah king of Judah began to reign. He was sixteen years old when he began to reign, and he reigned fifty-two years in Jerusalem ...' (2 Kings 15:1,2).

By all rules of exegesis, one would conclude that Uzziah was made king after the death of his father when he was 16 years old. This event happened in the 27th year of Jeroboam. Not so according to Thiele and others! A little arithmetic will show that it is rather difficult to be made king 8 years before you were born! For if you came to the throne when you were 16 but had been a viceroy with your father for 24 years already, you were made viceroy 8 years before you were born!

According to Thiele, McFall and others the text is incorrect. They say that it should read in the 3rd year of Jeroboam not the 27th.[11] By happy chance, by having Uzziah as viceroy for 24 years, Thiele can manipulate the rest of the numbers for Uzziah's reign without violating too many synchronisms. **There is no Biblical or sound logical reason for this amendment**.

Before we proceed to the next example, a little historical note is of interest. Thiele was not the first to propose Uzziah's imaginary viceroy relationship. It can also be found in a very old Bible produced around 1900 and in the 1909 *International Standard Bible Encyclopaedia* (*ISBE*).[12] The latter also postulates this non-existent viceroy relationship that Uzziah had with his father for the same 24-year period. However, it creates a 12-year viceroy relationship between Uzziah and his son, Jotham, and has Pekah becoming king in the 52nd year of Uzziah, as one would expect.

Unless one checked the Bible and found out that Pekah ruled for 20 years, one would not notice a problem. However, the *ISBE* chart shows Pekah coming to the throne in 736 BC This means his rule finished in 717 BC, four years *after* the fall of his kingdom of Samaria in 721 BC This is a tad ridiculous. No doubt some wag pointed out this piece of illogic to the theological 'experts' and this view was quietly dropped.

This brings us to the next example and how Thiele found another place to delete these 12 years from the chronology.

Second Biblical example

To delete the 12 years requires incredible ingenuity. Thiele worked on the reign of Pekah just as the *ISBE* had done many years earlier. Read the following Scripture texts carefully:

'In the thirty-ninth year of Azariah [Uzziah] king of Judah, Menahem the son of Gadi began to reign over Israel, ten years in Samaria' (2 Kings 15:17).

'And Menahem slept with his fathers. And Pekahiah his son reigned in his place. In the fiftieth year of Uzziah [Azariah] king of Judah, Pekahiah the son of Menahem began to reign over Israel in Samaria, two years. . . . But Pekah the son of Remaliah, a commander of his, conspired against him and struck him in Samaria, in the palace of the king's house, with Argob and Arieh, and fifty men of the Gileadites with him. And he killed him and reigned in his place. . . . In the fifty-second year of Uzziah [Azariah] king of Judah, Pekah the son of Remaliah began to reign over Israel in Samaria, twenty years' (2 Kings 15:22—27).

Tables 1&2. *The traditional view for the chronology of the Hebrew kings. Accession dating[13] is used in the above examples.*

Uzziah Regal Year	Northern Kingdom King	
39	Manahem	10 years (2 Kings 15:17)
50	Pekahiah	2 years (2 Kings 15:23)
52	Pekah	20 years (2 Kings 15:27

39	40	41	42	43	44	45	46	47	48	49	50	51	52	Years of Uzziah
	1	2	3	4	5	6	7	8	9	10				Reign of Manahem
											1	2		Reign of Pekahiah
												1		Reign of Peka

Tables 3&4. *Thiele and McFall's view of the chronology of the Hebrew kings.*

39	40	41	42	43	44	45	46	47	48	49	50	51	52	Years of Uzziah
	1	2	3	4	5	7	7	8	9	10				Reign of Menaham
											1	2		Reign of Pekahiah
	1	2	3	4	5	6	7	8	9	10	11	12	13	Reign of Pekah

Uzziah Regal Year	Northern Kingdom King	
38	Zechariah	6 months (2 Kings 15:8)
39	Shallum	1 month (2 Kings 15:13)
39	Menahem	10 years (2 Kings 15:17)
50	Pekahiah	2 years (2 Kings 15:23)
52	Pekah	20 years (2 Kings 15:27)

There are two views on how to understand this passage.

a. The traditional view

The traditional view based on a straightforward reading of the Bible, and not influenced by modern scholarship, is that: 1) Menahem reigned for 10 years, followed by his son, Pekahiah, who reigned for two years (Tables 1 & 2); 2) Pekahiah was murdered by his commander, Pekah, who in turn reigned for 20 years. By normal rules of exegesis, this would be the most normal way to understand the text.

b. The Thiele and McFall view

Both Thiele and McFall would instead have it look like Tables 3 & 4 (above).

No Biblical justification is given for starting the reign of Pekah in the 39th year of Uzziah. They say Pekah was a rival king in Gilead to both Menahem and Pekahiah and Pekah really started his sole reign in the 52nd year of Uzziah. The Bible says that Pekah was Pekahiah's captain, not a rival king reigning in Gilead. Further, the Bible says Pekah started to reign in the 52nd year not the 39th year of Uzziah.

Let us look at all the kings of the Northern Kingdom who were dated by the reign of Uzziah (Table 4).

By all rules of exegesis, one would think these kings in the Northern Kingdom reigned sequentially. Not so if you have the guide of enlightened scholarship. It is obvious that Menahem and Pekahiah's reigns overlap the first 12 years of Pekah's reign–or is it? Both Thiele and McFall contort the obvious meaning of the Bible (2 Kings 15:25, 27). **There is no Biblical justification for this**. Indeed, they use different rules when it suits them. In the first example we gave, they said the synchronization date referred to the time when Uzziah was made viceroy. In this case, they say the synchronization refers to the time when Pekah became sole king. You cannot have it both ways and, no matter which way Thiele and McFall go, they create logical inconsistencies in the text. Further, the 'just-so story' they created about Pekah is pure fiction and contradicts the Bible (2 Kings 15:25). Pekah was a commander of Pekahiah's and not a rival king to him!

Third Biblical example

Thiele holds to a synchronization for the year 701 BC to make it the 14th year of the reign of Hezekiah when Sennacherib invaded Judah. Thiele is forced to discard three synchronizations to do this. According to the Bible:

a. Hezekiah started to reign in the 3rd year of Hoshea (2 Kings 18:1, 2).

b. In the 6th year of Hezekiah and the 9th year of Hoshea, Israel was captured (2 Kings 18:10).

c. In the 12th year of Ahaz, Hoshea began to reign over Israel (2 Kings 17:1).

Thiele claims these are late amendments to the Biblical text, and is honest enough to admit he cannot make these verses fit his chronology. In forcing this synchronization, Thiele has the reign of Hezekiah and his son, Manasseh, co-reigning for at least 11 years. There is no Biblical evidence to support this, aside from this forced synchronization.

Thiele also runs into problems with the secular chronology of Babylon. The Bible says that Hezekiah was visited by representatives from Merodach-Baladan, the king of Babylon (2 Kings 20:12). According to our understanding of Ptolemy's canon, this king ruled in Babylon from 721—710 BC and then died. If Thiele did not try to force this connection with Sennacherib for the year 701 BC, he would not have had this problem.

According to Assyrian chronology, this *Sennacherib* went on and reigned for a number of years after his invasion of Judah. The Bible states he returned to his own land and was killed by his sons (2 Kings 19:36, 37). No great time is implied between the unsuccessful invasion and his untimely death. According to Tobit in the Apocrypha, Sennacherib returned and conducted some ethnic cleansing to rid the land of Jews. About 55 days after his return, he was murdered by his two sons (APC Tobit 1:15—22). Verse 15 states that Sennacherib's 'estate was troubled'. This may refer to the loss of the 185,000 men in the campaign against Hezekiah (2 Kings 19:35), and would account for Sennacherib's fury against any Jews he found.

McFall tries to salvage the synchronisms that Thiele discards by saying Hezekiah reigned as viceroy with his father for the first 16 years of his reign. Then he commenced his sole reign after the death of his father in 715 BC. Thereby, the synchronizations Thiele could not make fit, McFall does. (This solution is not new and was proposed 40 years ago in the *New Bible Dictionary*. Thiele never accepted it.) This creates some real exegetical problems, for in the 6th year of Hezekiah, Israel fell and in the 14th year Hezekiah was invaded by Sennacherib. By all rules of logic, you would assume about 8 years elapsed between these events. Wrong, according to this 'New Math'! Over 22 years elapsed if you use Thiele's dates of 723 BC for the fall of Israel and 701 BC for the invasion by Sennacherib! McFall tries to wiggle out of this by claiming the first date (6th year) was from the time Hezekiah was made viceroy with his father and the second date (14th year) was dated from the time Hezekiah became sole king. How would anyone know this if they were reading just the Bible?

Earlier Bible dictionaries, like the 1909 *ISBE*, did not require this synchronization and nor do we. The Biblical record does not list all the invasions and battles that Israel and Judah fought. Nations generally avoid documenting their disastrous defeats, so it should come as no surprise that the earlier ill-fated invasion is passed by in silence in the Assyrian records. As previously stated, the name for a particular person may not resemble the name given to him in another country. Ancient history abounds with examples of this.

Other issues

There are many more problems with Thiele's chronology (and McFall's amendments) which space does not permit us to deal with. How much time should be wasted refuting a defective system? Unless there are good Biblical answers for the alleged 24-year vice-regency of Uzziah and the 12-year overlap of Pekah with the other kings of Israel, not to mention the many conflicts introduced by these changes, we should not surrender the older, longer chronology of the Bible.

Since most historians for the Egyptian period have blindly accepted Thiele's dates, they are labouring under a 40- to 50-year error when they try to align Egyptian history with Biblical history. Egyptian history is challenging enough without being handicapped by the errors introduced by Thiele's dubious dating procedures! It is interesting to note the conjecture as to who the pharaoh of the Exodus was in 1446 BC when the Biblical date for the Exodus is actually closer to 1491 BC!

Conclusion

The arbitrary nature in which Thiele, McFall and others handle the Biblical text is obvious. Their methods are no different than the methods of those who came before them and amended the Bible based on what they thought the Assyrian records stated. All who do this create imaginary viceroy relationships when it suits them. Sometimes they count years from when a king became a viceroy, sometimes from when he became sole king. The only reason for this is to escape the logical contradictions created by their incorrect initial assumptions. The longer chronology consistently measures time from when a king became viceroy. This procedure is in accord with the oldest Talmudic understanding of how this was done. Thiele, McFall and others sweep aside methods of interpretation that are derived from the most ancient writers, in favour of a new capricious way of handling the text according to the external dictates of archaeology. Their work has indeed rendered the numbers of the Hebrew kings most mysterious.

Sennacherib, king of Assyria, seated upon his throne before the city of Lachish, and receiving tribute.

Christians have largely abdicated the fields of history and archaeology to those who are worldly-wise. Many have been told, even in Bible colleges, that the historical portions of the Bible are unreliable. This is hardly faith-building! Fifty years ago, most Christians did not have ready access to the wealth of material we have today concerning science and evolution. We can thank Dr Henry Morris and others who have followed in his steps for this. We do not have all the answers about Assyrian chronology and how it fits with the Bible. However, we must learn the same lesson about *history* as we learnt about *science*. True science does not conflict with the Bible. Likewise, true history agrees with and does not refute the Scriptures. Pray that God will raise up Christians in the field of history to help us write a true history that honours the Bible.

Lewis Dabney[14] was a 'voice crying in the wilderness' 140 years ago. He recognized most clearly the problems, and sounded a warning against the dangers of science, *falsely so called*, to the church. No one listened, and the church madly pursued a course of compromise which, but for the grace of God, would have destroyed her. At that time, he said concerning attacks made by geologists against the Bible:

'The authority of the Bible, as our rule of faith, is demonstrated by its own separate and independent evidences, literary history, moral, internal, prophetical. It is found by the geologist in possession of the field, and he must assume the aggressive, and positively dislodge it from its position. The defender of the Bible need only stand on the defensive. That is, the geologist must not content himself with saying that his hypothesis, which is opposed to Bible teachings, is plausible, that it cannot be scientifically refuted, that it may adequately satisfy the requirements of all the physical phenomena to be accounted for. All this is naught, as a successful assault on us. We are not bound to retreat until he has constructed an absolutely exclusive demonstration of his hypothesis; until he has shown, by strict scientific proofs, not only that his hypothesis *may be* the true one, but that *it alone can be* the only true one; that it is impossible any other can exclude it.'[15]

What applies to attacks on the Bible from geology applies equally to attacks from historians and archaeologists. The Bible is the only book that provides a continuous history from Creation up to the death of Nebuchadnezzar (and to early AD). More importantly, the Bible is the inspired Word of God and is without error. Assyrian chronology is not inspired and is fraught with errors. Both Thiele and McFall have too low a view of inspiration. If what they claim is true, why should we ever trust any historical portion in the Bible until it has been interpreted by the 'sure word' of the archaeologist? If we cannot trust the numbers in the Bible, why should we trust the words between the numbers? Are we to trust the fallible word of sinful fallen men who have yet to get their first theory right? Or are we to trust the infallible Word written by God, who has yet to make his first mistake and never will![15]

Addendum:

The author strongly suggests to any critics that before responding to this item, they first download the work cited in footnote 16 and ensure that their arguments are derived from and based on the authority of the Bible.[16]

References

1. Thiele, E., *The Mysterious Numbers of the Hebrew Kings*, University of Chicago Press, Chicago, 1951.

2. Thiele, E., *The Mysterious Numbers of the Hebrew Kings*, William B. Eerdmans Publishing Co., Grand Rapids, 1965.

3. Thiele, E., *The Mysterious Numbers of the Hebrew Kings*, Zondervan Corp., Grand Rapids, 1983.

4. McFall, L., A translation guide to the chronological data in Kings and Chronicles, *Bibliotheca Sacra* **148**(589):3—45, 1991.

5. Thiele, Ref. 3, pp. 103, 104; Thiele, Ref. 2, p. 66; Thiele, Ref. 1, p. 62.

6. Entry, Shalmaneser, Black Obelisk of, *New International Dictionary of Biblical Archaeology*, Zondervan Publishing House, Grand Rapids, p. 409, 1983

7. Faulstich, E.W., *History, Harmony & The Hebrew Kings*, Chronology Books, Spencer, Iowa, pp. 143—157, 1986.

8. Faulstich, Ref. 7, entry, Qarqar, p. 376.

9. Ussher, J., *Annales Veteris Testamenti*, J. Flesher & L. Sadler, London, p. 139, 1650. (This work is in Latin. On the new English translation that is being prepared for publication, the paragraph number is 908.)

10. Thiele, Ref. 3, p. 16; Thiele, Ref. 2, p. vi; Thiele, Ref. 1, p. vi.

11. Thiele, Ref. 3, p. 119; Thiele, Ref. 2, p. 83; Thiele, Ref. 1, p. 68—70. Each edition treats this matter in less detail than the previous edition.

12. Article, Chronology of the Old Testament, *The International Bible Encyclopaedia*, vol. 1, Hendrickson Publishers, Peabody, MA, p. 640, 1929. (The original publication was published in 1909–Editor).

13. Accession dating means that a king did not start counting his years of reign until the Jewish New Year was past. So the length of his reign is really given in the number of Jewish New Years he celebrated. According to the Bible this was in Nisan (Exodus 12:2). According to Thiele and McFall, the godly Southern Kingdom used Tishri (about October) and the ungodly Northern Kingdom used Nisan (about April.) No convincing proof is given except that they say *it works*.

14. Robert Lewis Dabney (1820—1898) was a Presbyterian minister, theologian and author, and was Professor of Theology at Union Theological Seminary, Virginia, for over thirty years.

15. Dabney, R.L., *Discussions of Robert Lewis Dabney*, vol. 3, Banner of Truth Trust, Carlisle, PA, p. 136, 1982.

16. A detailed outline of the longer chronology is available from the author and is available for download. In it, he considers all the numbers in not just Kings and Chronicles but from the prophets as well. All popular problems with the chronology are addressed in detail. This article includes Ussher's Time Line for the Divided Kingdom and Archaeology and the Bible.

Larry Pierce publishes biblically related material as one of his hobbies, and enjoys the study of ancient history. He is retired and lives with his wife, Marion, in Winterbourne, Ontario.

Thoughts and Things………

Appendix B

From Adam

To

The Exodus

Name	Lived (Yrs)	Had Son	At Age		AY YEAR Year Born	Biblical Reference
Adam	930	Seth	130	Creation Yr	1	Gen 5:3
Seth	912	Enosh	105		131	Gen 5:6
Enosh	905	Cainan	90	Methusalah	236	Gen 5:9
Cainan/Kenan	910	Mahalalel	70	Dies	326	Gen 5:12
Mahalalel	895	Jared	65	1657	396	Gen 5:15
Jared	962	Enoch	162	Creation	461	Gen 5:18
Enoch	365	Methuselah	65	Year of Flood	623	Gen 5:21
Methuselah	969	Lamech	187	1657	688	Gen 5:25
Lamech	777	Noah	182	Shem Birth	875	Gen 5:28
Noah-600 @ Flood	950	Shem	502	1559	1057	Gen 5:32
Shem-Gen 11:10-Lived 600 yrs	600	Arphaaxed	100	Arphaaxed Birth	1559	Gen 11:10
Arphaaxed-Born 2Yrs after flood	438	Salah	35	1659	1659	Gen 11:12
Selah	433	Eber	30	Abram Covenant	1694	Gen 11:14
Eber	464	Peleg	34	1729	1724	Gen 11:16
Peleg	239	Reu	30	Abram 75 when	1758	Gen 11:18
Reu	239	Serug	32	enters Canaan	1788	Gen 11:20
Serug	230	Nabor	30	2024	1820	Gen 11:22
Nahor	148	Terah	29	Terah died in	1850	Gen 11:24
Terah	205	Abraham	70	2084	1879	Gen 11:26
Abraham...75 entered Canaan	175	Isaac	100	Abram 100 when	1949	Gen 21:5
Isaac	180	Jacob & Esau	60	Issac born	2049	Gen 25:26
Jacob	147	Joseph	91	2049	2109	See Below
Joseph	110				2200	Gen 50:22

Joseph sold into slavery at age 17 — 2217 / 1728

13 Yrs later at age 30 he is called before Pharoh (Gen 41:46)............. — 2230 | 2230 | 2230 / 1715

7 Years of Plenty follow — 2237 / 1708

Followed by 7 by years of famine — 2244 / 1701

Jacob moves to Egypt at age 130 in second year of famine.......... — 1689 ; 2239 | 2239 / 1706

Jacob lives for 17 Yrs in Egypt, then dies at age 147 [enters at 130, (130 +17)]=147 — 2256 | 2256 | 2256 / 1689

Joseph lives to age 110, and then dies in Yr — 2310 | 2310 / 1635

Now, Abram left at age 75 — 2024 / 1921

It is exactly 430 years to the day that Exodus starts....... — 2454 | Julian Yr.. 1491 / 1490

Since Exodus was in year .... 2454 | 1490 | 2454 | Hence, Creation Year is.. 3944

Moses was born in year.......... 2374 | 1570

The number of years between Josephs death & Moses birth is — 64 | 64

Moses born in Julian Year...... — 1570

Aaron was 3 Years younger, Born i 2371

Note that Terah, Abram's father died in Yr .. — 2084

Abram entered Canaan second time the same year...

...Exodus exactly 430 Yrs later in 2454

	AY	Year
Joseph dies in:	2310	1635
Exodus in	2454	1490
Moses born in:	2374	1570
Adam Expunged	1	3944

Abram born in Yr 1949

Abram 75 when leaves Canaan (Gen 12:4) year............ 2024 | Exodus in Year................. 2454

Abram has Issac 30 yrs later year............. 2049 | Covenant of Circumcision with Abram

Isac Blessed five yrs & name change at age 99 in year................... 2048 | Gen 17:1

later Yr............ 2054 | Abram is 86 when Ishmael born to Hagar.............. 2035 | Gen 16:1

Ishmael was 13 yrs old when circumsized, and abraham w 2048 | Gen 17: 24-25

Exodus in Year................. 2449

Issac born when Abraham was 100 (Gen 21:5)..... 2049

Terah was 205 when he died in Haran (Gen 11:32). 2084 | This proves that Abraham

Abram was age 75 when he left Haran (Gen12:4) i 2024 | left Haran as soon as his father

Therefore, Terah was age 130 when Abram born 2009 | Died

Abram promly left Haran for Canaan when Terah his father died..(Gen 12:1)

Abram is 75 when he leaves Haran | 2084 | 1920

430 years to Exodus — Abram departure to death of Joseph

Joseph dies in.................................. | 2370 | 1634 | 286 | 286

From birth of Moses to Exodus is 80 years | 2513 | 1491 | 366

Subtracting 366 from 430=.. | 64 | Years

From Joseph's death to Moses birth is 64 years

Note: Noah had Shem at age 500, at the year of the flood he was age 600 Shem was age 100 at year of the flood. The flood began in the second month, and Noah was in the ark for one year and 17 days...7 days before rain came (Gen 7:10) Rain began on 17th day of 2cd month (Gen 7:11), and left the ark on 27th day of 2cd month (Gen 8:14)...over one year later. Noah is age 601 and Shem is age 98 when the flood sojourn ended. Two years laer, Shem had Arphaxad. Shem is now 103 .

Note...Gen 5:32 says that Noah had "Shem Ham and Japeth at age 500". However, the order of birth was Japeth, Shem and Ham.Shem was born when Noah was age 502. Shem was age 98 at the year of the flood.

Shem-Ham-Japeth (Gen 5:32, Gen 9:23)

Gen10:21....... Japeth born first

Gen 9:24...... Ham is the Youngest

...Japeth 2 years older than Shem

APPENDIX C

A Compilation of AY Years

And

Julian Calendar Years

For Important Chronological Events

With

Sabbatical and Jubilee Years

Block 1

1	2	3	4	5	6	7
1 3944 3943	2 3943 3942	3 3942 3941	4 3941 3940	5 3940 3939	6 3939 3938	7 3938 3937
8 3937 3936	9 3936 3935	10 3935 3934	11 3934 3933	12 3933 3932	13 3932 3931	14 3931 3930
15 3930 3929	16 3929 3928	17 3928 3927	18 3927 3926	19 3926 3925	20 3925 3924	21 3924 3923
22 3923 3922	23 3922 3921	24 3921 3920	25 3920 3919	26 3919 3918	27 3918 3917	28 3917 3916
29 3916 3915	30 3915 3914	31 3914 3913	32 3913 3912	33 3912 3911	34 3911 3910	35 3910 3909
36 3909 3908	37 3908 3907	38 3907 3906	39 3906 3905	40 3905 3904	41 3904 3903	42 3903 3902
43 3902 3901	44 3901 3900	45 3900 3899	46 3899 3898	47 3898 3897	48 3897 3896	49 3896 3895

Block 2

1	2	3	4	5	6	7
50 3895 3894	51 3894 3893	52 3893 3892	53 3892 3891	54 3891 3890	55 3890 3889	56 3889 3888
57 3888 3887	58 3887 3886	59 3886 3885	60 3885 3884	61 3884 3883	62 3883 3882	63 3882 3881
64 3881 3880	65 3880 3879	66 3879 3878	67 3878 3877	68 3877 3876	69 3876 3875	70 3875 3874
71 3874 3873	72 3873 3872	73 3872 3871	74 3871 3870	75 3870 3869	76 3869 3868	77 3868 3867
78 3867 3866	79 3866 3865	80 3865 3864	81 3864 3863	82 3863 3862	83 3862 3861	84 3861 3860
85 3860 3859	86 3859 3858	87 3858 3857	88 3857 3856	89 3856 3855	90 3855 3854	91 3854 3853
92 3853 3852	93 3852 3851	94 3851 3850	95 3850 3849	96 3849 3848	97 3848 3847	98 3847 3846

Block 3

1	2	3	4	5	6	7
99 3846 3845	100 3845 3844	101 3844 3843	102 3843 3842	103 3842 3841	104 3841 3840	105 3840 3839
106 3839 3838	107 3838 3837	108 3837 3836	109 3836 3835	110 3835 3834	111 3834 3833	112 3833 3832
113 3832 3831	114 3831 3830	115 3830 3829	116 3829 3828	117 3828 3827	118 3827 3826	119 3826 3825
120 3825 3824	121 3824 3823	122 3823 3822	123 3822 3821	124 3821 3820	125 3820 3819	126 3819 3818
127 3818 3817	128 3817 3816	129 3816 3815	130 3815 3814	131 3814 3813	132 3813 3812	133 3812 3811
134 3811 3810	135 3810 3809	136 3809 3808	137 3808 3807	138 3807 3806	139 3806 3805	140 3805 3804
141 3804 3803	142 3803 3802	143 3802 3801	144 3801 3800	145 3800 3799	146 3799 3798	147 3798 3797

⋮   ⋮   ⋮

Block 51

1	2	3	4	5	6	7
2451 1494 1493	2452 1493 1492	2453 1492 1491	2454 1491 1490	2455 1490 1489	2456 1489 1488	2457 1488 1487
2458 1487 1486	2459 1486 1485	2460 1485 1484	2461 1484 1483	2462 1483 1482	2463 1482 1481	2464 1481 1480
2465 1480 1479	2466 1479 1478	2467 1478 1477	2468 1477 1476	2469 1476 1475	2470 1475 1474	2471 1474 1473
2472 1473 1472	2473 1472 1471	2474 1471 1470	2475 1470 1469	2476 1469 1468	2477 1468 1467	2478 1467 1466
2479 1466 1465	2480 1465 1464	2481 1464 1463	2482 1463 1462	2483 1462 1461	2484 1461 1460	2485 1460 1459
2486 1459 1458	2487 1458 1457	2488 1457 1456	2489 1456 1455	2490 1455 1454	2491 1454 1453	2492 1453 1452
2493 1452 1451	2494 1451 1450	2495 1450 1449	2496 1449 1448	2497 1448 1447	2498 1447 1446	2499 1446 1445

Block 52

1	2	3	4	5	6	7
2500 1445 1444	2501 1444 1443	2502 1443 1442	2503 1442 1441	2504 1441 1440	2505 1440 1439	2506 1439 1438
2507 1438 1437	2508 1437 1436	2509 1436 1435	2510 1435 1434	2511 1434 1433	2512 1433 1432	2513 1432 1431
2514 1431 1430	2515 1430 1429	2516 1429 1428	2517 1428 1427	2518 1427 1426	2519 1426 1425	2520 1425 1424
2521 1424 1423	2522 1423 1422	2523 1422 1421	2524 1421 1420	2525 1420 1419	2526 1419 1418	2527 1418 1417
2528 1417 1416	2529 1416 1415	2530 1415 1414	2531 1414 1413	2532 1413 1412	2533 1412 1411	2534 1411 1410
2535 1410 1409	2536 1409 1408	2537 1408 1407	2538 1407 1406	2539 1406 1405	2540 1405 1404	2541 1404 1403
2542 1403 1402	2543 1402 1401	2544 1401 1400	2545 1400 1399	2546 1399 1398	2547 1398 1397	2548 1397 1396

Block 53

1	2	3	4	5	6	7
2549 1396 1395	2550 1395 1394	2551 1394 1393	2552 1393 1392	2553 1392 1391	2554 1391 1390	2555 1390 1389
2556 1389 1388	2557 1388 1387	2558 1387 1386	2559 1386 1385	2560 1385 1384	2561 1384 1383	2562 1383 1382
2563 1382 1381	2564 1381 1380	2565 1380 1379	2566 1379 1378	2567 1378 1377	2568 1377 1376	2569 1376 1375
2570 1375 1374	2571 1374 1373	2572 1373 1372	2573 1372 1371	2574 1371 1370	2575 1370 1369	2576 1369 1368
2577 1368 1367	2578 1367 1366	2579 1366 1365	2580 1365 1364	2581 1364 1363	2582 1363 1362	2583 1362 1361
2584 1361 1360	2585 1360 1359	2586 1359 1358	2587 1358 1357	2588 1357 1356	2589 1356 1355	2590 1355 1354
2591 1354 1353	2592 1353 1352	2593 1352 1351	2594 1351 1350	2595 1350 1349	2596 1349 1348	2597 1348 1347

The Jordon River was crossed by Joshua in March/April of 1450.
Joshua took a little over 6 years to conquer the land to the point when he
divided it up. The entire army then moved the tabernacle to Siloh and constructed
a temple in spring of 1444. The tribes were then sent home and the
Sabbatical year count started. The first Sabbatical year was Sept 1438-Sept 1437.

59

	1			2			3			4			5			6			7		
1	2843	1102	1101	2844	1101	1100	2845	1100	1099	2846	1099	1098	2847	1098	1097	2848	1097	1096	2849	1096	1095
2	2850	1095	1094	2851	1094	1093	2852	1093	1092	2853	1092	1091	2854	1091	1090	2855	1090	1089	2856	1089	1088
3	2857	1088	1087	2858	1087	1086	2859	1086	1085	2860	1085	1084	2861	1084	1083	2862	1083	1082	2863	1082	1081
4	2864	1081	1080	2865	1080	1079	2866	1079	1078	2867	1078	1077	2868	1077	1076	2869	1076	1075	2870	1075	1074
5	2871	1074	1073	2872	1073	1072	2873	1072	1071	2874	1071	1070	2875	1070	1069	2876	1069	1068	2877	1068	1067
6	2878	1067	1066	2879	1066	1065	2880	1065	1064	2881	1064	1063	2882	1063	1062	2883	1062	1061	2884	1061	1060
7	2885	1060	1059	2886	1059	1058	2887	1058	1057	2888	1057	1056	2889	1056	1055	2890	1055	1054	2891	1054	1053

60

	1			2			3			4			5			6			7		
1	2892	1053	1052	2893	1052	1051	2894	1051	1050	2895	1050	1049	2896	1049	1048	2897	1048	1047	2898	1047	1046
2	2899	1046	1045	2900	1045	1044	2901	1044	1043	2902	1043	1042	2903	1042	1041	2904	1041	1040	2905	1040	1039
3	2906	1039	1038	2907	1038	1037	2908	1037	1036	2909	1036	1035	2910	1035	1034	2911	1034	1033	2912	1033	1032
4	2913	1032	1031	2914	1031	1030	2915	1030	1029	2916	1029	1028	2917	1028	1027	2918	1027	1026	2919	1026	1025
5	2920	1025	1024	2921	1024	1023	2922	1023	1022	2923	1022	1021	2924	1021	1020	2925	1020	1019	2926	1019	1018
6	2927	1018	1017	2928	1017	1016	2929	1016	1015	2930	1015	1014	2931	1014	1013	2932	1013	1012	2933	1012	1011
7	2934	1011	1010	2935	1010	1009	2936	1009	1008	2937	1008	1007	2938	1007	1006	2939	1006	1005	2940	1005	1004

61

	1			2			3			4			5			6			7		
1	2941	1004	1003	2942	1003	1002	2943	1002	1001	2944	1001	1000	2945	1000	999	2946	999	998	2947	998	997
2	2948	997	996	2949	996	995	2950	995	994	2951	994	993	2952	993	992	2953	992	991	2954	991	990
3	2955	990	989	2956	989	988	2957	988	987	2958	987	986	2959	986	985	2960	985	984	2961	984	983
4	2962	983	982	2963	982	981	2964	981	980	2965	980	979	2966	979	978	2967	978	977	2968	977	976
5	2969	976	975	2970	975	974	2971	974	973	2972	973	972	2973	972	971	2974	971	970	2975	970	969
6	2976	969	968	2977	968	967	2978	967	966	2979	966	965	2980	965	964	2981	964	963	2982	963	962
7	2983	962	961	2984	961	960	2985	960	959	2986	959	958	2987	958	957	2988	957	956	2989	956	955

66

	1			2			3			4			5			6			7		
1	3186	759	758	3187	758	757	3188	757	756	3189	756	755	3190	755	754	3191	754	753	3192	753	752
2	3193	752	751	3194	751	750	3195	750	749	3196	749	748	3197	748	747	3198	747	746	3199	746	745
3	3200	745	744	3201	744	743	3202	743	742	3203	742	741	3204	741	740	3205	740	739	3206	739	738
4	3207	738	737	3208	737	736	3209	736	735	3210	735	734	3211	734	733	3212	733	732	3213	732	731
5	3214	731	730	3215	730	729	3216	729	728	3217	728	727	3218	727	726	3219	726	725	3220	725	724
6	3221	724	723	3222	723	722	3223	722	721	3224	721	720	3225	720	719	3226	719	718	3227	718	717
7	3228	717	716	3229	716	715	3230	715	714	3231	714	713	3232	713	712	3233	712	711	3234	711	710

72

	1			2			3			4			5			6			7		
1	3480	465	464	3481	464	463	3482	463	462	3483	462	461	3484	461	460	3485	460	459	3486	459	458
2	3487	458	457	3488	457	456	3489	456	455	3490	455	454	3491	454	453	3492	453	452	3493	452	451
3	3494	451	450	3495	450	449	3496	449	448	3497	448	447	3498	447	446	3499	446	445	3500	445	444
4	3501	444	443	3502	443	442	3503	442	441	3504	441	440	3505	440	439	3506	439	438	3507	438	437
5	3508	437	436	3509	436	435	3510	435	434	3511	434	433	3512	433	432	3513	432	431	3514	431	430
6	3515	430	429	3516	429	428	3517	428	427	3518	427	426	3519	426	425	3520	425	424	3521	424	423
7	3522	423	422	3523	422	421	3524	421	420	3525	420	419	3526	419	418	3527	418	417	3528	417	416

69	1			2			3			4			5			6			7		
1	3333	612	611	3334	611	610	3335	610	609	3336	609	608	3337	608	607	3338	607	606	3339	606	605
2	3340	605	604	3341	604	603	3342	603	602	3343	602	601	3344	601	600	3345	600	599	3346	599	598
3	3347	598	597	3348	597	596	3349	596	595	3350	595	594	3351	594	593	3352	593	592	3353	592	591
4	3354	591	590	3355	590	589	3356	589	588	3357	588	587	3358	587	586	3359	586	585	3360	585	584
5	3361	584	583	3362	583	582	3363	582	581	3364	581	580	3365	580	579	3366	579	578	3367	578	577
6	3368	577	576	3369	576	575	3370	575	574	3371	574	573	3372	573	572	3373	572	571	3374	571	570
7	3375	570	569	3376	569	568	3377	568	567	3378	567	566	3379	566	565	3380	565	564	3381	564	563

82	1			2			3			4			5			6			7		
1	3970	25	26	3971	26	27	3972	27	28	3973	28	29	3974	29	30	3975	30	31	3976	31	32
2	3977	32	33	3978	33	34	3979	34	35	3980	35	36	3981	36	37	3982	37	38	3983	38	39
3	3984	39	40	3985	40	41	3986	41	42	3987	42	43	3988	43	44	3989	44	45	3990	45	46
4	3991	46	47	3992	47	48	3993	48	49	3994	49	50	3995	50	51	3996	51	52	3997	52	53
5	3998	53	54	3999	54	55	4000	55	56	4001	56	57	4002	57	58	4003	58	59	4004	59	60
6	4005	60	61	4006	61	62	4007	62	63	4008	63	64	4009	64	65	4010	65	66	4011	66	67
7	4012	67	68	4013	68	69	4014	69	70	4015	70	71	4016	71	72	4017	72	73	4018	73	74

A Table of Sabbatical and Jubilee Years

The Jordon River was crossed by Joshua in March/April of 1450. Joshua took a little over 6 years to conquer the land to the point when he divided it up. The entire army then moved the tabernacle to Siloh and constructed a temple in spring of 1444. The tribes were then sent home and the Sabbatical year count started. The first Sabbatical year was Sept 1438-Sept 1437.

First Jubilee..1395-1394

Sabbatical Years							Jubilee Yr	Cycle	Sabbatical Years							Jubilee Yr	Cycle
1	2	3	4	5	6	7			1	2	3	4	5	6	7		
1438	1431	1424	1417	1410	1403	1396	1395	1	1389	1382	1375	1368	1361	1354	1347	1346	2
1340	1333	1326	1319	1312	1305	1298	1297	3	1291	1284	1277	1270	1263	1256	1249	1248	4
1242	1235	1228	1221	1214	1207	1200	1199	5	1193	1186	1179	1172	1165	1158	1151	1150	6
1144	1137	1130	1123	1116	1109	1102	1101	7	1095	1088	1081	1074	1067	1060	1053	1052	8
1046	1039	1032	1025	1018	1011	1004	1003	9	997	990	983	976	969	962	955	954	10
948	941	934	927	920	913	906	905	11	899	892	885	878	871	864	857	856	12
850	843	836	829	822	815	808	807	13	801	794	787	780	773	766	759	758	14
752	745	738	731	724	717	710	709	15	703	696	689	682	675	668	661	660	16
654	647	640	633	626	619	612	611	17	605	598	591	584	577	570	563	562	18
556	549	542	535	528	521	514	513	19	507	500	493	486	479	472	465	464	20
458	451	444	437	430	423	416	415	21	409	402	395	388	381	374	367	366	22
360	353	346	339	332	325	318	317	23	311	304	297	290	283	276	269	268	24
262	255	248	241	234	227	220	219	25	213	206	199	192	185	178	171	170	26
164	157	150	143	136	129	122	121	27	115	108	101	94	87	80	73	72	28
66	59	52	45	38	31	24	23	29	17	10	3	5	12	19	26	27	30
33	40	47	54	61	68	75	76	31	82	89	96	103	110	117	124	125	32
131	138	145	152	159	166	173	174	33	180	187	194	201	208	215	222	223	34

APPENDIX D

A Compilation

of

Judges

And

Years of Reign

		Julian Year Dates			Duration		AY Years	
							Sept/Oct	Sept/Oct
Exodus	April	1490	April	1489	40	Exodus	2454	2455
		1451		1450			2494	2495
Joshua	April	1450	April	1449	25	Joshua	2494	2495
	April	1426	April	1425			2519	2520
Elders	April	1425	April	1424	20	Elders	2519	2520
	April	1406	April	1405			2539	2540
Judges	April	1405	April	1404	40	Othiniel	2539	2540
		1386		1365			2579	2580
	April	1365	April	1364	80	Ehud	2579	2580
		1286		1285			2559	2560
	April	1285	April	1284	40	Deborah	2659	2660
		1246		1245			2699	2700
	April	1245	April	1244	7	Mideonite Opression	2699	2700
		1239		1238			2706	2707
	April	1238	April	1237	40	Gideon	2706	2707
		1199		1198			2746	2747
	April	1198	April	1197	3	Abimilech	2746	2747
		1196		1195			2749	2750
	April	1195	April	1194	23	Tola	2749	2750
		1173		1172			2772	2773
	April	1172	April	1171	22	Jair	2772	2773
		1151		1150			2794	2795

		Julian Year Dates					AY Years	
							Sept/Oct	Sept/Oct
Judges	April 1150 1145	April	1149 1144	6	Jephthah		2794 2799	2795 2800
	April 1144 1138	April	1143 1137	7	Ibzan		2800 2806	2801 2807
	April 1137 1128	April	1136 1127	10	Elon		2807 2816	2808 2817
	April 1127 1120	April	1126 1119	8	Abdon		2817 2824	2818 2825
	April 1119 1100	April	1118 1099	20	Sampson		2825 2844	2826 2845
	April 1099	April	1098	1	No King		2845	2846
	April 1098 1096	April	1097 1095	3	Samuel		2846 2848	2847 2849
	April 1095 1058	April	1094 1057	38	Samuel & Saul		2849 2886	2850 2887
Kings	April 1057 1056	April	1056 1055	2	Saul		2887 2888	2888 2889
	April 1055	Sept	1055		Transition 6 Months		2889	2890
	Sept 1055 1016	Sept	1054 1015	40	David		2890 2929	
	Sept 1015 976	Sept	1014 975	40	Solomon		2930 2969	
		Divided Kingdom.......................... 975-974				AY 2970		

Exodus to Solomon's 4th Yr	479
Exodus to Solomon's 40th Yr	515

Sept/Oct AY 2454		March/April AY 2494		March/April AY 2539		March/April AY 2659		March/April AY 2706		March/April AY 2749		March/April AY 2794
	March/April AY 2454			March/April AY 2519		March/April AY 2579		March/April AY 2699		March/April AY 2746		March/April AY 2772
6 Mos	Exodus from Egypt	Jordan River Crossed	25 Yrs	20 Yrs	40 Yrs	80 Yrs	40 Yrs	7 Yrs	40 Yrs	3 Yrs	23 Yrs	22 Yrs
			Joshua Rules	Elders Rule	Othniel	Ehud	Deborah & Shagmar	Mideonite Opression	Gideon	Abimilech	Tola	Jair
	Conquest of Heshbon late in the 39th year of the Exodus led by Moses			Joshua 24:31	Judges 3:11	Judges 3:30-31	Judges 4-5	Judges 6:1	Judges 6-8	Judges 9:22-5	Judges 10:1-2	Judges 10:3
					Assyrian Opression 8 Yrs	Moabite Opression 18 Yrs	Cannanite Opression 20 Yrs					Ammonite Opression 18 Yrs
					Judges 3:8	Judges 3:14	Judges 3:11	300 Years (Judges 11:15-26)				Judges 10:6-9
6 Mos	40 Yrs											

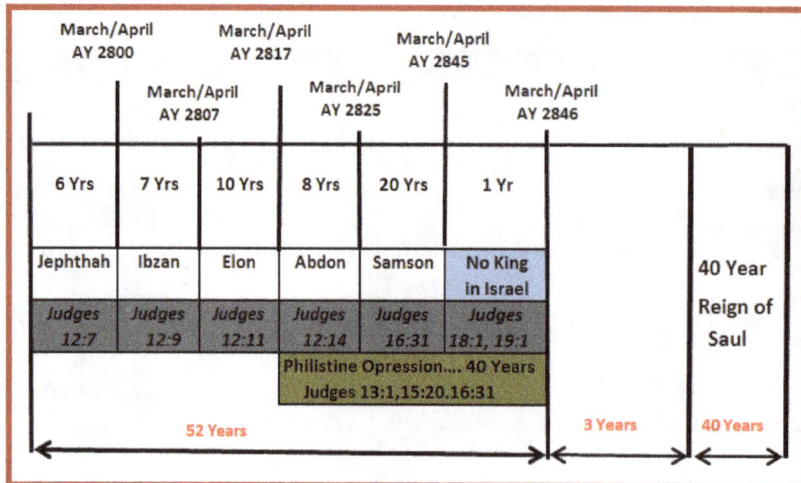

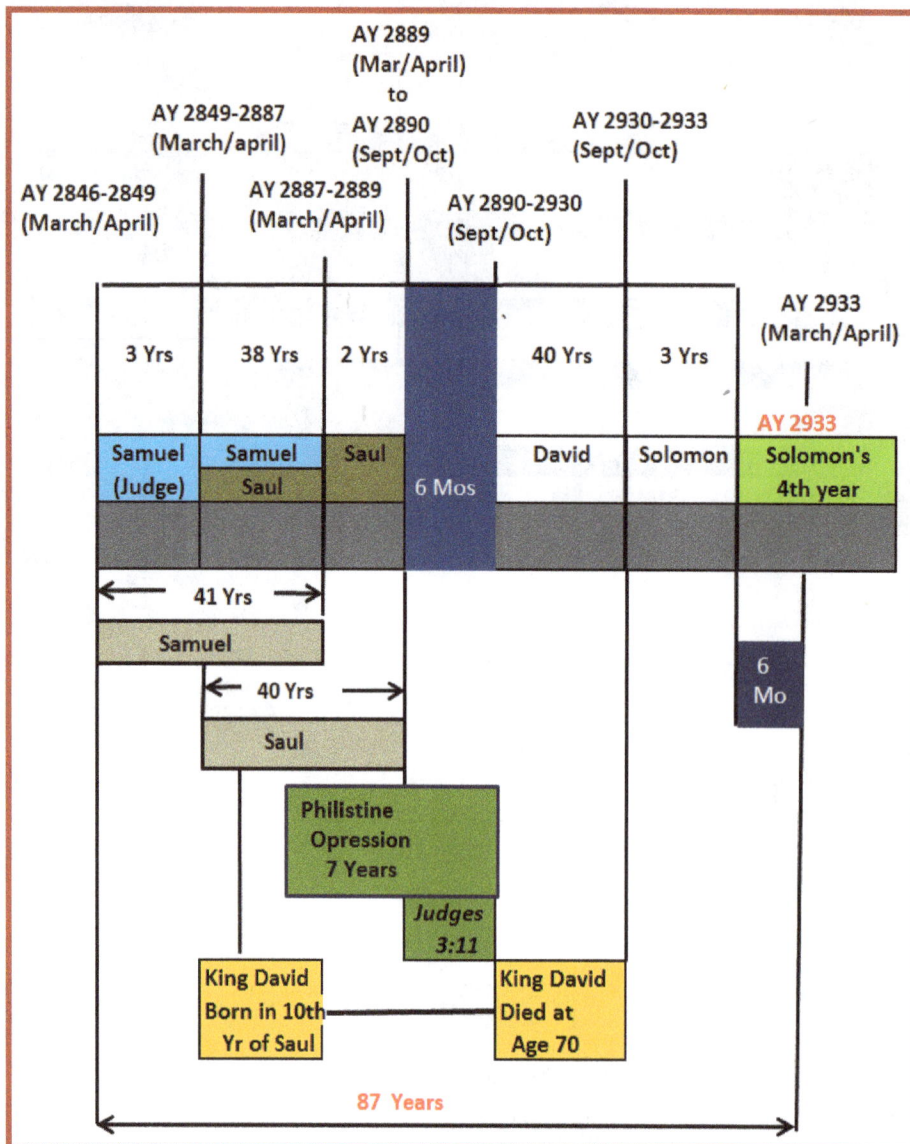

170

APPENDIX E

A Record of Kings

and

When They Reigned

Southern Kingdom Kings			
Name of King Duration of Reign			
Rehoboam	17	Years	I Kings 14:21
Abijah	3	Years	I Kings 15:1-2
Asa	41	Years	I Kings 15:9-10
Jehosephat	25	Years	I Kings 22:41-42
Jehoram	8	Years	II Kings 8:16-17
Ahaziah	1	Years	II Kings 8:25-26
Athaliah	6	Years	II Kings 11:1-21
Joash	40	Years	II Kings 11:17-20, II Kings 18:1
Amaziah	29	Years	II Kings 14:1-2
Uzziah	52	Years	II Kings 15:1-2
Jotham	16	Years	II Kings 15:32-33
Ahaz	16	Years	II Kings 16:1-2
Hezikiah	29	Years	II Kings 18:1-2
Manasseh	55	Years	II Kings 21:1
Amon	2	Years	II Kings 21:19
Josiah	31	Years	II Kings 22:1
Jehoahaz	1	3 Months	II Kings 23:31
Jehoakim	11	Years	II Kings 23:34
Jehoiachin	▮▮▮	3 Months, 10 Da	II Kings 24:8
Zedekiah	11	Years	II Kings 25:17-18

The Divided Kingdom: *The Southern Kingdom of Judah*

King	Years Reigned	AY Years	Julian Years (Sept-Sept)	Year Count
Rehoboam	17	2970-2986	975-958	1-17
Abijah	3	2987-2989	958-955	18-20
Asa	41	2990-3030	955-914	21-61
Jehosephat	25	3031-3055	914-889	62-86
Jehosephat co-ruled with his son Jehoram for the last 4 years of his reign. This is very clear from II Kings 8:16 and synchronization				
Joram/Jehoram	8	3052-3059	893-885	83-90
Ahaziah	1	3060	885-884	91
Athaliah	6	3061-3066	884-878	92-97
Joash/Jehoash	40	3067-3106	878-838	98-137
Amaziah/Ahaziah	29	3107-3135	838-809	138-166
Uzziah/Azariah	52	3136-3187	809-757	167-218
Jotham	16	3188-3203	757-741	219-234
Ahaz	16	3205-3220	741-725	235-250
Hezikiah	29	3221-3249	725-696	251-279
Manasseh	55	3250-3304	696-641	280-334
Amon	2	3305-3306	641-639	345-336
Josiah	31	3307-3337	639-608	337-367
Jehoahaz	3 Mo (1 Yr)	3338	609-608	368
Jehoiakim	11	3339-3349		368-378
Jehoiakin	3 Mo, 10 days			
Zedekiah	11	3350-3360		379-389

Top chart

Rehoboam (Judah)	Yr	Sept–Sept span	April–April span	Jeroboam (Israel)	Yr
			April 975	Jeroboam	1
Rehoboam	1	Sept 975 – 974	April 974		2
	2	Sept 974 – 973	April 973		3
	3	Sept 973 – 972	April 972		4
	4	Sept 972 – 971	April 971		5
	5	Sept 971 – 970	April 970		6
	6	Sept 970 – 969	April 969		7
	7	Sept 969 – 968	April 968		8
	8	Sept 968 – 967	April 967		9
	9	Sept 967 – 966	April 966		10
	10	Sept 966 – 965	April 965		11
	11	Sept 965 – 964	April 964		12
	12	Sept 964 – 963	April 963		13
	13	Sept 963 – 962	April 962		14
	14	Sept 962 – 961	April 961		15
	15	Sept 961 – 960	April 960		16
	16	Sept 960 – 959	April 959		17
	17	Sept 959 – 958	April 958		18

Bottom chart

Judah King	Yr	Sept	April	Israel King	Yr	Reign
(Rehoboam)	17	Sept 959 – 958	April 958	Jeroboam	18	3 yrs
Abijah	1	Sept 958 – 957	April 957		19	
	2	Sept 957 – 956	April 956		20	41 yrs
	3	Sept 956 – 955	April 955		21	
Asa	1	Sept 955 – 954	April 954	Jeroboam	22	
	2	Sept 954 – 953	April 953	Nadab	1	
	3	Sept 953 – 952	April 952	Baasha	1 (2)	
	4	Sept 952 – 951	April 951		2	24 yrs
	5	Sept 951 – 950			3	

Abijah: 18th year of Jeroboam

(I King 15:1)

Abijah: 18th year of Jeroboam (I King 15:1)
1st year of Abijah is Sept, 959-Sept, 958
18th year of Jeroboam is April, 959-April, 958

Asa: 20th year of Jeroboam

(I King 15:9)

1st year of Asa is Sept, 956-Sept, 955
20th year of Jeroboam is April, 957-April, 956

Nadab: 2cd year of Asa (I King 15:25)
2cd year of Asa is Sept, 955-Sept, 954
Nadabs first year is April, 955 to April, 954

Baasha killed Nadab in the 3rd year of Asa and
immediately assumed throne(I King 15:28)

Baasha killed Nadab in the 3rd year of Asa
and in the 3rd year of Asa and immediately
assumed tl 1st year of Baasha is April, 954-April, 953

				950	950	April	4
	6	Sept	950	949			
			949	949	April		5
	7	Sept	949	948			
			948	948	April		6
	8	Sept	948	947			
			947	947	April		7
	9	Sept	947	946			
			946	946	April		8
	10	Sept	946	945			
			945	945	April		9
	11	Sept	945	944			
			944	944	April		10
	12	Sept	944	943			
			943	943	April		11
	13	Sept	943	942			
			942	942	April		12
	14	Sept	942	941			
			941	941	April		13
	15	Sept	941	940			
			940	940	April		14
	16	Sept	940	939			
			939	939	April		15
	17	Sept	939	938			
			938	938	April		16
	18	Sept	938	937			
			937	937	April		17
	19	Sept	937	936			
			936	936	April		18
	20	Sept	936	935			
			935	935	April		19
	21	Sept	935	934			
			934	934	April		20
	22	Sept	934	933			
			933	933	April		21
	23	Sept	933	932			
			932	932	April		22

Table 1

Asa	#					Baasha/Omri	#	Elah/Zimri	#
Asa	23	Sept 933	932						
			932 932	April			22		
	24	Sept 932	931						
			931 931	April			23		
Asa	25	Sept 931	930						
			930 930	April	Baasha	24	Elah	1	
	26	Sept 930	929						
			929 929	April	Omri	1	Zimri...7 day	2	
	27	Sept 929	928						
			928 928	April	2	2			
	28	Sept 928	927						
			927 927	April	3	3	Omri is in Tibni 4 yrs while half follow		
	29	Sept 927	926						
			926 926	April	4	4	Tibni and half follow		
	30	Sept 926	925						
			925 925	April	5	1	Omri		
	31	Sept 925	924						
			924 924	April	6	2			
	32	Sept 924	923						
			923 923	April	7	3	Omri prevails		
	33	Sept 923	922						
			922 922	April	8	4	and is King		
	34	Sept 922	921						
			921 921	April	9	5	for 8 years		
	35	Sept 921	920						
			920 920	April	10	6	in Jerusalem		

Elah: 26th year of Asa
(I Kings 16:6-23)

Zimri killed Elah in the 27th year of Asa...Zimri was
burned to death in his palace 7 days later by Omri,
who immediately assumes throne(I King 16:15)

During a short period of time , Elah (died)
Zimri (killed) and Omri (new King) were on
the throne of the Northern Kingdom (Israel)

Omri claimed 12 years as King. The *first 4 years*
were in fact in turmoil between him and
His first official year as soverign monarch was
in April of 926 BC -April, 925 BC , in the
31st year of Asa (II Kings 16:23)
Omri was in Tibney for 6 years...2 years as King.
Than he reigned for 6 years in Jerusalem.

Table 2

Jehosephat	Asa	#					Ahab/Omri	#	Ahab	#
	Asa	36	Sept 920	919						
			919 919	April	11	7				
	Asa	37	Sept 919	918						
			918 918	April	12	8	Ahab	1		
		38	Sept 918	917						
			917 917	April		2				
		39	Sept 917	916						
			916 916	April		3				
Jehosephat Pro Rex		40	Sept 916	915						
			915 915	April	Ahab	4				
Pro Rex		41	Sept 915	914						
	Asa		914 914	April		5	25 yrs			
Jehosephat Sole Rex		1	Sept 914	913						
			913 913	April		6				
		2	Sept 913	912						
			912 912	April		7				
		3	Sept 912	911						
			911 911	April		8				
		4	Sept 911	910						
			910 910	April		9				
		5	Sept 910	909						
			909 909	April		10				
		6	Sept 909	908						
			908 908	April		11				
		7	Sept 908	907						
			907 907	April		12				

Ahab: 38th year of Asa
(I King 16:29)
Asa was diseased in his feet

Asa diseased in his feet
in his 39th year. Possibly
sugar diabetes(II Chron 16:12)
Jehosephat: 4th year of Ahab
(II King 22:41-42)

Top table

Judah (notes)	Judah King	Judah Yr	#	Sept Yr	April Yr	Israel King	Israel Yr	Notes
			8	Sept 907	906 / April		13	
			9	Sept 906	905 / April		14	
			10	Sept 905	904 / April		15	
			11	Sept 904	903 / April		16	
			12	Sept 903	902 / April		17	
			13	Sept 902	901 / April		18	
			14	Sept 901	900 / April		19	
			15	Sept 900	899 / April		20	
			16	Sept 899	898 / April		21	
Joram must have assumed the role of pro-rex in year 17 to satisfy II Kings 1:17.	Joram /Jehoram Pro-Rex		17	Sept 898	897 / April	Ahab 22	Ahaziah 1 (2 yrs)	Ahaziah: 17th year of Jehosephat (I Kings 22:51) (I King 22:51) Ahaziah: 2cd year of Joram: (II King 1:17)
			18	Sept 897	896 / April		Joram / Jehoram 2 (1)	
			19	Sept 896	895 / April		2	
	Jehosephat	20	20	Sept 895	894 / April		3	
		21	21	Sept 894	893 / April	Joram 4	3 (12 yrs)	Joram: 18th year of Jehosephat (II Kings 3:1)...Joram(Israel) in 18th year of Jehosephat(Judah)
Joram / Jehoram 1		1	22	Sept 893	892 / April		5	Joram(Judah) began reign in the 5th year of Joram (Israel) (II Kings 8: 16-17) (8 yrs)
Co-Rex 2		2	23	Sept 892	891 / April		6	
3		3	24	Sept 891	890 / April		7	Joram is the only King that is specifically identified as a Co-Rex (II Kings 8:16, 1:17)
Joram / Jehoram 4		4	25	Sept 890	889 / April		8	

Bottom table

Judah (notes)	Judah King	Judah Yr	#	Sept Yr	April Yr	Israel King	Israel Yr	Notes
During his last two years he had an incureable disease in his bowels. (II Chronicles 21: 18-19)			5	Sept 889	888 / April	Joram	9 (1 yr)	Ahaziah reigned in 11th yr of Joram (Israel) II Kings 9:29 Ahaziah reigned in 12th yr of Joram(Israel) II Kings 8:25
			6	Sept 888	887 / April		10	
			7	Sept 887	886 / April	Joram	11	
Ahaziah 1 (Jehoahaz) 0			8	Sept 886	885 / April		12	Jehu 1 — Jehu killed Joram, Ahaziah and all in kingly line but baby Joash II Kings 10:36 just says Jehu reigned 28 years
Age of Joash → 1	Athaliah 1	1	1	Sept 885	884 / April	Jehu 1	2	
2		2	2	Sept 884	883 / April		3	
3		3	3	Sept 883	882 / April		4	
4		4	4	Sept 882	881 / April		5	
5		5	5	Sept 881	880 / April		6	
6		6	6	Sept 880	879 / April		7	
7	Joash/Jehoash 1	1	1	Sept 879	878 / April		8	
			2	Sept 878	877 / April		9	
Jeoash was annointed as King at age 7, at the beginning of Athaliah's 7th year in the 7th year of Jehu (Israel)			3	Sept 877	876 / April		10	
			4	Sept 876	875 / April		11	
			5	Sept 875	874 / April		12	

Jehu Kills Ahaziah and then Joram(Israel) between Sept, 885 and April, 884
There is now now King in either the Northern or Southern Kingdoms.
Athaliah moves to killl all of her sons and assumes the throne immediately....but
little Joash, her youngest son, is hidden and saved. Jehu continues to war....
also killing Jezebel. He declares himself King of Israel in 885.
In 7th year of Jehu, Joash began to reign..(II King 12:1, II Chron 12:1)
Joash took throne between April-Sept of 878 BC
Josepus recorded that Joash was less than 1 year old when hidden by Jehosheba (Ahaziah's sister and wife of High Priest Jehodia (Antiq 9:7:1)

King (Judah)	Yr	Sept				Ruler (Israel)	Yr	Note
Joash/Jehoash	6	Sept 874	873					
		873	873	April			13	
	7	Sept 873	872					
		872	872	April			14	
	8	Sept 872	871					
		871	871	April			15	6 yrs
	9	Sept 871	870					
		870	870	April			16	
	10	Sept 870	869					
		869	869	April			17	
	11	Sept 869	868					
		868	868	April			18	
	12	Sept 868	867					
		867	867	April			19	
	13	Sept 867	866					
		866	866	April			20	
	14	Sept 866	865					
		865	865	April			21	
	15	Sept 865	864					
		864	864	April			22	
	16	Sept 864	863					
		863	863	April			23	
	17	Sept 863	862					
		862	862	April			24	
	18	Sept 862	861					
		861	861	April			25	
	19	Sept 861	860					
		860	860	April			26	
	20	Sept 860	859					
		859	859	April			27	
	21	Sept 859	858					
		858	858	April	Jehu	28	
Joash / Jehoash	22	Sept 858	857					
		857	857	April	Jehoahaz	1	17 yrs
	23	Sept 857	856					
		856	856	April		2	
	24	Sept 856	855					
		855	855	April		3	

Athaliah siezed the throne when when her son Ahaziah was slain by Jehu, sometime between Sept 886-Sept 885.

Jehoahaz: 23rd year of Joash (II Kings 13:1)

Jehoahaz suddenly switched to an acession year system

King (Judah)	Yr	Sept			Ruler (Israel)	Yr
Joash / Jehoash	25	Sept 855	854			
		854	854	April	Jehoahaz	4
	26	Sept 854	853			
		853	853	April		5
	27	Sept 853	852			
		852	852	April		6
	28	Sept 852	851			
		851	851	April		7
	29	Sept 851	850			
		850	850	April		8
	30	Sept 850	849			
		849	849	April		9

177

Table 1

Judah King	Judah Yr		Year	Year		Israel King	Israel Yr	Note
	31	Sept	849	848				
			848	848	April		10	
	32	Sept	848	847				
			847	847	April		11	
	33	Sept	847	846				
			846	846	April		12	
	34	Sept	846	845				
			845	845	April		13	
	35	Sept	845	844				
			844	844	April	Jehoahaz	14	
Joash / Jehoash	36	Sept	844	843				
			843	843	April		15	
	37	Sept	843	842				
			842	842	April		16	Jehoash Pro Rex
	38	Sept	842	841				
			841	841	April		17	Pro Rex
	39	Sept	841	840				
			840	840	April	Jehoash Sole Rex	1	
	40	Sept	840	839				16
			839	839	April		2	
Amaziah/ Ahaziah	1	Sept	839	838				
			838	838	April		3	
	2	Sept	838	837				
			837	837	April		4	
	3	Sept	837	836				29
			836	836	April		5	
	4	Sept	836	835				
			835	835	April		6	
	5	Sept	835	834				
			834	834	April		7	
	6	Sept	834	833				
			833	833	April		8	
	7	Sept	833	832				
			832	832	April		9	
	8	Sept	832	831				
			831	831	April		10	

Jehoash (Israel) began to reign as Pro Rex with his father Jehoahaz in the 37th year of Jehoash' reign. He became sole ruler after two years. Synchronization with all the other Kings of Judah and Israel demand this interpretation.

In 2cd year of Joash/Jehoash (Israel) Amaziah began reign. He reigned 29 years in Jerusalem (II Kings 13:10)

Table 2

(left)	Judah King	Judah Yr		Year	Year		Israel King	Israel Yr	Note
		9	Sept	831	830				
				830	830	April		11	
		10	Sept	830	829				
				829	829	April		12	
		11	Sept	829	828				
				828	828	April		13	
		12	Sept	828	827				
				827	827	April		14	
		13	Sept	827	826				
				826	826	April		15	
	Ahaziah	14	Sept	826	825				
				825	825	April	Jehoash	16	
1		15	Sept	825	824				
				824	824	April	Jeroboam II	1	41 yrs
2		16	Sept	824	823				
				823	823	April		2	
3		17	Sept	823	822				
				822	822	April		3	
4		18	Sept	822	821				
				821	821	April		4	
5		19	Sept	821	820				
				820	820	April		5	

Jeroboam II: 15th year of Amaziah (II King 14:23)

Amaziah year 15: Sept, 825-Sept, 824

Amaziah lived 15 years after the death of Joash (II Chron 25:25)

Joash must have died early in his 16th (last) year

178

Top table

	King	Yr						Jeroboam II	
6	Ahaziah	20	Sept	820		819			
					819	819	April		6
7		21	Sept	819		818			
					818	818	April		7
8		22	Sept	818		817			
					817	817	April		8
9		23	Sept	817		816			
					816	816	April		9
10		24	Sept	816		815			
					815	815	April		10
11		25	Sept	815		814			
					814	814	April		11
12		26	Sept	814		813			
					813	813	April		12
13		27	Sept	813		812			
					812	812	April		13
14		28	Sept	812		811			
					811	811	April		14
15		29	Sept	811		810			
					810	810	April	Jeroboam II	15
	Uzziah / Azariah	1	Sept	810		809			
					809	809	April		16
		2	Sept	809		808			
					808	808	April		17
		3	Sept	808		807			
					807	807	April		18
		4	Sept	807		806			
					806	806	April		19
		5	Sept	806		805			
					805	805	April		20
		6	Sept	805		804			
					804	804	April		21
		7	Sept	804		803			
					803	803	April		22

52

Uzziah…In 15th year of Jeroboam II Uzziah was annointed King at age 6. Uncapable of reigning untill he matured, Uzziah did not become sole monarch until he was age 18 in the 27th year of Jeroboam II (ii Kings 15:1-2)

Bottom table

	Yr						Jeroboam II	
	8	Sept	803		802			
				802	802	April		23
	9	Sept	802		801			
				801	801	April		24
	10	Sept	801		800			
				800	800	April		25
	11	Sept	800		799			
				799	799	April		26
	12	Sept	799		798			
				798	798	April		27
Uzziah/ Azariah	13	Sept	798		797		Jeroboam II	
				797	797	April		28
	14	Sept	797		796			
				796	796	April		29
	15	Sept	796		795			
				795	795	April		30

King	Yr		Sept yr	Green yr	April	King (N)	#	
	16	Sept	795	794				
			794	794	April		31	
	17	Sept	794	793				
			793	793	April		32	
	18	Sept	793	792				
			792	792	April		33	
	19	Sept	792	791				
			791	791	April		34	
	20	Sept	791	790				
			790	790	April		35	
	21	Sept	790	789				
			789	789	April		36	
	22	Sept	789	788				
			788	788	April		37	
	23	Sept	788	787				
			787	787	April		38	
	24	Sept	787	786				
			786	786	April		39	
	25	Sept	786	785				
			785	785	April		40	
	26	Sept	785	784				
			784	784	April	Jeroboam II	41	
Uzziah/ Azariah	27	Sept	784	783				
			783	783	April		1	
	28	Sept	783	782				
			782	782	April		2	
	29	Sept	782	781				
			781	781	April		3	
	30	Sept	781	780				
			780	780	April		4	
	31	Sept	780	779				
			779	779	April		5	
	32	Sept	779	778				
			778	778	April		6	
	33	Sept	778	777				
			777	777	April		7	
	34	Sept	777	776				
			776	776	April		8	
	35	Sept	776	775				
			775	775	April		9	

Most chonologists record a 10-12 year interregum here, but it is more likely that Zachariah had an unrecorded reign of 11 years.

The Holy Scriptues simply state that "Zachariah reigned 6 months in the 37th year of Uzziah"

	Yr		Sept yr	Green yr	April	King (N)	#	
	36	Sept	775	774				
			774	774	April		10	
	37	Sept	774	773				
			773	773	April		11	
	38	Sept	773	772				
			772	772	April	Zachariah	6 Months	
	39	Sept	772	771			Shallum	1 Month	
			771	771	April	Menahem	1	10
	40	Sept	771	770					
			770	770	April		2	
	41	Sept	770	769					
			769	769	April		3	
	42	Sept	769	768					
			768	768	April		4	
	43	Sept	768	767					
			767	767	April		5	

Zachariah reigned 6 months in the 38th year of Uzziah (II King 15:8)
Shallum killed Zachariah: reigned 1 month in the 39th year of Uzziah (II King 15:13)
In 39th year of Uzziah: Menahem killed Shallum and assumed the throne after the assassination (II King 15: 17). Menahem claimed the full year of Spring 771-Spring of 770 using Acession year logic The Assyrian King PUL came aginst Menahem early in his reign. (II King 15:19)

Uzziah was struck down by with leprosy by God for burning incense on the Alter of Incense in the temple. Jotham "served as a judge" for Uzziah until he died (II Chronicles 26: 18-23)

Jotham Pro Rex — Served as a Judge

Jotham was 25 years old when he became sole monarch (II Chron 27:1). He reigned as a pro rex and a judge for his father Uzziah who was confined to his room as a leper. It is not likely that Jotham was an accepted judge before he was 18 years old, so he likely served for over 6 years until Uzziah died.

Menaham early in his reign. (II King 15:19)

Pro Rex	King	Yr	Sept	BC	BC	April	North	Yr
		43	Sept	768	767			
				767	767	April		5
		44	Sept	767	766			
				766	766	April		6
		45	Sept	766	765			
				765	765	April		7
		46	Sept	765	764			
				764	764	April		8
1		47	Sept	764	763			
				763	763	April		9
2		48	Sept	763	762			
				762	762	April		10
3		49	Sept	762	761			
				761	761	April	Pekahiah	1
4		50	Sept	761	760			
				760	760	April		2
5	Uzziah	51	Sept	760	759			
				759	759	April	Pekah	1
6		52	Sept	759	758			
				758	758	April		2
	Jotham	1	Sept	758	757			
				757	757	April		3
		2	Sept	757	756			
				756	756	April		4
		3	Sept	756	755			
				755	755	April		5
		4	Sept	755	754			
				754	754	April		6
		5	Sept	754	753			
				753	753	April		7
		6	Sept	753	752			
				752	752	April		8
		7	Sept	752	751			
				751	751	April		9
		8	Sept	751	750			
				750	750	April		10
		9	Sept	750	749			
				749	749	April		11
		10	Sept	749	748			
				748	748	April		12

Pekahia began to reign in Uzziah's 50th year II Kings 15:23) — 2 yrs

Pekah began to reign in the 52cd year of Uzziah II Kings 15:27 — 20 yrs

Jotham began to reign in 2cd year of Pekah II Kings 15:32-33 — 16 yrs

Left	King	Yr	Sept	BC	BC	April	North	Yr
		11	Sept	748	747			
				747	747	April		13
		12	Sept	747	746			
				746	746	April		14
		13	Sept	746	745			
				745	745	April		15
		14	Sept	745	744			
				744	744	April	Pekah	16
		15	Sept	744	743			
				743	743	April		17
	Jotham	16	Sept	743	742			
				742	742	April		18
	Ahaz	1	Sept	742	741			
				741	741	April		19
		2	Sept	741	740			
				740	740	April	Pekah	20
		3	Sept	740	739			
				739	739	April	Hoshea Pro-Rex	1
20	Ahaz	4	Sept	739	738			
				738	738	April		2
		5	Sept	738	737			
				737	737	April		3
		6	Sept	737	736			
				736	736	April		4

Ahaz: 17th year of Pekah (II Kings 16:1) — 16 yrs

Ahaz seemed to rule both kingdoms during this period of time (II Chronicles 28:19-27) The Years between 739 BC-729 BC were evidently ruled by Ahaz.

Hezikiah began reign April-Sept,726 which is in 3rd year of Hoshea. Using the Acession year system, Hezikiahs first regnal year is Sept, 726 BC to Sept, 725 BC.....

II Kings 18:1 Hezikiah's 1st year was in 3rd year of Hoshea
II Kings 18:9...Hezikiah's 4th year was in 7th year of Hoshea
II Kings 18:10 Hezikiah's 6th year was in 9th year of Hoshea
II Kings 17:1 Hoshea began reign in 12th year of Ahaz
II Kings 17:6 Samaria fell in the 9th year of Hoshea's reign

Name	Yr		Year	Year		Hoshea	No.	Yrs
Ahaz	12	Sept	731	730				
			730	730	April		10	
	13	Sept	730	729				
			729	729	April	Hoshea Sole-Rex	1	9 yrs
	14	Sept	729	728				
			728	728	April		2	
	15	Sept	728	727				
			727	727	April		3	29 yrs
	16	Sept	727	726				
			726	726	April	Hoshea Sole-Rex	4	
Hezikiah	1	Sept	726	725				
			725	725	April		5	
	2	Sept	725	724				
			724	724	April		6	
	3	Sept	724	723				
			723	723	April		7	
	4	Sept	723	722				
			722	722	April		8	
	5	Sept	722	721				
			721	721	April		9	
	6	Sept	721	720				
			720					
	7	Sept	720	719				
	8	Sept	719	718				
	9	Sept	718					

Hoshea gained enough support to function as King in 12th year of Ahaz in the summer of 730 BC. Using the acession year system Ahab was credited as king between April 730-April 729 BC (II Kings 17:1)

Hezikiah : 3rd year of Hoshea (II Kings 18:1-2)

Shalmanezar besieged Samaria in 4th year of Hezekiah, and in the 7th year of Hoshea. At the end of 3 yrs, Samaria fell in the 6th year of Hezikiah and in the 9th yr of Hoshea. (II Kings 18:9-10, II Kings 17:6)

Shalmanezar..started siege in Sept/Oct of 723 He died during the seige in 722 BC...Sargon II took over and continued the seige for another 2 years
Year 1- Fall of 723 BC-Fall of 722 BC (Shalmanesar V)
Year 2-Fall of 722 BC-Fall of 721 BC (Sargon II)
Year 3-Fall of 721 BC-Summer of 721 BC (Sargon II)

II Kings 17:6 Samaria fell in Hoshea's 9th year of reign
II Kings 18:1 Hezikiah's 1st year was 3rd year of Hoshea

	Yr		Year	
	10	Sept	717	716
	11	Sept	716	715
	12	Sept	715	714
	13	Sept	714	713
	14	Sept	713	712
	15	Sept	712	711
	16	Sept	711	710
	17	Sept	710	709
	18	Sept	709	

The Northern Kingdom fell in late Summer of 721
Hoshea is credited with his last and 9th year as April, 721-April, 720
W.F.Albright & Jones both date the fall of Northern Kingdom to 721
Duration of Northern Kingdom
Northern Kingdom formally started in Summer of 975 with the death of King Solomon....Finnegan also proposes that Israel fell in the summer of 721 BC. From summer of 775 BC to Summer of 721 BC was 254 years. If measured from the death of Solomon: 454.5 yrs

Sennacherib invaded Judah in 14th year of Hezikiah (II Kings 18:13). In the 14th year of Hezikiah, he was sick to death. At that time God promised him that he would get well and added 15 more Years to his life. As a sign, the sundial Ahab had built went backward in time 10 degrees (II Kings 20:10).

		18	Sept	709 708
		19	Sept	708 707
		20	Sept	707 706
		21	Sept	706 705
Sargon was assassinated in 705 BC. His successor was Sennacherib		22	Sept	705 704
		23	Sept	704 703
		24	Sept	703 702
		25	Sept	702 701
		26	Sept	701 700
		27	Sept	700 699
		28	Sept	699 698
		29	Sept	698 697

Manasseh	1	697	696	
	55	643	642	
Amon	1	642	641	
	2	641	640	
Josiah	1	640	639	
	31	610	609	
Jehoahaz	1	609	608	3 Mo.
Jehoiakim	1	608	607	
	11	598	597	
Jehoiachin				3 Mo,10 days
Zedekiah	1	597	596	
	11	587	586	

183

Josiah was only 8 years old when he began to reign...(II Kings 22:1). Reigned 31 Years	

Josiah died in his 31st year of reign at Meggido in month of Tammuz, 609 BC

  Month of Tammuz (Tammuz 1=June 24 - Tammuz 29=July 23)

  Last year is Tishri 1, 610-Tishri 1, 609 BC.... (Sept 21, 610-Oct, 19, 609)

Jehoahaz reigned only 3 months (II Kings 22:30), but his last month of reign allowed him to assume the throne

  on Tishri 1, 609 Bc. This allowed him to claim the year 609 BC-608 BC as a full regnal year.

  Month 1 Tammuz (June 25-Jul 609 BC

  Month 2 Ab (July 24-Aug 22) 609 BC

  Month 3 Elul (Aug 23-Sept 20) 609 BC

Jehoiakim accession year was Tishri (Sept 21-Oct 19)-End of Elul (Sept 9), 608 BC

  Year 1   Sept 10, 608 BC to Sept 28, 607 BC

  Year 2   Sept 29, 607 BC to Sept 18, 606 BC

  ....

  Year 10   Sept 29, 599 BC to Sept 17, 598 BC

  Year 11   Sept 18, 598-Sept 6, 597

Jehoiakim died in late Fall 598 BC.....Likely Dec 16, 598 BC

Jehoiakin became King likely on Dec 17, 598 and reigned 3 months, 10 days

  Month 1 (Dec 17, 598 BC -Jan 16, 597 BC)

  Month 2 (Jan 17, 597 BC -Feb 15, 597 BC)

  Month 3 (Feb 16, 597 BC- 22-Mar 15, 597 BC)

..... Jehoiakin flees from Jerusalem and is captured 10 days later on Mar 25, 597

..10 days: Dec 16, 597 BC-Mar 25, 597 BC

Since Jehoiakin was following an accession year system, and his 3 Mo, 10 day reign fell entirely within the

  last year of Jehoiakim, He never achieved a Tishri 1 Regnal start date. When Zedikiah started his reign in late

  spring of 597 BC he honored the ongoing last (11th) regnal year of Jehoiakim (Sept 18, 598 - Sept 6, 597 BC). His

  first officcial regnal year started Tishri 1, 597 BC.

Zedekiah reigned 11 years

  Year 1   Sept 7, 597 BC to Sept 26, 596 BC

  Year 2   Sept 27, 596 BC to Sept 14, 595 BC

  Year 3   Sept 15, 595 BC to Sept 3 , 594 BC

  Year 4   Sept 4, 594 BC to Sept 22, 593 BC

  Year 5   Sept 23, 593 BC to Sept 12, 592 BC

  Year 6   Sept 13, 592 BC to Sept 1, 591 BC

  Year 7   Sept 2, 591 BC to Sept 19, 590 BC

  Year 8   Sept 20, 590 BC to Sept 8, 589 BC

  Year 9   Sept 9, 589 BC to Sept 28, 588 BC

  Year 10   Sept 29, 588 BC to Sept 17, 587 BC

  Year 11   Sept 18, 587-Sept 6, 586

Zedekiah was taken prisoner in June/July of 586, and his last year of reign

  was given as Sept 18, 587 BC to Sept 17, 586 BC

The date that Jerusalem fell is well known as July 18, 586 BC

Bibliography

Africanus, Julius, *Chronographies*, Grand Rapid, Michigan: 1978 reproduction of 1867 version.

Agee, M. J., *The End of the Age*, Avon Books, New York, NY,1994.

Albright, W. F., *The Chronology of the Divided Monarchy of Israel*, American School of Oriental Research, 1945

Anderson, Sir Robert, *The Coming Prince*, 1882

Anderson, Sir Robert, *The Coming Prince*, Kregel Publications, Grand Rapids, Michigan, 1988.

Anstey, M., *The Romance of Biblical Chronology*, London Marshall Brothers, 1913.

Archer, Gleason, *A survey of the Old Testament,* Moody Press, Chicago, 1974

Babylonian Talmud, Rosh Hashana and Arakin Tract.

Barnhouse, Donald Grey, *Revelation*, Zondervan Publishing House, Grand Rapids, Michigan, 1871.

Booker, Richard, *Jesus in the Feasts of Israel*, Destiny Image Publishers, Shippinsburg, Penn., 1987.

Bright, J., *A History of Israel*, Westminister Press, Chicago, Illinois, 1959.

Bullinger, E. W., *The Companion Bible*, Kregal Publishing Co., Grand Rapids, Michigan, 1990.

Finis Jennings Dake, *Dake's Annotated Reference Bible,* Dake Bible Sales, Inc., Lawrenceville, Georgia, 1974.

DeHaan, M.R., *Daniel the Prophet*, Zondervan Publishing House, Grand Rapids , Michigan, 1947.

Dewitt, Roy Lee, *Teaching From the Tabernacle*, Baker Book House, Grand Rapids, Michigan, 1991.

Encyclopedia Judaica, Keter Publishing House, Jerusalem, Israel, 1971.

Finnegan, Jack, *Handbook of Biblical Chronology*, Revised Edition, Hendrickson Publishing Co., Peabody, Maryland,1998.

Faulstich, Eugene, http://biblechronologybooks.com/

Fuchs, Daniel, *Israel's Holy Days*, Loizeaux Brothers, Neptune, New Jersey, 1985.

Galil, Gershon, *The Chronology of the Kings of Israel & Judah*, E. J. Brill Publishing Co., New York, NY, 1996.

Gaster, Theodore H, *Festivals of the Jewish New Year*, Morrow Quill Paperbacks, New York, NY, 1978.

Glaser, Zhava and Mitch Glaser, *The Fall Feasts of Israel*, Moody Bible Institute, Chicago, Illinois, 1977.

Good, Joseph, *Rosh Hashanah and the Messianic Kingdom to Come*, Hatikva Ministries, Port Arthur, Texas, 3rd Edition, 1970.

Hales, William, *A New Analysis of Chronology*, 2cd Edition, London, England, 1830.

Hislop, Alexander, *The Two Babylons*, Loizeaux Press, New Jersey, 1916.

Hoehner, Harold W., *Chronological Aspects of the Life of Christ*, Zondervan Press, Grand Rapids, Michigan, 1977.

Horn, H. H., and L. H. Wood, *The Chronology of Ezra 7*, TEACH Services, Inc., Second Edition, www.TEACHServices.Com, 1970.

Http://www.olive-tree.net, *A Summary of Edwin Theil's Work*, 5/3/2007

Ice, Thomas, http://www.pre-trib.org/

Ironside, Henry A., *Daniel*, Loizeaux Brothers Inc., Oakland, California, 1920.

Jeffrey, Grant R., *Armageddon: Appointment with Destiny*, Toronto, Canada, Frontier Research, Inc., 1988

Jones, Floyd Nolan, *The Chronology of the Old Testament*, Master Books, Third Printing,: May, 2007

Josephus, Flavius, *The Works of Josephus*, Hendrickson Publishing Company, 1987.

Lahaye, Tim, *Revelation*, Lamplighter Books, Zondervan Publishing House, Grand Rapids, Michigan,1975.

Larkin, Clarence, *The Greatest Book on Dispensational Truth in the World*, The Clarence Larkin Estate, Glenside, California, 1918.

Lenski, R. C. H., *Lenskie's Commentary on the New Testament*, Augsbury Fortress Press, 1964.

Levitt, Zola, *The Seven Feasts of Israel*, Zola, P. O. Box 12268, Dallas, Texas, 75225, 1979.

Lindsay, Gordon, *16 Volume Revelation Series*, Published by Christ for the Nations, Dallas, Texas, 1982.

Lindsey, Hal, *The Late Great Planet Earth*, Zondervan Publishing Company, Grand Rapids, Michigan, 1970.

Lukenbill, D.D., *Ancient Records of Assyria and Babylon*, Greenwood Press, New York, N.Y., 1968.

Newton, Sir Issac, *The Chronology of Ancient Kingdoms*, London, England, 1728.

McDowell, Josh, *Prophecy: Fact or Fiction*, Here's Life Publishing Company, San Bernadino, California, 1981.

McFall, Leslie, http://www.btinternet.com/~lmf12/

McGee, J. Vernon, *Daniel*, Thomas Nelson Publishers, Nashville, Tenn., 1975.

Morris, L.C., *The Gospel According to Luke*, William B. Eerdmans Publishing Company, Grand Rapids, Michigan, 1982.

Nee, Watchman, *Come Lord Jesus*, Christian Fellowship Publishers, New York, NY, 1976.

Pentecost, Dwight D., *Parables of Jesus*, Zondervan Publishing.

Pentecost, Dwight J., *Things to Come*, Zondervan Publishing, Grand Rapids, Michigan, 1973.

Phillips, Don T., *The Book of Revelation: Mysteries Explained*, Second Edition, 2012.Virtualbookworm.com Publishing Co., PO Box 9949, College Station, Texas, 2004.

Phillips, Don T., *The Birth and Death of Christ*, Virtualbookworm.com Publishing Co., PO Box 9949, College Station, Texas, 2004.

Phillips, John, *Exploring Revelation*, Moody Press, Chicago, Illinois, 1987.

Pickle, Bob, http://www.pickle-publishing.com/papers/

Pink, A. W., *The Antichrist*, Kregel Publishing, Grand Rapids, Michigan, 1988.

Pratt, John P., *Divine Calendars Testify of Abraham, Isaac and Jacob*, Meridian Magazine, Sept 11, 2003.

Prideaux, Humphrey, *The Old and New Testament: History of the Jews*, 25th Edition, London, England, 1858.

Rawlinson, George, http://en.wikipedia.org/wiki/George_Rawlinson

Rice, John R., *The King of the Jews (Matthew)*, Sword of the Lord Publishers, Murfreesboro, Tenn, 1971.

Rice, John R., *The Son of Man (Luke)*, Sword of the Lord Publishers, Murfreesboro, Tenn., 1971.

Ritchie, John, *Feasts of Jehovah*, Kregel Publications, Grand Rapids, Michigan, 1982.

Rosenthal, Marvin, *The Pre-Wrath Rapture of the Church*, Thomas Nelson Publishers, Nashville, Tenn., 1990.

Ryrie, Charles C., *Ryrie Study Bible*, King James Version, Moody Press, Chicago, Illinois, 1978.

Ryrie, Charles C., *Ryrie Study Bible*, New King James Version, Moody Press, Chicago, Illinois, 1985.

Salerno, Donald A., *Revelation Unsealed*, Virtualbookworm.com Publishing Co., PO Box 9949, College Station, Texas, 2004

Sedar Olam, Roman & Littlefield Publishing Company, New York, New York, 2005.

Shea, William H., Andrews University Seminary Studies, Summer 1988, Vol. 26, No. 2, 171-180.

Shepard, Coulso, *Jewish Holy Days*, Loizeaux Brothers Publishing Co., 1961.

Shodde, George H., *The Book of Jubilees*, Artisan Publishers, 1980.

Spurgeon, Tommie, The 7 Spirits of God, http://www.americaisraelprophecy.com/thesevenspiritsofgod.html

Strauss, Lehman, *God's Prophetic Calendar*, Loizeaux Brothers, http://www.google.com/Publishing Co. , 1987.

Strong, James, *Strong's Concordance of the Bible*, World Bible Publishers, Iowa Falls, Iowa, 1986.

Thiele, Edwin R., *The Mysterious Numbers of the Hebrew Kings*, Zondervan Press, Grand Rapids, Michigan, 1983.

Thiele, Edwin R., *A Summary of Edwin Thiele's Work*, http://www.olive-tree.net

Thomas, Robert, *Revelation 1-7: An Exegetical Commentary, Moody* Press, Chicago, Illinois, 1992.

Thomas, Robert, *Revelation 8-23: An Exegetical Commentary*, Moody Press, Chicago, Illinois, 1992.

Ussher, James, *Annals of the World*, Master Books, London, England, 1658.

Van Kampen, Robert, *The Sign*, Crossway Books, Inc., 1992.

Vine, W.E., *The Expanded Vines Dictionary of New Testament Words*, Bethany House Publishers, Minneapolis, Minn.,1994.

Wacholder, Ben Zion, *The Calendar of Sabbatical Cycles During the Second Temple and the Early Rabbinic Period*, Hebrew Union College Annual 44 (1973), pp. 153-196